PRAISE FOR NADIA DAVIS

"A powerful example of following our light within to break a cycle of trauma and consciously choose a life of happiness. Nadia is a true warrior spirit and champion for the fight against injustice."
—Chris Gardner, author of *The Pursuit of Happyness*, also a major motion picture

"Nadia Davis is a brilliant writer, attorney, and crusader for causes. Her book, *Home Is Within You*, encompasses her journey from crisis to redemption. It's truly a compelling read."
—Leigh Steinberg, American sports agent and author

"The courage of Ms. Davis to share her journey in her book is an incredible demonstration of selflessness. Ms. Davis has lived through challenges of addiction and recovery, and she has survived. By sharing her story, Ms. Davis has removed the shame and loneliness that plagued her and has plagued so many others. Her personal reflections and work are presented in her book and can give hope and success to others who find themselves in similar human conditions."
—Nancy O'Malley, Alameda County district attorney, founder of Alameda County Family Justice Center

"I have followed Nadia's journey from the time she was the wunderkind Santa Ana school board member doing courageous things such as supporting charter schools and have followed her successful effort to overturn a wrongful conviction of a defendant who was a convenient fall guy for a crime he didn't commit. Nadia's extraordinary book tells how she rose to great heights, took quite a hit, and successfully battled back. Inspiring story!"

—Richard Reisman, publisher and CEO,
Orange County Business Journal

"Writing a book, any book, requires commitment, focus, and fortitude. To write a book like *Home Is Within You* requires all that along with a level of honesty, belief, and vulnerability that is nothing short of extraordinary. For anyone who knows Nadia, of course, it's not the least bit surprising, since she has always committed herself to those who need help or feel helpless. I first became aware of her when she was as an attorney tirelessly working for the release of a young man convicted of a crime he did not commit—a 'lost cause' she eventually won. That's the Nadia Davis her friends know, a woman of generosity and grace who readers can trust to help guide them home."

—Steve Lowery, former editor, *OC Weekly*

"I have known Nadia since she was a little girl. Inspired by her father, Wally Davis, a close mentor and friend who was a pillar in our community, she carried on his legacy of public service, improving the lives of others in more ways than one. Here in California Hispanic leadership circles, we never doubted her comeback story would strike the world with hope!"

—Ruben A. Smith, Esq., attorney and former president,
Hispanic Bar Association of Orange County

"It takes courage to tell your story, and Nadia Davis has acted with such courage and transparency in telling her story in a creative and conscientious way. We who have experienced trauma can all learn from her bravery and raw honesty."

—Casey Gwinn, Esq., president of
Alliance for HOPE International

"This is a can't-put-it-down book that will keep readers engaged from the beginning to the very last word. Nadia has masterfully woven such beauty and grace into her first memoir. By exploring her family's cultural background, her passion for those in need, her legal advocacy, and a string of addiction-fueled choices that resulted in chaos and trauma for herself and her family, Nadia has woven together rigorous honesty and unrelenting grace in a way rarely seen in contemporary memoirs. Nadia tells her story with such passion while managing to tap into broader societal issues related to her Mexican and Native American roots, gender dynamics, and personal trauma that led to a promising young attorney spiraling down and ultimately crashing in a very public way. But that's only the beginning of her story. The real story is one of compassion, resilience, love, and eventually recovery. As a professor and clinical therapist, I plan to refer to this book often with students, clients, and friends."

—Michelle Martin, PhD; MSW; therapist;
associate professor, Department of Social Work,
California State University, Fullerton

"Nadia Davis's memoir is a deeply personal story of addiction and motherhood and the heart-wrenching, almost debilitating shame and stigma uniquely borne by women with addictive disorders. Nadia's resilience is a testament to the power of a mother's love and to her inner spirit, which fought to reclaim not just her personal dignity but also justice for anyone shamed in the middle of a mental health breakdown."

—Ahbra Kaye Schiff, producer, REEL Recovery Film
Festival, and director of operations, Writers in Treatment

"Arthur Carmona was my son. Nadia shares the fight for the truth in her book. Arthur and I were blessed to have her take on this monumental case. During that journey, Nadia's

compassion and dedication to fighting for the truth regardless of the challenges amazed me. Hope came in the form of a woman named Nadia Maria Davis. I highly recommend *Home Is Within You* as a must read. It is a rare opportunity to journey with Nadia as she shares her truth. The book allows you to feel her emotions about her victories as well as her hardships."
—Ronnie Sandoval Carmona, cofounder of the Arthur Carmona Center for the Wrongfully Convicted

"Nadia is a testament to the power of trauma work and breaking through the bonds of our minds that separate us from our core true innocence and being."
—Mariam Paul, MFT, trauma specialist

"Nadia's journey of recovery is deeply admirable. I commend her as a mother, a professional, and a former spouse for having the courage to share her journey in order to help others."
—Bill Lockyer, former Attorney General and Treasurer, State of California; Nadia's former longtime spouse

"I have had the honor and privilege of witnessing the many twists and turns on Nadia's journey from being utterly lost to finding her way to her own inner home, where she belongs unconditionally. I am in awe of her perseverance, integrity, and conviction in spite of the cascade of adversities she has faced in her life. Through *Home Is Within You*, she now inspires countless others to seek that unconditional home that resides within them. This book is a must read!"
—Priya Jain, spiritual life coach; kundalini yoga trainer; founder of Seventh Chakra Yoga Institute of Spiritual Sciences; author of *Awakening Sutras of Japji Sahib*

"Very few of us have the courage to write about the challenges life throws our way. Nadia's courage and strength—not only

to endure so much but also to share so that others can heal—
are beyond heroic. I have personally known Nadia for decades,
since she first hit the ground advocating for improving the
lives of others less fortunate. Even after her near-death car
accident, I witnessed her being in the hospital, still unable to
walk, and yet going through paperwork to help others. She is
an inspiration to women all over the world, regardless of color,
heritage, religion, and financial status. I never doubted she'd
make it through the hardships, and I am beyond grateful that
she survived and now thrives."

—Bethzabe Martinez, founder and president of
Nuestro Pueblo; human resources manager

HOME IS
WITHIN YOU

HOME IS WITHIN YOU

A Memoir of Recovery and Redemption

NADIA DAVIS

Foreword by Nancy O'Malley

GIRL FRIDAY BOOKS

 GIRL FRIDAY BOOKS

Published by Girl Friday Books™, Seattle
www.girlfridaybooks.com

Produced by Girl Friday Productions

Design: Paul Barrett
Production editorial: Laura Dailey
Project management: Kristin Duran

Image credits: Cover photograph © John Gilhooley

ISBN (paperback): 978-1-954854-94-9
ISBN (ebook): 978-1-954854-95-6

Library of Congress Control Number: 2022917265

This memoir is dedicated to my three sons,
Diego, Harrison, and Elijah.
May you always remember that home is within you.

CONTENTS

FOREWORD

For most of my adult life, I have worked supporting victims of crime, victims of interpersonal violence, and victims of human trafficking. I have also worked supporting those who have struggled in life, who go through childhood trauma, mental health challenges, substance-use disorders, and other circumstances that directly interfere with their quality of life.

I have worked with individuals who are emotionally stalled or immobile; with individuals who feel like their life can't change; and with others whose circumstances have led to self-destructive behavior. In addition, I have worked with many who have found the courage to reach out to another person or to organizations to seek support, guidance, spirituality, or enlightenment. It is inspiring to be a witness to such beautiful transformation and growth.

I have known Nadia Davis for several years. She is a woman of compassion, care, and great intelligence. She is also a woman who has been brave and selfless in sharing her own personal struggles and her journey through traumas, through substance use, recovery, relapse, and recovery again. Ms. Davis's book, *Home Is Within You*, provides tremendous insight for anyone and everyone, regardless of their circumstances.

Ms. Davis's courage to share her journey in her book is an incredible demonstration of selflessness. She has lived through challenges, and she has survived. By sharing her story, she has removed the shame and loneliness that plagued her and that plague so many others.

Having worked with Nadia, she as the Director of the Family Justice Center and an elected Supervisor, I have borne witness to the inspiration that she provides to anyone who desires transformation led by hope, trust, support, and strength. Her story can give hope and a pathway to success for others who find themselves in similar human conditions.

Nancy O'Malley
Alameda County District Attorney
Founder, Alameda County Family Justice Center
National Victims' Rights Advocate

PREFACE

The concept of home evokes many different things in each of us. In childhood, when we are able to be free and in our element, our memories evolve through authentic play and exploration of all the wonders in the world. Thoughts of home during youth may include playing in the backyard with friends, a reliable warm embrace, the smell of our pillow as we lie down to rest, or that special homemade meal on a familiar plate. As we enter adulthood and take on responsibilities, our relationships, work, and family life add to these personalized experiences, shaping our concept of home. They transform four walls into that singular physical place we go to that is set apart from the rest of the world.

Home Is Within You is a memoir written about a deeper, non-physical, divine, infinite space—an expanse that offers refuge, serenity, and clarity—which anyone can obtain within their heart. For much of my life, I survived entirely on a set of mental intrigues based on fear and judgment of myself and others. I did not yet know that my mind was running the show, or that we are all fractals of something miraculously timeless, healing, and empowering beyond this physical life. Most of us do not learn this concept when we are young, let alone before bad things start to happen and shape our minds. We simply do our best, and often thrive, in varying survival modes, praising the grit, blood, and sweat it takes to succeed in daily life.

I did this far into adulthood. It worked well for a while,

until trauma and losses reared their ugly heads, back-to-back and out of the blue. There, all along, my soul and deep core wounds had been crying out in vain to be heard, but I barely recognized their voices. I drowned them out. That approach landed me in addiction and further trauma, which many of us are far too familiar with.

Thankfully, I eventually found mentors, therapists, a healing yoga spiritual family, and a sober fellowship of individuals who offered tools and a way out of darkness and shame. I learned that I had a choice every day between fear and love—love that looks like acknowledging my and others' true selves. I discovered that anything anyone does in this physical life is either a cry for love or an act of love. I came to believe that the only truth that matters is that we are all infinite beings, whole, perfect, and complete, and we are simply doing the best we can in this finite life. That said, we have a grand choice: to live ruled by our minds' attacking thoughts on self and others, or to change the game and use our minds to our benefit, discovering our true selves and gaining solace within on a daily basis.

You too can discover and cultivate a "home within" where you are elevated beyond troubles, where everything begins to resolve itself on its own, and where you can let go of trying to figure things out based on your thoughts alone. It is a space to connect to anytime, anywhere, and under any circumstances. By taking refuge in this space, all pain and suffering disappear, and this adventure we call life becomes a journey of simply further discovering our hearts and souls through the ups and downs, thereby walking authentically and wholeheartedly side by side with others.

When I began writing *Home Is Within You*, words flowed onto paper from the depths of my heart as a mother to my three sons. My sole intention was to guide them into a different, more fulfilling way of living in this world. The process evolved into a humbling, blessed opportunity to guide and help others on their own roads of recovery and redemption, no matter their reasons or circumstances. This memoir is for all those seeking to heal and grow—for anyone wanting and needing a place free of judgment, where all forms of shame are banned, and internal sources of strength and freedom are nurtured.

Every chapter includes intimate letters to my sons. Some of these letters provide guideposts to the subjects that follow, as well as golden moments of wisdom when past, present, and future intertwined while I was writing. The letters contain lessons to be learned; reassurances of love; encouragement to be true to oneself; warnings of dangers; and messages of heritage, justice, and hope.

I'm not sure whether 1) my life created the story, 2) my children's lives made and saved mine, or 3) my children inspired who I truly was all along. I'd like to think that all three symbolically co-exist herein in an ever-evolving, beautiful way.

This narrative begins with my father's story, as his spirit is mine, and he arises throughout the book. His story is followed by a chronicle of my childhood and young adult life, which includes the legal-justice case of Arthur Carmona, a wrongfully convicted youth whose fight for freedom captivated the nation. While I had the honor of assisting him as a young attorney, decades later, it was the inspiration from his strength and courage to fight for the truth that eventually saved my life in the darkest hours.

As a precaution, please know I also share much that is deeply personal and painful herein. Some parts may be very difficult to read, as they include my experiences of trauma, addiction, and loss. My main reasons for including those are to take a stand against all sources of public shaming of mental health and addiction struggles, and to genuinely offer a relatable, safe, judgment-free place in my story where everyone's truth is acknowledged and internal sources of strength and peace are nurtured. I humbly ask you to continue through the difficult parts till you arrive at the last page. The gems of spiritual truth and a way out of darkness exist therein.

This is my story. I am home. I am finally home within.

May you find your own personal path to the one true home within.

Dear Son,

when I visited the angels,

you were there.

My father's inspiration carried me through years when I thrived working in my element. A little brown girl who simply wanted to save the world, I became a passionate attorney and school board member in the city he grew up in.

"Young, smart, and beautiful," they said, "an up-and-comer."

I wanted to bring warmth and light where the dark was winning.

So when a desperate mother begged me to help free her innocent son, I went on autopilot. Many said I was crazy. Well, frankly, I am. At least now, I happily admit it.

"A young, inexperienced lawyer? Who the hell does she think she is?" they asked. *Um, sir, doing the right thing doesn't require permission or tenure,* I thought.

Go ahead and call me nuts. But the truth isn't, and it had

to win. The fight to free a wrongfully convicted kid was off and running. Hundreds joined the effort and the press followed.

Yet it all could have come to an end the night of the accident. A big rig hit my car, hauling it off into a triple flip, landing in an embankment out of sight. I wasn't breathing when they finally found me. Twenty-two broken bones, a punctured lung, and a bleeding brain later, it took a mighty toll I'd fail to recognize for years to come.

Dear Son,

You were there that night I died, long before any human idea of you ever came to be. Engulfed in an infinite, formless warmth, love, and light, "It" is where no fear or judgment exist. "It" is a magnificent and all-knowing peace. My father's soul and innumerable others shined and thrived whole, perfect, and complete. I didn't want to leave.

But then a message came so clear, "Now is not the time." An indelible mark of that home within was etched into my being.

Another's breath was forced inside me and a thump of my heart was heard again. My soul returned to a body that would struggle for years to survive.

But now I know the reason it did. It was to carry your life.

Truth is, I had no clue how to live in this life before my body was shattered. Navigating emotional, mental, and physical pain thereafter was beyond difficult and my choices were not all smart.

Any normal person would've taken time to heal before returning to public life. Me? No, I had to prove my worth. And thoughts are crappy things when you believe they are really you. My mind was alive and kicking before I could even take a step. Fueled by a hospital IV line of morphine, *tap, tap, tap*, it rang. *Just accept you're a broken body. You'll never walk again.*

Outside, rumors fueled the agony. "She'll never be the same. She's a goner now, out of our way." I didn't know any better then and responded inside, *Screw you and screw that. Hey! Watch me now. I'll get back on my feet again, just like my daddy did.*

Plus, an innocent kid was still behind bars, and I was still free.

Sure enough, my body got up and walked again. Years of hard work brought prestigious titles, awards, and accolades. Then I ended up in the arms of the most powerful man in the State of California. But none of that erased the fact that I was struggling deep inside. I was so gravely ill-prepared for all that would happen in my life next.

Tragedy after tragedy hit, back-to-back, and out of the blue. Death and trauma reared their ugly heads, and I never could seem to catch up. Perfect fodder for a sociopath and highly addictive drug, I fell into a swamp of terror and saw absolutely no way out.

Worse, the press marred the truth and turned my agony into a scandal. The system denied justice and the hell only continued. Shame consumed my entire being and I nearly let it kill me too. All connection back to the truth within was stuffed down deep and forgotten. I was once the "up-and-comer," but now my life became treatment, jail, and hospitalizations. Bumps and falls, hopes and gains, the road to recovery was filled with challenges.

All along there you were, dear Son, waiting for Mommy to get better. To say I am sorry will never be enough. All I can do is strive to give you a healthier parent and the things I have learned today.

It was only in you that hope and commitment remained.

It was only through you that I could barely breathe again.

It was only from you that I saw glimpses of that home within.

It saved my life in the darkest hour, as I cried on my knees.

Please, oh please, please, infinite one, please show me how to live. I've tried so hard. I've tried so long. I've tried every possible way. Please take away this shame and pain. My children need me thriving again. Please show me the truth of what I am, please bring me back to that home within for them.

And there "It" came, dear Son, to break down the chains. I saw what was real, illusions erased. "It" whispered so gently, *Wipe your tears now. Get back on your feet. Your true self and home are right there within you. Step by step, walk again. Remember, you did it before. This time, remember there are lights along the way always there to guide you. It's time to free yourself now, dear, just like you did for that kid back then.*

Everything changed. A seven-year journey came to an end. Another phase of life began, thankfully now in wholehearted living.

Dear Son,

Please stay here with me,
knowing the one and only truth within.
We are infinite beings of love, light, and
warmth,
that nothing can change or hide.
It is here where your true self remains the
same,
no matter what anyone says or does.

It is here where your life's challenges
hold purpose and beautiful rhythm.
And it is here, dear Son, where we first met,
and will forever hold hands in time.

CHAPTER 1

Dear Son,
poverty is not living in a small house,
it is living in a small world.

There he was, flying through the air, adjusting his body so he would land on his own two feet, barely missing the shards of glass and manure in the pile below. *Hijo, que suerte,* he thought. *Boy, how lucky!* A flood of feelings and thoughts ran wild. He felt both unimportant and invisible, as if no one cared, but it didn't matter.

"I'll get out of this hole," he said to himself, and he did.

Wallace (Wally) Robert Davis was born March 21, 1935, of Native American, Spanish, Irish and Mexican descent in the "La Colonia 17" barrio in West Santa Ana. His haven, there he found self-worth and respect on his own in a tiny space of shelter with a wood-burning stove, outhouse, and no water heater.

Surrounded by fields, animals, and poor farmers, the

neighborhood was rich with family values, respect, loyalty, honor, and an ethic of hard work. Enriched with Mexican customs, neighbors helped one another and left their doors wide open. Martinez Hall, the social hotspot, was on the northwest corner, across from Tony Acosta's service station. Families survived on credit at the local grocery store run by a generous Asian immigrant family, the Matsunagas. Yes, there were gangs, but it didn't interfere with life. The battles were over girls and face-to-face. Hands and knives were the norm rather than guns and drive-bys.

He and his friends found treasures in sticks and stones as toys. Along with a few plastic soldiers, they'd cross seas to battle afar or find chests of gold in a puddle nearby. After swimming at the local water tank, they'd gather on front porches and listen intently to elders' stories. These friendships would last a lifetime.

"Do You Remember"
My dear friend Bob
How close we were. Closer than
　　brothers—you told me so.
How we shared our toys. How we shared
　　our joys.
How we shared our sorrows then, some
　　50 years ago.
Do you remember?
We were five or six in our barrio.
Every year, we exchanged Christmas gifts.
I can remember the handmade little cars,
　　pennies,
nuts, baseball cards in those little boxes—
　　hand-delivered with love.
How little did we know they were price-
　　less—those little things that expressed

our fondness for each other. I couldn't buy
    one now.
We shared the fruits of prejudice thrown
    at us from the outside world.
How clear it came. "No Mexicans al-
    lowed!" But we knew better.
You were proud of your Mexico—I was
    proud of my "Southwest."
We volunteered to serve our country
    nonetheless.
But the music that we shared would last
    forever.
Remember the clarinet duet, the school
    bands,
"The Continentals," the "Bob Garcia's
    Group."
How you loved it. The sax would put you
    in a trance—like me.
The later years took us apart, my friend.
You went your way, and I went mine.
We didn't talk, we didn't share in later
    years.
But it didn't matter, my friend.
I ask you now—do you remember? I do.
The nicest memories include you in my
    youth.
That steady, quiet, patient friend of my
    youth.
No, you're not dead.
I feel your presence, yet.
Do you remember?
    —Wally Davis

Little Wally's mother, Margaret E. Kirker ("Margarita"), was a beautiful, lanky, stylish woman and a mix of Southwest gem genes, born in New Mexico of Native American (Navajo/Apache), Mexican (Eliseo), and Irish descent.

I never got to meet her, and I sometimes envy those with lots of grandmother stories. But that doesn't help anything a bit. I can still hold on to the memories of watching my father's eyes fill with fondness, love, and sympathy every time he gazed upon a photo of her. It somehow permeated a connection to her spirit, eventually creating a bridge through which she visited me various times in life.

When my father was seven, his world was torn apart when Margarita was stricken with tuberculosis while his father was away serving in the U.S. Navy with World War II in full force. His mother was abruptly sent away to a sanatorium in another state, so little Wally was removed from his home and placed in foster care with strangers.

Daddy,

Did you know she had no choice, and they made her leave? Or did you think she chose to just get up and go? My God, the pain that would bring. Did you give up hope? Or cry alone? Did anyone explain what was really going on? Could they? Should they? What could've been said to help you through? Because, Daddy, I went through the same thing as a mother too.

Rosa and Mr. Castellan thought the kid would only be there for a few days. But weeks had passed and, sure enough, he was still there. So when little Wally accidentally spilled his water, Mr. Castellan blew his cork, grabbed him by his suspenders, and threw him out the back door.

It was this flight in the air and landing that Wally remembered vividly the rest of his life. Mr. Castellan had unintentionally given Wally the unique ability to always land on his own two feet. For the rest of his life, he would.

Uncle Bobby, Robert Kirker, finally came one day to get him, picked him up, propped him on his shoulder, and said, "Come on, Wallitas, we're going home." Wally scanned the room with his deep, dark brown eyes. He wanted to take it all in. He had a gut feeling he'd never return or ever want to come back even if Rosa had given him love as best she could. He was going home at last.

Wally's mother got better for a little bit, and there were glimpses of hope she'd survive. Upon her return to California, she quickly had another son with a different man. But her disease lay latent, and a few days after giving birth, her little boy died. Shortly thereafter, she joined him in heaven.

Little Wally served as an altar boy for the first time at his mother's funeral mass, along with his childhood friend Frank Martinez. No one knows what happened to her baby boy's body. She was buried in an unmarked grave at Holy Sepulcher Cemetery in Orange, where Wally would one day be buried too.

Daddy,

What does it feel like to lose a mommy?
Did you get to say goodbye?
What memories did you hold on to when
you missed her and cried?
You knew she loved you dearly. You knew
she walked with grace.
You believed she did her best as a mother,
isn't that right?

Please tell me, Daddy. I need to know. I am
so scared, I feel so low.
My son is scared, and he does not know the
truth.
Please tell me what to do to prevent a
broken heart.
And Daddy, oh Daddy, what is it like to
lose a little brother too?
Did you ever get to look in his eyes?
Were they like yours? Like yours are mine?
Did you know that my son is a big brother
now too?
Did you visit him when he was so sad and
blue?
And what did they do with your little
brother's body?
Did they even let your mother say goodbye
to her baby?
Did they just throw it away, like they did
with mine?
And Daddy, oh Daddy, are our babies'
souls with you too?

Eventually, Wally returned to the loving arms of his grand-parents, "Mama Candi" (Predicanda Eliseo Serrano) and "Papa Leandro" (Serrano), his step-grandfather from Zacatecas, Mexico. Mama Candi was born and raised in New Mexico, of mixed southwestern heritage. She had several children with Robert Kirker, including Robert Jr., Henry, and Oscar, who all served in the military and became Wally's treasured uncles.

A very Indigenous-looking woman, she somehow thought her lighter half sister was more beautiful. But Mama Candi was indeed a beauty inside and out, with a gregarious sense of humor and sarcastic wit that lit up the room. Her homemade chili con carne and tortillas filled Wally's hungry tummy. I am blessed to have her stone corn grinder in my home today.

Every day after school and during summer vacations, little Wally worked as a child laborer in the fields of Garden Grove, Fountain Valley and Santa Ana. He'd hear stories and share conversations with Papa Leandro as they picked chili peppers, tomatoes, potatoes, and oranges. He felt mighty every time Papa Leandro gave in and pulled him up high onto the tractor's seat so he could hold the wheel a few seconds, every time pretending he ruled the land and was entering in a horsed carriage.

Papa Leandro was Wally's refuge and rock. He had three years of grade school yet a mind of endless wisdom and a heart of gold. He gave meaning to the words "respect" and "honesty," instilling in his boy the idea that maybe he could break through to the outside world. It wasn't because there was any reason to leave. Rather, it was because there was something in Wally that the world needed to receive.

"Mientras yo pueda arrastrar por los files, mi hijo va a ir a la escuela," said Papa Leandro, or "While I can slug through the fields, my son is going to school." The inspiration planted a tiny yet powerful seed in little Wally that eventually became a lush forest of inspirational words my father used in speeches to hopeful students later in life.

Thank you, Papa Leandro.

Thank you for being a mighty man and son and hero to my father. It is you who gave so much to his home within. It did not matter that the outside world perceived there was so little to give in an impoverished surrounding.

Today I hold snippets of Daddy so close to
my heart. His handwritten notes on yellow pad
pages. His tethered and torn old briefcase. The
saved cards from admirers and cut-out sayings.
The folded pages of law books and his fine black
marker pens. They are all I have of him in finite
form. But because of you, his words live on.

"There was a flood once and we had to go up the hills so our homes wouldn't be washed away," my father said to my brother Mark much later in life—May 9, 1977, when he was forty-two, to be exact. It was for a history assignment, another paper I found in my father's belongings.

"When Delano Roosevelt died, I heard it on the radio and went in the backyard and cried because he meant so much to me," he said, and "I can remember when my Japanese friends were taken away to concentration camps during the war and the arguments over dropping the bomb on Hiroshima. We drove our car with the headlights off so we wouldn't be seen by planes. At the end of WWII, everyone was celebrating. I remember seeing my uncles coming back from the war."

Oh how I wish I'd taken the time to ask him so much more.

My great-grandfathers, including Wallace Wayne Davis, were all attorneys originally from Tennessee who landed in Southern California during the Prohibition Era. With their stylish suits, hearty business goals, and minds of alcoholic underground outlaws, they made a mark and a name for themselves in more ways than one.

A routine pattern of practicing law, drinking booze, and illegal smuggling of alcohol made for an interesting, stressful, and unhealthy life. They literally were originators of the term "bootlegging," or the concealing of liquor-filled flasks in one's boot tops when trading with Native Americans.

But they took things a step further. Native American women also caught their eyes. Some of the Southern California Indigenous beauties were impregnated by the Davis crew, and a perfect pot of hearty alcoholic genes manifested for me.

Dear Son,

I could blame a few of my diseases on genes alone. I got 'em. And I got 'em bad. A line of depressed self-medicating drinkers on both sides of the family surely sent a blueprint our way.

Still, there is nothing to be afraid of. Knowing this is power.

Mental health and substance abuse are complicated to understand and even harder to navigate. Worse, admitting them is difficult in a shame-making world. It is letting shame rule that you should fear, not the "diseases," dear Son.

It is through sharing my personal process of recovery that you might receive a fair view into them, and more importantly, an ounce of hope and wisdom to help yourself or another human being should they ever occur.

So herein, I share a heck of a lot. Like a lot a lot.

It may be too much. It may not be enough. It may be embarrassing, disturbing, and cause moments when you feel distraught. Please breathe as you go and know my intentions were good. And, most of all, promise me you'll read it to the end.

Love, Mom

When Lucy Rios, my great-grandmother of Acjachemen/ Juaneño Band of Mission Indian descent, was impregnated by my great-grandfather, she was very young and had no parents, both of whom had died from foreign diseases when she was just three. She had thus been raised by her aunt and uncle, Antonia and Antonio Eliseo, also of Acjachemen/Juaneño Indian descent.

She and the baby in her belly were abandoned by my great-grandfather. She ended up giving birth to my grandfather, Wallace Carlos Davis, in her aunt and uncle's home, but tragically died shortly thereafter. Thankfully, the Eliseos, in their elderly age, also raised my grandfather.

While my grandfather had the loving arms of his great-uncle and -aunt, nothing erased the gnawing self-doubt and emptiness churning inside him from having an absent father. When he was just a small child, my grandfather actually walked straight into the Davis brothers' law office and blatantly asked my great-grandfather, "Are you my father?"

I do not know what response he received. Nor do I know if it helped my grandfather fill the hole in his heart, if even a little bit. All I do know is that my grandfather became a depressed alcoholic too.

Daddy,

Imagine the weight of questions your father already carried so young in his mind, so very heavy they compelled him to do such a thing. How does the child of a dead mother and absent alcoholic father learn how to live?

They say people who do not know their genetic father often grow up with identity problems. They attribute all personality characteristics they cannot trace or understand to the father they never knew. As a result, those traits are less strongly felt as being their own. How very confusing. No wonder he spent his entire life drunk, searching and searching for answers, the truth, and a foundation. No wonder he never became aware of the home within him. I'm sure his mother Lucy would've said, holding him close to her heart, "Oh dear Son of mine, I love you so dearly, I'll love you for all time."

And how could he have known how to be a father to you if he never had one himself? Perhaps he did the best he could while drinking away his sadness just to get by. Perhaps he was really a good person deep down inside. I do know indeed that you thought this too.

Eventually, the Davis brothers became a headline scandal. They were caught red-handed along with crooked police officers in the depths of their illegal bootlegging scheme. Tragically, the day it hit the front page on newsstands, my great-grandfather shot and killed himself, leaving my grandfather, who had no present father, fatherless.

Daddy,

Perhaps I wasn't the biggest Davis scandal after all?!

Or is this just wishful thinking because I fell down so hard and far?

Labeled an "alcoholic" and "criminal" permanently in ink is a recipe for suicide. Shame and self-pity are overwhelming. Prospects of rebuilding a life seem nonexistent. I know this all too well. And it almost killed me too. It took everything in me to find my way back to that refuge and home within.

My father spoke only Spanish until he was seven years old. But with a last name like "Davis," when it was time for him to begin school, officials assumed he was Anglo and assigned him to an all-white classroom. So there was little Wally, in all the glory of his dark brown skin, walking into a classroom, excited and proud to begin his education as Papa Leandro so distinctly wished for him. He sat down in his seat to begin class like all the other students. But there was a delay. A weird, awkward one. Soon enough, an authority figure entered, stood at the door, and announced before the class, "Wallace Davis? Yes, you," he said, pointing at my father, the only brown child in the room. "You're in the wrong classroom. Please come with me," he demanded.

Little Wally obliged and was escorted far down a hall and into another classroom. When he entered, he couldn't help but notice it was filled with only poor brown Spanish-speaking children like him.

What goes through a child's mind when their outside traits determine where they must be? Perhaps a message, "You are just a body," a finite thing, and "All that matters is the physical space your skin and bones take." A clear message: "Who gives a damn what you think, feel, and believe."

Do fear and anxiety consume their entire being? Maybe, if they are unclear about the actual boundary lines, as in "I better not step there, or maybe there, nor even let them see."

How can a kid freely play, explore, and learn in
such terrain?
 When did my father know in his gut some-
thing wasn't right? Did the words "unfair," "un-
equal," or "unjust" enter his mind as a child?

Yep, that was my daddy, my dear sons' grandfather. One
of millions of children throughout the nation segregated in
schools simply due to the color of their skin. Well, it took a bit,
a long bit that is, for the Constitution to reach California, let
alone the South. The Westminster School District ended up as
defendant in the groundbreaking *Mendez v. Westminster* case.
Five Mexican American families sued on behalf of thousands
of students who were forced to attend substandard segregated
schools within the district. Ultimately, the court ordered that
students of Mexican descent be allowed to attend schools pre-
viously reserved for white students.

After the Mendez case, Governor Earl Warren led the
call for full integration of California public schools. The
case was actually an important precursor to the desegrega-
tion of schools across the nation, including *Brown v. Board
of Education.* Thurgood Marshall authored an amicus curiae
brief in favor of integration on behalf of the NAACP, citing the
Mendez case, and later argued the merits before the Supreme
Court. Time was on equality's side too. The untimely death
of Chief Justice Vinson during the Court's recess resulted in
the ascendancy of Earl Warren to the position of Chief Justice,
who made the favorable ruling in *Brown* possible.

***

"Poverty is not living in a small house, but living in a small
world," my dad always said later in life. To him, one's world

could only be reduced by self. Another's impositions and limitations upon you can be debunked and smashed.

There were several teachers in little Wally's schools that believed this too. And they made all the difference in the world. Mr. Bailey at Hoover actually went to Wally's house and told Mama Candi and Papa Leandro how much Wally bonded with music and instruments. Mr. Winters, a counselor in junior high, gave Wally words of encouragement, telling him, "You can be anything you want to be."

It wasn't until my father was fourteen that officials finally moved all children into "mixed" classes in schools. And like Papa Leandro had hoped for, Wally's world "opened up" to a myriad of possibilities and dreams. He was now "with sons and daughters of doctors, lawyers, and business owners," so why couldn't he too be one someday? All the while, Papa Leandro's words stuck in Wally's mind: "Yes, there is work in the fields, but you, my son, are still going to school."

Junior high and high school began a whole new phase. Now thoughts lingered on fads like "peggers," flashy colored pants that narrowed at the bottom. His classmates had flattops and mohawks. Cars were always lowered so "the body was near the ground and Rock 'n' Roll could be played louder." Wally soon also gained an appetite for banana splits. Still, the building of "mini houses without plans" upset him, "mostly because it was taking up all the clear land" he still dove his hands into.

The sense that "home" was falling between his fingertips was magnified when Papa Leandro tragically passed away. The loss hit Wally very hard. He was just fifteen years old and a junior at Garden Grove High School. He hadn't yet shown Papa Leandro how big his dreams were and that he'd reach them. He hadn't yet become a grown man with enough financial means to someday support his grandmother, now all on her own and without a dime in her pocket.

He had no choice but to drop out of school to work and

support them both, he thought, but only for a split second. Instead, it became a self-described "turning point" in Wally's life. He went on autopilot and into overdrive. He found a job in a shoe factory, worked full-time at night, and managed to continue high school in the day.

To further support his family, he played music on the weekends and created his own dance orchestra called The Continentals. On top of that, he was first-string quarterback on the football team, first-string guard on the basketball team, and served as senior class president.

He also serendipitously became the school band's leader. It was "by accident," Wally said. I guess the band director, Mr. Gill, was also a volunteer firefighter. One day, near the end of a music concert at school, there was a fire alarm. So Mr. Gill handed Wally the baton, instructed him to take over the band, and left abruptly. Wally remained in the position from there on out. Later he said, "The other students were special to me because they all received good grades and were very hard workers."

Later in life, my father admitted in speeches he didn't know how he managed to do it all back then. He said he merely equated it to being "dream driven" and learning "not to waste time."

> *Hmm, dear Son, sound a bit like your mom?*
> *Well, it caught on to you too.*

***

Segregation and discrimination were blatantly obvious throughout the nation, state, and Southern California at this time. In Orange County, one merely had to open their actual eyes to see hate screaming. As a result, even though he was popular, my father held his best friends close, like Bob Garcia, Pete Perez, Robby Rose, and Bob Chandos, among others.

At the Gem Theatre, Wally had to sit in the last four rows because his skin was brown. The owners wouldn't let him sit anywhere else, even when the rows were empty elsewhere. In the Broadway Theatre, the "brown-skinned" had to sit upstairs. Black people weren't even allowed in. At the West Coast Theatre, "No Mexicans Allowed" signs were front and center. Brown- and Black-skinned people were banned from all swimming pools except one in Orange City Park, where they were only allowed on Wednesdays. Deeds of purchase had "No brown-skinned" inscribed on them. When Wally's uncle actually had finally earned and fronted the money to buy a home, the bank and sellers refused him.

Sometimes I wonder what messages this sent to my father and his friends. I mean, I can easily surmise what they might've been. "Hey, brown kid, you are not worthy of your very life," or something close. Sometimes I am in awe they ever dreamed at all. But more often, I'm simply grateful they had each other and a miracle road map.

When asked to share his story later in life, my father somehow found a way of describing the discrimination and segregation he experienced with candor and honesty while also singing the glories of American patriotism.

He pointed out the bad while feeling and feeding pride through the good.

He uncovered the truth in such a clever way that opponents could not respond.

"Don't misunderstand me," he'd say in speeches after sharing a brief example of discrimination he'd experienced. "I love America. It has the best system of government and freedom of opportunity in the world. I'd die for my country. As long as we have people involved, the flaws and imperfections can be mended. Remember that. And never forget, every little victory counts."

Thus, his favorite patriotic song was "America the Beautiful," not the national anthem. Why? Simply stated, the second verse is "America, America, God mend thine every flaw. Confirm thy soul in self-control, thy liberty in law."

He claimed and convinced others that pointing out flaws in America is patriotic. "Faults are like headlights. Those of others seem more glaring than ours. In the history of the USA, people who pointed out its flaws were called Communists and unpatriotic. It took great courage to stand up and say, 'There is a flaw in America and let's correct it.' The forefathers foresaw this and created freedom of speech.

"This is why I admire the League of United Latin American Citizens, as an organization. They have stood up for civil rights even when it wasn't fashionable. Individuals like this are true patriots of the American system. They will receive their true reward in their minds, conscience, and lives to come."

In 1969, while in the trenches of his work and community advocacy, Wally got a call from the *OC Register* asking him if he was a Communist. His reply? "No. Actually, I'm a Catholic, a U.S. veteran, and my ancestors lived here over one thousand years ago. Where did you come from?" To which the caller gave no answer.

***

Ironically, my father also experienced reverse racism from his own people. Carrying the last name Davis as a "brown-skinned" child and youth never ceased to result in being questioned about who and what he was, often shedding light on the frequency of stereotypes.

"Davis?" they'd ask him.

"Yes," he'd reply.

"Pero es Mexicano? Why did you change it?" As though the color of his skin invalidated his birth name. Still, not a big deal, and an understandable question. A simple explanation of the Davis name latching on to Indigenous blood seemed to do the trick. But when he was called names like the "Hidden Hispanic," well, that was a whole other matter. Still, my father would simply say, "I am who I am," roll it off his shoulders, and move on.

It's like he had this overflowing reserve of self-respect and preservation. He had honed a non-apologetic, straightforward individuality and thrived on it.

His notes:

To our students, we're here to give you hope and encouragement. Dream big . . . mentally, socially, financially. Don't let anyone steal it. Always remember, a dream without effort is a hallucination.

"There is no failure except in not trying. No defeat except from within. Don't be discouraged. Be positive. Everyone else is facing the same pressure. The real winners are not first. It is a process, a marathon.

"If you cheat, you cheat yourself. One day at a time and you'll be ok. Consult with successful people. Never stop learning. We don't receive wisdom. We must discover it for ourselves after a journey only we can take.

"You are our hope for the future. You are going to be helpers of God, to identify, remove the flaws in America, and make it even better. You don't have to do it publicly. The most notable acts aren't publicized or glorified. You

can do it by being a good citizen, a strong spir-
itual person, a good mother, father, relative, or
friend, by simply being a decent, honest human
being. Your goal ought not be to do better than
others, but to do better than ourselves, better
today than yesterday.

***

At his high school graduation in 1954, Wally was flooded with support and encouragement to continue onwards. Selected as the "Most Worthy Argonaut" and "Outstanding Music Student of the Year," he received the Elks Leadership Award and a scholarship from the Junior Red Cross. The Gemini Club, a Hispanic group, gave him a small scholarship that to Wally was "symbolically very big" community support, telling him, "Wally, you can do it."

At one point, he had to argue with some family members about whether or not to attend college. He "shut their mouths up by continuing to work and attend school," beginning his higher education at Long Beach City College, then transferring to California State Long Beach with a major in Political Science.

But there soon came a point in time when Wally was "tired and confused." Music? Law? Both? The law seemed like a "distant dream," and required three to four plus years while working. It didn't seem practically doable at the time.

So he joined the United States Army during the Korean conflict and served for two years as a special services band leader. Later he was recruited as a troop-information officer lecturing against Communism. He was able to pick up credit for half a year of college during his service, but it also gave him time to think about his future.

In my father's notes, I discovered that he "had a dream" one night. I never got to ask him about it, but somehow it solidified his conviction to become an attorney and in 1958, at the age of twenty-three, he was honorably discharged and returned to Mama Candi in La Colonia 17 and his studies at Cal State Long Beach.

Soon enough, reality kicked in and financial stressors were disabling. My father insisted that it wasn't going to stop him. He searched and searched for the "perfect" solution and discovered his alma mater high school had a position open for a full-time janitor. It didn't matter that he was once the school's academic and athletic star. *Screw pride. My dream's gotta win,* he thought.

There Wally was again, but this time a grown man, attending school during the day, working full-time at night, studying and playing in his band on the weekends, just like he did as a child.

At times he was exhausted, dismayed, and humiliated. After studying all day, night after night he cleaned the grime from the pool, picked up wet socks, and washed dirty gym floors. Students would make degrading comments to him, totally unaware of his prior honors as a student. One time, after he had just received his paycheck, he laid it down on the counter to wash cleaning chemicals off his hands. Eager to get back home to Mama Candi, give her the check, and eat, he forgot to pick it back up. When he returned, someone had taken it. He just fell to the floor and cried. "Two weeks of hard work down the drain," he wrote. It cut like a knife.

My father continued to drag himself through the halls class after class, just like he and Papa Leandro had in the fields. He held on to the little but big things that happened here and there, which convinced him to keep going.

Like when he was chosen by his university's student body to meet and introduce Hubert Humphrey. The tears that fell on the bathroom ground from a lost check were quickly re-placed with tears of joy and newfound hope. He sensed Papa Leandro was looking down on him from heaven every step of the way.

He just kept going, one foot in front of the other, day after day.

The one place he could escape and find comfort was in his music. His Latin jazz band The Continentals performed regularly at El Rancho Alegre dance hall in the center of La Colonia 17. Men who could dance were the machos of the night. Women who spun and swayed with grace, the beautiful ones. Everyone dressed up to a T with honor.

Here, nothing else mattered but the handwritten music sheets in front of him. Here, he could get lost in time and space using his breath and instrument. Here, his eyes would close in a rhythmic meditation. Here, he felt an abundance of love and respect, surrounded by neighbors.

Dear Son,

Music always was my father's best friend.

Remember recently you told me the music videos you made?

How you captured the essence of a song's rhythm in pictures of friends?

That is a piece of "Opi," your grandfather, in you.

Your knack for reading music with black-framed glasses like his.

Today, I hold his old records, tuning fork, and handwritten music gems. They are in safe boxes near his baby grand, my clarinet, and your violin.

I'll always remember watching his large hands and long fingers play.

My long, lanky, brown fingers, a blueprint of his.

I knew it was time to leave for church when Opi started to play piano.

I knew he'd had a drink if he started playing the saxophone.

Because of him, we gained an ear for music and perfect pitch.

There is so much about music that reminds me of him.

There is so much about his love of music that carries on through you.

Love, Mom

Late one evening, after a long, exhausting day of school and work, Wally paused just outside the front door, where Mama Candi was waiting. It was as though he heard a voice, maybe his, maybe Papa Leandro's, maybe one of his supportive teachers, maybe his best friend's.

He took a deep breath, straightened his shoulders, then closed his eyes. He did not ask the universe what was next. Rather, he asked the infinite if he could be front and center in order to improve the world.

Miles and miles away from La Colonia 17, the safe, loving migrant community surrounded by fields and filled with loving memories, stood UCLA Law School. It was far beyond the prior imposed boundary lines and back seat rows of segregation. *Tonight I will tell Mama Candi I am applying,* he thought. He surprised even himself.

A few days later, standing in front of the mailbox with his completed application in hand, Wally paused and prayed. He "made a deal with God," sealed the envelope, and dropped it in the mailbox.

Thankfully, God indeed was listening, and my father's dream came true.

> *How does a poor, orphaned child field laborer,*
> *shoe factory worker, and full-time janitor be-*
> *come one of the first "Mexicans" and Native*
> *Americans to ever be accepted into and grad-*
> *uate from UCLA Law School? My daddy did it!*
> *Yep, that is him.*

***

During the summer before his first year in law school, Wally and his bandmates had just finished a gig and decided to grab a bite at one of their regular spots in Garden Grove, Belisle's.

There she was, a stunning Marilyn Monroe look-alike, natural and carefree, with a class like no other woman he'd ever seen. Immediately upon placing his eyes on her, he announced to his bandmates, "I'm going to marry that woman."

> Two shall be born the whole wide world
>   apart . . .
> shall blend each wandering step to the
>   end,
> that one day out of darkness they shall
>   meet
> and read life's meaning in each other's
>   eyes.
> (Words on my father's gravestone.)

She was in her early twenties at the time, and all my beautiful mother had known prior was a life clear across the Atlantic Ocean in her homeland, Germany.

Irmgard Wally Herman was born in Frankfurt, Germany, on June 12, 1935, four years before WWII began, in the center of Hitler's all-consuming hatred. She had two older sisters, Inge and Eleonor.

Yes, her middle name is really "Wally." I know it's super-weird. But it was indeed given to her at birth. Even stranger, it's her mother's first name.

My grandmother, Oma, Wally Herman, was born the middle of three children on March 22, 1915, also in Frankfurt, Germany. Her father was a furniture maker prior to the ravages of the war, so they were able to live in a small house. According to my mom, that meant you were a "middle-class" family.

Oma was a strong, gregarious, outspoken, and playful woman. She and Tante Irene, my great-aunt, shared a unique sister camaraderie, often with the thrill of their own language in silly sayings, the cool kind that uses metaphor to describe a complex situation in seconds. I wish I knew more.

In German she'd say, "Wear your shirt inside out, then the witches can't get you," referring to evil or bad people out there. Geez, I should wear my shirt inside out more often. I remember Oma saying, "Ein gedanke, und zwei aschlocher," or "One thought, two assholes."

Opa, my grandfather Phillip Herman, was born and grew up in the same area. He was a charming, often quiet, and emotional man. A butcher by trade, Opa became a chef for a large outfit at the local train station. He liked to escape in his drink before, during, and after the war. I remember how his face would flush in various shades of red. Just like the Davis bloodline, alcoholic genes run wild on this side of the family.

Growing up in the center of a world war wasn't easy, or simple, for my mother, especially when she was a passenger on a freight train of hate she never decided to be on in the first place. She was only four years old when the war began, and just ten when it ended. Even so, the hardest battle for the family started inside their four walls.

My mother's sister Inge became very ill. Oma and Opa told everyone that she had heart problems, but in reality, they didn't want people to know she had tuberculosis. Oma invested much of her time and energy trying to save her daughter. But she passed away after a year or so of battle when she was just nine years old.

My mother was only six when her sister died. She remembers it like it was yesterday. In fact, my mom got sick immediately after Inge passed away and was in the hospital the day of her sister's funeral, eerily put in the exact same bed her sister had died in days before.

No one knew what was wrong with her. Oma and Opa thought they'd lose her too. Oma expressed how bad she felt, thinking she had neglected her other daughters while focusing on Inge. Sadly, Oma and Opa came to appreciate that little Irmgard's illness shifted their focus away from Inge's death.

But Opa never got over his daughter's death. My mom said he always cried and cried when he talked about it. Shortly after, heartbroken, Opa was notified he had to join the Nazi army. No man was allowed otherwise. So he lied about his eyesight to bypass battle and working in the camps. For a while there, he served as a chef for the services.

My mom saw very little of him for several years. The handful of times he was able to visit, he arrived with a suitcase of smuggled meat to give to their neighbors in hiding. He never said a word about it. He just did it and kept his mouth shut.

Toward the end of the war, Opa was taken out of the kitchen and sent to battle in Normandy, along with all the other men the Nazis could muster. My mother said he was never the same.

Oma took the risk of carrying a radio around. Listening to the airways was forbidden by the Nazis. The Americans streamed informational messages about what Hitler was up to next. She knew when bombs would soon hit, and they had to run down to the basement for shelter.

My mother and her sisters would scuttle down quickly and wait, sitting on their hands, until the rumbling and shaking stopped. As soon as it did, like clockwork, they'd run up the stairs and out to the street, searching for the biggest bomb scrap possible, a child's made-up war game. They'd compare their findings with neighboring little ones, surrounded in rubble.

Eventually, Irmgard and her sister Eleonor were taken, separated, and sent away to farmland along with all the other children. In shock, confused, and dismayed, my mother cried for weeks. She did her best to remain a little girl under the circumstances.

Thankfully, the sisters were eventually reunited and able to live together on the same host family's farm. During the day, they had to work in the fields. All the while, American planes would fly above and shoot at anything that moved. So they'd freeze and hide in fright as best they could until they passed. They gazed into each other's eyes and tried to smile amidst the world's screwed-up mess.

Little Irmgard found refuge from the strife in the barn house, caring for the pigs and cows, making their beds extra cozy. She eventually also gained a friend with the host family's daughter, Waltraut.

All the while, Oma was deeply sad, alone, and distraught back at home. She thought, *Well, if we're going to die, we might as well die together.*

So she literally hopped on a train and headed to the farms in the middle of bombings, eventually walking barn to barn in search of her children. Almost ready to give up and in tears, she finally found them. They embraced with both glee and fear but soon enough had to leave quickly. She grabbed their hands and ran back to the tracks. The trains were barely still going at that time and they got lucky when one came by and slowed enough to hop on.

British and American warplanes shot at the windows on the ride. Anything that moved was aimed at. Little Irmgard and her sister scampered quickly and lay down on the ground under the seats. They made it home safely, but my grandmother was reported to the Nazis. If the war had not been at its tail end, who knows what would've happened to her.

When the war ended, after several months, my mother eventually returned to "berus schule," or grade school. Two years passed quickly, and in addition to regular school in the day, she began trade school. She dreamed of becoming a fashion designer in France and selected certification as a seamstress.

So there she was, my beautiful mother when not quite a teenager, hopping on the streetcar a few times a week after school for a one-hour ride to sewing class. After a couple years, practical training began under the wing of a woman Oma had once worked for.

But being a seamstress isn't merely putting string in needles and punching holes in fabric. They were tested repeatedly, given sewing projects to complete to perfection, and books of trade lingo to memorize and understand. Her hard work paid off and Irmgard completed school and was certified when she was only fifteen.

Soon thereafter, my mother started her own business as a seamstress and ran it from the family apartment, paying taxes and keeping records. Eventually she was so good, Oma let her take over her own customers. A teenage girl with her own business, she had big dreams ahead.

When she was still a teenager, Irmgard and her sister went to a small dance event. A male musician six years her senior by

the name of Walter noticed my mom. Apparently, my father
Wally wasn't the first musician that pursued my mother.

They started dating and after four years were engaged. But
my mother said he was often absent and never did a thing to
make it real. She tried to break up with him several times, but
he wouldn't allow it. When he came back from a work trip, my
mother found some pictures of him and another woman. She
broke off the engagement immediately.

She had given Walter nine years of her life as a teenager
through young adulthood and was now twenty-four years
old. Opa said, "Why don't you go visit your sister in America?
She's homesick." Eleonor had married a GI and moved to
the States—Garden Grove, Orange County, California, to be
exact. My mom thought, *Ok, I'll just leave to get away from
him for now, then return in a month or so to pursue my dream
in fashion design school.*

When she said goodbye to her parents at the airport,
Walter stood there with them. As she started to walk away,
Walter said out loud, "I'll never see her again," knowing he had
lost her forever. For once, he actually was right.

***

When Irmgard first stepped foot on American soil, no one
would have suspected she couldn't speak English. Nor that she,
rather than my father, was actually the immigrant. She looked
like an "all-American girl" with her blond hair, blue eyes, and
healthy curves. Stereotypes are tricky.

A few weeks after she arrived, she sent Walter a goodbye
letter and returned the engagement ring. Over the next couple
of months, she sent multiple letters to Oma and Opa describing her days, expressing how much she missed them.

On the night she walked into the same restaurant my

father and his bandmates were in, her three-month stay was coming to an end. She was a tad anxious and distracted with her plans to return home. More importantly, she couldn't have cared less about the stranger across the room making lifelong plans in his head.

Wally's gaze was relentless. He couldn't keep his eyes off her. "That man keeps staring at me. He's crazy," she told her sister.

Wally tried to catch her eyes for more than a second, but she kept deflecting. Eventually, annoyed, she stood up and headed toward the restroom. Wally immediately did the same. He tried to catch her before she escaped but to no avail. Her sister noticed, pulled him aside, and gave Wally her phone number and address.

Bam! One little act would change the course of history.

Over the next few days, Wally left flowers and notes for Irmgard at the doorstep. Still, she wanted nothing to do with him. But he didn't stop, and her sister kept begging her to just talk to him. *Ok, then he'll go away,* she thought.

They went on a short outing to a local pizza joint. With her broken English, they awkwardly tried to communicate with the help of a dictionary in tow. They connected at the core.

Wally quickly convinced Irmgard to stay a little longer.

Within a week, she was the first woman he ever brought home and introduced to Mama Candi. Mama Candi was overjoyed and said something to Wally in Spanish.

"What did she say?" Irmgard asked.

"She told me if you ever hurt that girl, I will never forgive you."

Irmgard fell in love with both of them. She saw in Wally a man of values, respect, love for family, hard work ethic, and, let's face it, great looks and personality.

One week became a couple months and summer quickly ended.

Clear across the Atlantic Ocean, a letter arrived to Opa

and Oma with words from their daughter expressing how she had met "a really nice man, that he was Native American." She "wanted them to know and was concerned because he wasn't 'a white person.'" In response they simply wrote, "All we want is for you to be happy."

It is most certain my mother had no inkling she'd end up staying in the States the rest of her life and have seven children in a nine-year span with Wally.

Dear Son,

Every Christmas, the one touch we had with my mother's homeland Germany was through an annual Christmas box of goodies sent by Oma and Opa. German chocolate bars, butter cookies, gummy bears, Opa's favorite gum, and more. My mom somehow portioned it out equally between seven children over the course of months. We'd each get a little square of the pre-wedged bars after dinner. Thinking of the distance it had traveled and the care put into wrapping it, we knew the box was priceless. Pieces of home for my mother, pieces of joy for us.

Early last year, my mother said to me, "Nadia, I'm going to live till I'm one hundred years old. And we're going to do a lot more talking." She hopes to live to meet your children too, she said, if that is the path you so choose. How cool would that be? To have them pick her brain too? Whatever life brings, I'm so grateful you've had time with your sweet Oma. We need to do more of that soon.

Love, Mom

When it was time for Wally to begin law school in Los Angeles, Irmgard decided to stay with Mama Candi while he studied and did handyman work during the week. Every weekend he came back to La Colonia 17 to spend time with Irmgard, although it was minimal with his need to study and work as a musician.

They were married within a year on July 15, 1961, happy to drive off in Wally's Volkswagen for a road trip honeymoon with nothing but a friend's loaned gas card. Irmgard became my father's unwavering solace and stability while he pursued his dreams. He was one of the luckiest men on earth to have won her heart.

Eventually, they moved into a small apartment near UCLA, and she gave birth to the first of their seven children. Very low on money, they decided to manage apartments while she also worked part-time as a seamstress to make ends meet. Irmgard quickly became pregnant again. Wally began to think he would not be able to finish law school.

During this time, Wally's long-estranged father was living in Arizona with his second wife. A retired veteran, he'd fallen into a deep depression and alcoholism. Barely able to get himself up, he'd lost his will to live. His wife was bitter and left him alone. Upon hearing of his condition, in the height of academic and financial stress, my father flew out to visit him and found a distraught, neglected, dying man.

My father immediately flew him to California and made arrangements for his admission into Long Beach Memorial Hospital. He thought, *This way I can visit him and stay on top of his care at least.* But my grandfather lived for only a short time thereafter, having already failed at his attempt to smother his depression with alcohol. I just know in my gut there was an unspoken "I get you" connection between the two of them and that my father had compassion for him.

My father never said anything to me about his father.

Dear Son,

I didn't know I'd never get to ask my dad how he felt when his father died. Would it have prepared me more for his death?

Would I have spent more time visiting with him on study breaks?

Would I have asked more questions about the Davis name?

I'll try to explain how it felt.

How I'd handle it differently if I could go back.

I don't know if it will prepare you more for a parent's death.

But I think it may prevent regret, that stupid awful feeling we get.

Love, Mommy

Wally eventually received his Doctorate of Law in 1963 and passed the California State Bar Exam. He proudly and graciously called all his old teachers to thank them. My parents moved back to the Santa Ana area.

You can take the boy out of the barrio but not the barrio out of the boy, Wally thought. He was one of only a handful of Spanish-speaking attorneys in California.

He began his practice at the Law Office of James E. Walker, who had been in Santa Ana for over thirty years. Within a year, Wally was made full partner and the firm became "Walker & Davis." When Mr. Walker semi-retired in 1968, Wally became the managing partner, and Mr. Walker gave my father his entire law library, which I have today. Mr. Walker's mentorship was another guiding light on Wally's path to become a legacy in the practice of law.

***

At some point in his very early days practicing law, Wally heard that the majority of Hispanic children were again being placed in separate classes than their white peers. *Wait, what?* he thought. *But that was back then, how could that be now?*

So my father started investigating. Sadly, the reality of discrimination in schools was still very alive and kicking. Spanish-speaking children were being misdiagnosed by officials as "mentally retarded," a shame-based label and an excuse to segregate.

How? Aptitude was only being tested for in English. As a result, the true abilities and intelligence of these children were disregarded and ignored. Thousands upon thousands of Spanish-speaking brown children across the United States were being segregated in schools through "discriminatory ability grouping." Would you pass a test given to you in a language you do not understand? No.

My father didn't waste a minute nor blink an eye. He went on autopilot and fought for their rights. After months of research, further investigation, and gathering evidence, he filed a lawsuit against Santa Ana Unified School District, citing the *Mendez v. Westminster* case, the same case that had opened his world as a child.

And guess what? Little Wally, the orphaned field worker turned attorney, was victorious! If that's not progress, then I don't know what is. The landmark 1968 California State Supreme Court case changed the law in the entire state, finding that Santa Ana's then English-language-only achievement tests were inappropriate for Spanish-speaking students. The true level of intelligence of all children thereafter had to be measured with culturally neutral entrance exams. Following the lawsuit, New Mexico, Arizona, Texas, and others used his case as a model to make similar changes.

My father eventually became a law partner with Al Stokke, who would become his longtime best friend and my mentor. Together they built a large firm, adding many other partners and practices along the way. They shared innumerable friends throughout the county and state, but it was one-on-one conversations they treasured most.

I think Al Stokke probably knew my father best. I would have loved to have been a fly on the wall in their office. Today, Al is a highly respected defense attorney. Judges and prosecutors know that what he is offering is both fair for his client as well as in the best interests of the public. This helps when you are seeking even an ounce of justice. If I had anything close to a real uncle, it is Al Stokke.

Daddy,

Do you know Al advised me when I fought for the freedom of a kid?

Do you know I would've gone to you if I had had that chance instead?

Oh how wondrous that would've been, fighting for justice with you. But oh my dear Daddy, I fell down after you died, years later, so hard.

Was it you who sent Al to help me there behind bars? Were you shocked and ashamed that your little girl was so scared?

I am so sorry, Daddy, I am so ashamed indeed.

Please give me this chance to bring back honor to your legacy.

Please tell me you still love and believe deeply in me.

For the next thirty years, my father set legal precedents, transformed public education policy, and enabled positive change throughout Orange County and California. He gained extensive experience in the areas of land, environmental, business, contract, and real estate law. He tried multi-million-dollar lawsuits, conducted numerous legal seminars, and consulted on bank formations and business, including the Orange City and Santa Ana Banks. He formed the Orange County Hispanic Bar Association, Hispanic Chamber of Commerce, and County Democratic Party, even with some of his best friends being on the other side of the political aisle.

And his community efforts were tireless. From police abuse to voting rights, immigration, education, farm workers, and equal opportunity matters, he led it or was there. He organized Banco Del Pueblo, a grassroots institution in Santa Ana owned by over 1,300 local shareholders, and founded Los Padrinos y Las Marinas, whose objective was to increase the number of Latino students at UCI Medical School. He served on the boards of the Garden Grove Boys & Girls Club, Veterans Charitable Foundation, Legal Aid Society of Orange County, Santa Ana Bank, Orange City Bank and so many more. He was Chairman of the Mexican American Political Association and Urban Resources Center at University of California Irvine and a U.S. Delegate to the Third International Meeting of the US-Mexico Border Governors.

Little Wally from La Colonia 17 eventually got to meet and sit at the tables of U.S. presidents, governors, and leaders such as Cesar Chavez, all of whom consulted with him regularly.

***

I doubt my mom knew what she was signing up for when she married my father. In a matter of hours, our home would evolve into a place filled with leaders who cared about others' best interests and positive change in the world. A single "Sure, we can host" became multiple times after many years.

I wanted to be in the middle of it all, part of the change efforts, at a very young age. It opened up my world and expanded my dreams to save it. Little did I know that I would organize many large events later in life. From the delivery of rented chairs and tables, to the stage and speaker setup in the backyard, to my mom literally hand making every single appetizer, I loved observing it all and often tried to contribute in any little way I could. I'd help my mom spread cream cheese on thin slices of ham, put a green olive in the middle, roll it up and stick it with a toothpick, over and over again.

I remember one day Governor Jerry Brown arrived at our house with an entourage of security. I didn't understand what all the commotion was about, that is, until I saw Linda Ronstadt. I knew who she was even then despite my young age. She was of Mexican and German heritage like me. My father adored her album *Canciones de Mi Padre*, songs sung to her own father, crooned to her as a child.

***

My father's ancestors, the Acjachemen, are the Indigenous people of Southern California. They traditionally lived in what is now Long Beach, Orange, and Northern San Diego counties. Their name was changed by Spanish colonizers to Juaneño following their baptisms at Mission San Juan Capistrano in the late eighteenth century. As a people, they had no concept of land ownership. However, once the Spaniards attached a paper to any given area, the Indigenous people were robbed of and removed from the land. Many who had lived and thrived along the coast were forced inland to relatives living in the hills. Food became scarce and foreign disease reared its ugly head. Worse, during the Ranchero Period, more title papers were drafted. Proving "ownership" and a consistent existence on any one mass area of land thus became nearly impossible decades later during federal recognition efforts.

In the twentieth century, the Juaneño Band of Mission Indians, the Acjachemen Nation, was organized and recognized by the State of California. However, lack of federal recognition has prevented the Acjachemen from accessing, protecting, and restoring their ancestral lands and sacred sites. The great irony is that the Los Rios Historic District is considered the oldest continuously inhabited community in California. Some of my ancestors are buried at the mission's cemetery. Remember Lucy Rios, who raised my grandfather? She is a direct descendant.

My father had a lasting impact on his fellow Acjachemen descendants. He taught them their rights, how to work within the system, to be brave when faced with adversity and never give up.

Once, the tribal chairwoman, my third cousin Sonia, had to go to court to represent the Juaneños. Wally asked her how it went and she replied, "There were butterflies inside me the entire time."

"We all have butterflies in the beginning, but we just do it and move forward. We just don't give up," he replied.

Thankfully, during my first year of law school, my father was aware of my efforts to assist our people and research my Acjachemen heritage.

After his death, Sonia told me about a conversation she had with him shortly before he passed away. They apparently were talking about my future. She said, "He was so excited about working with you," and that he said something she'll never forget. "Nadia . . . she's the one, just wait and see, she's going to do great things."

Dear Son,

Oh, and by the way, my father was an "alco-holic." I didn't see any reason to mention it. Why? It doesn't reflect the good person he was nor his living spirit. The label sucks and is viewed derogatorily beyond fellowship circles.

Yes, the physical disease kills, like it did my grandfather. But the crappy label can too, like it did my great-grandfather. My forever hero father deserved to thrive in the blessing of anonymity. Shame is a bitch and often wins. In fact, it kicked my ass. Beyond my own self-imposed whippings, I let it win.

But you can bet, dear Son, I will never let that happen again.

Love, Mommy

CHAPTER 2

Dear Son,
you are not a body
nor the thoughts your mind makes.

I wasn't supposed to be born.

After all, the womb that carried me had done the same for six children prior. In fact, my mother had seven children in a nine-year span. By the time I was conceived, she not only had a raging kidney infection, her uterus was kaput and sitting on her bladder. Major medications were necessary yet a threat to her growing baby.

Mama Candi had wished her last grandchild would be blond and blue-eyed. I was anything but. When the nurse walked into the after-birthing room with a chubby, brown, dark-eyed, native-looking baby, after seeing my mother, she stopped in her tracks, looked down at me, looked back up at her, then turned around and walked straight out. My beautiful blond, blue-eyed mother began cussing at the lady in German and shouting, "My baby, my baby! Bring back my baby!"

I doubt that my mother ever thought her little baby girl would grow up to be a mother screaming those same words in despair.

My mother had to stay in the hospital for her infection when I was first sent home. She thought her medications caused a birthmark on the right side of my face. Silly stories we make. Or maybe it isn't. Who knows? It really doesn't matter.

My father later told me it was shaped like a heart and made me special. And I believed him. The more I'm in the sun, the heart mark comes out. I thought it meant to keep my head up and look toward the sky with pride.

Still, mean kids at school tried to convince me otherwise.

Today, I admittedly put mineral makeup over it to even out the skin tone. Yes, I am self-conscious about it. No one has ever told me it's cool. When someone stares at or asks me a question about it, bad memories that come are yucky too. I don't try to hide it from those closest to me. They see it regularly and as part of me like I do.

***

Having lots of detailed childhood memories is not a blessing of mine. My brain is strange. To be frank, it actually was ripped off.

I envy those who can easily spew off the "Do you remember when" stories, those they somehow stored as videos in their heads. It's proof they were alive back then, like a reference point. The more details they share, the more I am astonished. Don't get me wrong, I'm happy for them. It must be so cool to be able to remember a lot. It's just something I don't get to have or do much.

I either never had such memories, they were blocked out, or they were erased by head injuries. Thinking about it sometimes brings me down, or used to. I often felt like I was floating in time before, without a home base. And that what must've been a list of good ones got ripped from my brain. Now at least I know the cause is a combo of things.

The memories I do have fall into two different categories.

The first type are actually more like relived memories that I feel both emotionally and physically, as though I am there in a very specific room or place and position. To say there is a beginning and end would be inaccurate. It's more like a couple seconds repeat themselves. They are stuck in time. Sometimes, they return in an instant. I am right back there and don't realize it right away. It just happens.

This first type are so familiar to me, so organic to living this life, that they have basically shaped my perception of the world outside and within me. My mind is like a canvas of deeply engraved imprints. They taught me I am in constant danger, can trust no one, and am completely alone, unlovable, and abandoned. I learned to please and save others to cope with these feelings. As long as I was doing those things, my mind convinced me I was safe and worthy. This very quickly became lack of self-care and placing myself in harm's way. My memory bank was off and it took me years to crawl out of it.

The second set of memories are not organic to my brain. They were implanted in my head as though they were completely mine. A sibling or friend shares an experience that I apparently was a part of. Sometimes it initiates remembering my own parts, but more often than not, I just hop on their ride. I know you can relate, right?

Cool thing is that this library can be added to at any time if someone I trust sheds the light. I pray more and more are added by loved ones so my canvas can have great memories I think were always there. I also have boxes filled with old pictures and journals going way back. Like colorful, varied, unsorted puzzle pieces, they meant I finally was able to get a good picture of what happened back then.

As a child, my nickname was "Poobie." I apparently was a nice, chubby queen of an island floating in the sky with a song and "chair" made just for me.

My oldest brother, Mark, says it all came from a fourth-grade class assignment. Students were asked to create their own fictional country and to make up rules, customs, whatever. They had to put together a presentation of their country for the entire class. Mark's was "Poobieland."

He tells me it was a small island country located up on a cloud in the sky. I was the queen and "Poobies, Poochabies, and Poonabies" all lived there. "They did not get along," he said and "there was political tension." The "Poobies" were chubby and nice. The "Poonabies" were "the skinny ones and mean." He doesn't remember much about the "Poochabies."

Sitting on the "Poobie Chair" meant resting on top of someone's folded arms facing outward from their chest, legs bent and hanging over.

There was a big rock star on the island too. Mark doesn't remember what he named him. Sometimes I think he's just saying that to avoid admitting he actually named him Mark, who did become a rock star. *Just kidding, Brother.*

The rock star whose name he can't remember had a hit song called "Yeah Man Koolabandool" that likely was the country's national anthem. Mark even created a map of Poobieland by gluing a piece of paper to represent the land on top of a bed of cotton balls, or clouds. When presenting his "country" to class, Mark held up the map, took a deep breath, then proudly sang the song with his glorious voice.

> Yeah man koolabandool
> Oh-oh-ah-oh, it's not very nice for the
> Poobabawies.

Now, the Poobabawies have to be chubby
    and they have to have big eyes.
Just like me. I am a Poobie, I'm not in
    disguise.
Yeah man koolabandool
Oh-oh-ah-oh, it's not very nice for the
    Poobabawies.
    —Mark Davis

I'm still "Poobie" in my family's eyes. I hope so at least.

My siblings were the Brady Bunch before I was born. With three older brothers and three older sisters, I pretty much shattered that concept. But we were all very close in age, only a year to a year and a half apart.

There was always a lot going on in and around the house. Being "Poobie," you'd think I must've been in the middle of it all. That may very well be true before I was five. I just don't have my own memory of that in my head.

After about five, it felt more like a whirlwind was happening outside my solitude. Maybe because the oldest were teenagers and in the middle of puberty. Maybe because they were now in the real world and had more important problems. Maybe because my two oldest brothers bonded over music. Or because my three older sisters liked to share clothes.

Today I know it's because things happened to me that none of them could've known. And that those things caused little Nadia to feel separate inside. Perhaps things in their lives made them feel the same.

Every single one of my siblings are amazing and unique human beings. Together, they're an astonishingly beautiful plethora of personalities, shades, skills, and experiences too vast to share here. Anja ("Schatzie"), Mark, Luke, Marisa ("Peanie"), Sabrina ("Pudge"), and Erik ("Le Le").

I wish we knew each other more deeply, that we spent more time together, that we knew the truth in each other's story. Still, I truly believe we understand each other in a way that no one else could. Being one of seven children born in a nine-year span is, well, different. There's an undeniable, unspoken "I get it" kind of thing between us. And, well, each of us, like most people, has our own struggles.

On top of that, my parents took in my sister Anja's friend Monica temporarily after her parents kicked her out for dating a Black man. They also sponsored two Vietnamese refugees, Hoa and Thuy, who became more like sisters to us. We had three dogs, cats, rabbits, and who knows what else. To say it was an active environment is an understatement.

I didn't realize how lucky I was to grow up this way until I discovered very few do. I thought everyone had the blessing of multiple cultural influences under their roof. While this most definitely brewed a naive belief that all people are colorblind, it also made me colorblind without consciously knowing or trying.

I'm grateful to have some memories of my own from Christmas as a child. We'd celebrate on Christmas Eve with German pot roast, potato dumplings, and red cabbage alongside homemade tamales and egg rolls. Opening gifts always came after dinner, never in the morning. The a.m. treat was waking up to my father's chorizo and eggs, tortillas warmed up on Mama Candi's platter, and fresh pan dulce.

I miss those times so very much.

My Cabbage Patch doll and Barbie named "Natalia" were my angels. They both had pretty brown skin, dark eyes, and brown hair, my selections because somewhere inside, I must've thought they looked more like me. I don't remember thinking that inside then. It just happened that way automatically.

ET was my hero. John Travolta, my crush. Penny, stamp, and sticker collections, my hobbies. My siblings say we always

played with Little People, and I'm sure that's true. I don't remember much of it. Today, I most definitely am in heaven, re-
living with my little ones whatever I did back then.

By the time I was born, my father was doing better financially. We moved from an apartment to a fixer-upper home in
Fountain Valley. It was within walking distance to my older
siblings' school. I wasn't old enough to attend yet. They say my
playmates back then were twin boys, Roy and Swy.

Just before I started kindergarten, we moved again into the
suburbs of Orange County, right on the border of Orange and
Villa Park. All I can remember is that the ambiance and energy in the house changed. It seems interactions and playtime
with my siblings dwindled considerably. The older siblings
were teens after all.

I remember Anja as outgoing and popular. She seemed so
much older and more grown up than me. I thought she was
cool and had it all together. I'd observe from afar when she was
around, which didn't seem like much. But she was fourteen,
after all, and I was five, so maybe she was. We had two very
different worlds. I liked to peek at her shaving cream, razors,
and makeup. She had lots of friends and liked to have fun. Anja
is now married to Paul. They have four amazing sons.

Music was a big part of my childhood. Not only did my
father play the saxophone, clarinet, and piano, my two oldest
brothers were musicians and had a band called Clockwork.
They practiced regularly at our house inside the garage. The
hustle and bustle of the setup, instruments, and sounds often
surrounded me.

There was always music playing on the stereo too. I gravi-
tated to it, sat on the sidelines, and observed in awe. My father
and brothers have no idea how very much their written music,
favorite music, and library of tapes and CDs impacted me. The
songwriters and bands they liked are still my favorites—from
my father, Eydie Gormé, all the classics, oldies but goodies,

soul, rhythm and blues, and lots of jazz, mainly Latin. From my brothers, most of all U2, but also Bob Dylan, the Beatles, and more. Some of the modern bands had just come out with their first albums, and I got to watch them soar over the next several decades.

Mark is a gentle, kind soul and super-talented musician and songwriter and has been for years. He has written hundreds of amazing songs, each carrying his stunning voice and lyrics. He escaped in music both in and outside his room. I remember so clearly the day John Lennon was shot and killed. Watching basketball with my dad, the game was interrupted with the news flash. I could only think of my dear brother Mark and ran as fast as I could to his room. "John Lennon was shot! John Lennon was shot!" I yelled, startling him. He threw down his guitar in shock. He taught me how to play "Imagine" on my father's piano and I'll never forget that. The words of the song so pointedly represented my naive hopes for the world at the time. It is why I play the song often for my children and why I play it whenever I see a piano. Today Mark lives abroad, making music with his love, Karolina.

Luke is a calm and compassionate being and super-talented artist, instructor of art, and drummer. Some of my siblings say he was mean and made fun of them, but I only remember kindness. He not only has a great sarcastic sense of humor, he is patient, with a set of unique artistic talents. He got a scholarship to the Art Center in Pasadena and some of his three-dimensional pieces were not only acknowledged but many reflected my father's story with indirect messages about his life. Luke has an incredible daughter, Sadie. He is now a professor of art at various colleges.

Marisa always was and still is a funky, cool, very organized and hardworking chick. Maybe it's a middle child thing or something, she always seemed to do her own thing with an independent flair of confidence. She also has a knack for style. She loved beads and thrift store clothing and drove a Karmann Ghia. She met her husband in high school and they had two children, Sabina and Jake. She is very protective of her home and life. I had to follow her lead later in life to protect my heart. Her daughter Sabina is one of the kindest humans I know and a very talented artist and studies animal behavior. Jake, a genius.

Sabrina is a selfless, loving friend and super-talented writer who tutors children. When I was younger, I thought she looked like Katharine Hepburn. Shortest of the girls and on the shyer side, she appears delicate but is a warrior in her own right. We shared a room and thus interacted more until I left for college. She has an amazing daughter, Miquela, who is now a talented artist and teacher. We once all lived together. I drove Miquela to school, stopping by Dee's Donuts on the way. I credit Miquela for saving my life. She would not let me go anywhere unless I had my seat belt buckled.

My dear brother Erik. He is a gentle genius. I mean, a genius of geniuses, a quirky nerd with mounds of books and degrees. You could always tell he was thinking. He has a great sense of humor and is forever a faithful friend. He doesn't know this, but he is one of my lifetime heroes.

I adored watching how affectionate my parents were with each other. I know it's rare to see. "Mein schatz," my mom would say, rubbing my father's neck as he swayed his head back and forth.

My parents also gave us a strong example of giving back to the community. Their selflessness and humility shaped the person I am today. I can only hope to teach my children the same.

They sponsored and housed immigrant refugees, raised funds for a young burn victim named Tomas, and took us on annual trips to disperse toys donated from our church to a Mexican orphanage.

On one of the trips, my mom said I took off my shoes and handed them to a little girl who had none. Busy mingling with the orphans, I was apparently scooted away along with them, blending into the beautiful brown batch, shoeless myself. My family unknowingly took off in the motorhome without me. Minutes later, my mother noticed I was missing. Of course they went back for me.

But from there on out, my siblings joked with me that I was adopted. I admit, I kind of believed it. It helped me understand why I thought I looked different from them, although it wasn't quite true. More profound, it planted in me a desire to save all the brown kids in the world.

From an early age, I dedicated my life to helping others. Honestly, I have never been any other way. It's automatic and engrained. Whether it was taught or in my veins, it is me.

While my father worked tirelessly outside the house, my mom did the same tenfold inside it. I honestly don't know how she did it. She kept everything immaculately clean and organized, functioning like a machine. I think she found comfort and a sense of control among the chaos this way. I don't remember ever seeing her take a break before I was ten. And when she did, it was only to sit down and have a cup of her German coffee for a few minutes. Oh how I loved the smell, that smell of German coffee filling up the house in the afternoon! This is my own ritual today.

I loved going with my mom to Gemco and helping her keep a tally of the cost of groceries. I'd push the cart up and down the aisles as she carefully loaded item by item, counting. It was imperative to keep costs limited to two hundred dollars for a family of nine and she managed to do it.

On top of it, my mom heroically and miraculously coordinated the sponsoring of thirty-two Vietnamese refugee families following their treacherous migration across seas to safety here in the States.

Growing up, she showed me love through her actions. I could trust she was always there physically, always. Her discipline in creating an orderly house even gave me some needed sense of security, knowing what to expect next. I always knew there would be food on the table and clean clothes to wear the next day.

***

I don't remember one-on-one interactions with my parents as a young child. There is no recollection of ever sitting down on the ground and playing with them. I am sad that I can't remember them ever looking me in the eyes and giving me an "I see you. What's going on in there?" look. I just don't remember conversations of that sort ever happening.

Perhaps for some people, it doesn't matter to realize or acknowledge this. But for me, it did. It made all the difference in the world. It took my whole life to acknowledge and realize how this shaped me, my ability to create healthy connections, and my response to things.

And I do not blame them. It either wasn't possible, they weren't capable, or they didn't know any better from their own childhood experiences. How could they?

When bad things started to happen, I had no healthy attachment system in place to serve as a buffer. Our survival depends on the ability to be with and feel close to others. If that's in place, positive feelings about ourselves and the world around us flourish. Emotional resilience is built. Our innate instinctive defenses keep us safe when bad things happen. They don't overreact. On the other hand, when there is a lack of healthy attachment, there is no buffer between bad things that happen and our reaction to them. Without an ability to feel close to others, a belief there is no one to turn to and negative feelings about ourselves arise. There is little if any emotional resilience and our instinctive survival defenses overreact.

It was as though a blueprint was set deep into my entire identity and understanding of life. My sense of well-being, self-worth, and safety were based on it. Any instinctive defenses I had overreacted and became a habitual life pattern. Worse, as time passed, little Nadia was convinced she was just a "dirty little brown girl."

***

Dr. K. was his name. I was barely five years old, I think. My mother would take me to the office, but there was a point when she no longer stayed in the exam room with me. It wasn't until much later that I found out why.

For my entire life I had no detailed memories. Just a "scene" enters my head, a feeling in my gut, and a spacing-out phase. Then I am there.

> *I am looking at little me, lying down on an exam table. Frozen and thoughtless, by that point it's clockwork. I am not her, and she is not me. We are separate from that body, that being she must be.*
>
> *Everything outside those four walls is non-existent, a black hole.*
>
> *He walks in with a sick grin, and balding head.*
>
> *The gross shape of his mouth and thin lips I hate.*
>
> *I want to run, but I can't move a thing.*
> *"Live outside you," I scream at me.*
> *"Look down at her, don't be me."*

His eyes scream, "You're just a body. You dirty little girl."

His disgusting way inside me makes my tummy whirl.

I freeze yet want to fly. I cannot speak yet want to fight.

"Did I do something bad and must pay a price?"

Why does my entire existence end up here in a heartbeat? Present time falls through my fingertips and I can never get it back. I never understood why or how it happened. I never even asked myself. It just was and is. I never knew it wasn't normal. All I knew was that is how you live.

Innocence can't make sense of disgusting games, or evil ways. The mind claimed victory early over the once unmarked being full of dreams.

"The Brownies" is a story written by Juliana Horatia Ewing in 1870. In the story two children, Tommy and Betty, learn that children can be helpful, or Brownies, instead of being lazy "boggarts." It is the inspiration behind the Girl Scout program called the "Brownies."

In second grade, I became a proud member. There was an official Brownie uniform that consisted of a brown vest or sash that could be worn with a white shirt and khaki bottoms.

One day, I forgot to wear my uniform to school. My classmates said it was ok because "You're already a brownie. You don't need a uniform." *Oh, ok,* I thought. It didn't sink in, the reality of their intentions. I mean, there were a few other brown kids in my school, so ok. I chuckled along and moved on, like any little girl would, or try to.

But soon it became, "Hey Brownie, wash your face, it's dirty." *Huh? What do they mean? Oh yeah, that birthmark thing.*

Looking back, I wish I'd said, "It's called melanin, you dumb bitch. The sun brings it out when you sell cookies like a true 'Brownie.' Have you done that yet today? Probably not, I'm sure, not like I did. Why don't you take a closer look at the heart on my face? It's my own Brownie badge for me that you'll never get."

But instead, something shifted deeply inside me after that day. I hadn't really paid much attention to the birthmark on my face. I took a better look, then scratched and pulled. *What is that anyways? I know Daddy said something. But why do I have to be marked and branded?*

While my self-consciousness and fears grew, I tried to convince myself I didn't care what they said, that I liked who I was, and loved my brown skin. Then I skipped back to school and put a smile on my face but was only met with a much crueler thing.

A group of them walked up to me as I sat at the lunch table. They grabbed my lunch bag, dumped it out, then put something inside it. When they threw it back to me, I stumbled trying to catch it and a folded piece of paper fell out.

It was a handwritten letter. A big black sheep sticker was smack in the middle. In rainbow shaped lines above the sticker, they had written, "Baa Baa Black Sheep. We don't want you hanging around us anymore." Every single kid in my classroom had signed it.

Somehow, their cruel messages connected in my head to what that doctor did. *Nadia, baa baa black sheep, you dirty little brown girl, go home and hide,* my mind said. *No one likes you. You're damaged goods. But you'll get used to it like that.*

I hid in the closet for the next few days by pretending to leave for school out the front door, then sneaking back in through the garage. I had never done anything like that before. So I felt even worse inside. *See, they're right. You dirty little brown girl,* my mind went, over and over.

And the closet, oh that closet.

Being there is one of a few strong memories I have as a child. It's more of a general feeling kind of memory. But again, like the doctor's office, throughout my life, I am there in a heartbeat.

I am in her little body, sitting on the floor in the closet. The wheeled doors are on my left, wall is on my right, laundry room on the other side.

I bury my head in my arms and wrap them around my knees. It feels safer to be alone and not say a thing. "I don't know what to do with this inside me. What is it? What do I call it? Disgust at them, him? Or me?"

The feelings are fleeting yet scatter all around.

It's so very hard to decipher where and what the truth is.

The fear and aloneness are so potent, my foundation for living in this world.

She can hear the sounds outside and a lot is going on.

But no one knows what, where, or who she really is.

"Do they see me? Can they hear me? No, it's better to just hide."

"What would I say? I can't explain it. So I'll just keep it all inside."

"I don't think, feel, or speak up anymore. This is just how it is."

"It must be the truth, it must be you."

"Because I don't know anything else."

It's just a place I am at in my body or see myself at times.

Sometimes it's not me, it's little Nadia I look upon.

Sometimes the opposite, she looks at me from outside.

It's not by choice. I don't like it.

The hole inside my heart begs to be filled.

With what? I don't know where, who to turn to, or what to say.

Here it is at least familiar. I know what to expect.

I'm in control and will stay alone, all by myself this way.

Several days later, my sister found lunch bags on the closet floor. The letter was crumbled inside one of them with tear marks. I guess she showed it to my mother. We didn't talk about it. But soon we were standing in the school's office.

There she was, a five-foot-two, blond-haired, blue-eyed, German-accented woman holding the hand of her seven-year-old little brown girl and demanding to speak to the principal. She cussed them all out in German until someone started listening. "Verdammt (damn) scheissekopf (shithead)."

I'll never forget it. I had never seen anything come out of her like that before. *Who is this woman?* I thought.

The principal sat us down in his office, looked over the letter, gazed up at me, then looked at my mother, and asked, "This is your daughter?" Just as they had the day I was born.

"Yes, of course," she replied.

A stunned look on his face. He picked up the phone and began calling students individually over the intercom into his office. "Did you sign this?" he asked.

Most hesitated or made excuses until eventually, they muttered, "Um, yeah."

"Apologize," he ordered. And they did, one by one.

This was Orange County in 1978.

***

For some, being of mixed race can be confusing. Not me. I am a brown girl and have always identified as Native American and southwestern Mexican. Just like my father, people often ask me, "Why is your last name Davis?" I'm pretty sure this rarely happens to my brothers and sisters. Maybe it's because my skin is darker. Maybe it's the birthmark on my face. Maybe it's the fact I simply emanate more "ethnic" energy because the brown color of my skin was pointed out to me repeatedly as a child. Because it was engrained in my identity.

Perhaps none of the racial bullying crap would've changed a thing. Before I ever entered school, I simply automatically saw myself as brown. Who knows?

But it's an interesting thing to think about, that being of mixed race creates varying internally organic and outside influenced racial identifications. It's a reason being forced to check a particular race box on forms is all screwed up. No attempted accounting of racial percentages will ever be accurate.

And it doesn't bother me if full-blooded Hispanics, Latinos, or Mexican Americans deem me a "güera," or white woman. On the other hand, I do care if someone assumes I am Anglo. I don't always speak perfect Spanish, but "I am who I am," just like my father said.

***

Without a doubt, the bad doctor and racial bullying experiences created and intensified my calling to save the world. Before I was ten, reading about civil and human rights violations and efforts to stop them was an addiction. I scoured through my father's books and brothers' music magazines if bands like U2 were on the cover. Bono, Martin Luther King Jr., and Cesar Chavez influenced me a lot and were among my heroes.

I had to do something to distract my head and hurt, I had to support their causes. So I made flyers for babysitting services and passed them out door-to-door throughout the neighborhood. Sure enough, I landed two jobs within walking distance of our house. It was so lucrative, even my brothers and sisters started asking to borrow cash. Instead, I sent $200 to Live Aid for the starving children in Ethiopia and another $80 to Amnesty International for efforts to end apartheid.

When I received a T-shirt in return with the shape of Africa filled with a rainbow inside, I wore it like a badge of honor from the Brownie squad. I remember walking into my elementary school classroom with pride, thinking, *See, your hate can't stop me!*

Then the tomboy phase came. Yep, me, Nadia, the one they later called "Barbie." I chopped my hair off into a barely there pixie and only wore red corduroy pants. I have no idea why. But I remember the lead bully suddenly let me walk by her side.

My siblings called me "Eddie." We'd go out as a family to dinner and the waitress would say, "What would you like, son?" I liked it. It made me feel good. *Heck, maybe that'll help me in life,* I thought.

I was on a softball team called the Pickles, even though I was a klutz. Sometimes lousy, sometimes ok, I got darker and darker with every practice and game.

Strangely lanky and long, I just didn't have a bump or curve in sight. All the girls' bodies seemed to be changing but mine. I most definitely was the last to get a bra and menstruate. My mom and sisters never said a thing about either to me. But I would sneak and read the inserts in their boxes of pads.

I thought I was kind of pretty, but just "ok." It seemed the boys weren't interested in me at all. I was never asked to dance, ever, and it was rather embarrassing to be one of three standing alone on the side while everyone else swayed a foot away from each other to "Take My Breath Away." I thought, *I'm flat and brown. What did I expect would happen?*

During the summer and weekends, my brother Erik and I spent a lot of time together. It's not like we talked a lot. We just did a lot. Most of my memories with a sibling are with him. That bond would save both of our lives decades later.

When we swam, he'd shape his body into a ball and ask me to push him down so he could float back up by himself. I thought a few times it was a little strange. But it seemed to bring him comfort.

He'd sit on the computer for hours while I just sat on the floor, working on my projects. I liked doing weird things like pretending I was a dentist and giving him a "deep cleaning" because I was worried he'd lose his teeth from not brushing them.

We built a lemonade stand with parts of metal shelves from the garage. He put plastic wheels on it so when we tipped it over to lay it down, we could roll it to the corner with all our supplies inside. I laugh thinking about what it must have looked and sounded like. We made good money too. One time, a heck of a lot of money as truckers came back for seconds. We later discovered the homemade lemonade had fermented overnight.

***

Around this same time in life, when I was about ten, there was a flasher in the neighborhood. I didn't know and was alone at the lemonade stand one day. My brother had just left with my mom temporarily to get us lunch.

Within a minute after they took off, a Porsche pulled up.

I walked up to the window and leaned down, asking, "What would you like?" Bam! Right there in front of me was a large erect penis. His left hand stroking it, his right hand reaching out to me, he smiled and said, "You like it?"

I ran and hid behind the lemonade stand as best I could. Shaking, in my head, a flurry of pictures from the doctor's office. The entire world became a tiny bubble and no one else seemed to exist. Then he spoke, "Come on, come here," in a friendly, no big deal kind of tone. I didn't move. And then I heard it all.

Moaning, "Oh yeah, oh yeah, come here, baby," again and again, until I heard him in a last "ahhhh" ejaculating. I just sat there for what seemed like forever until he drove away. I couldn't figure out why he looked strangely familiar. I stayed down until my brother and mother returned. I felt five years old again. I didn't say anything. I still didn't know how.

I had my regular babysitting gig for a female tennis teacher who taught lessons in her backyard. One day, that same man came walking into the house for a lesson, acting like any other normal suburban Porsche-driving jackass. Ego driven and above the law, with his tennis racket in hand. At the same moment I saw his face, he saw my eyes. My face went white. His smirk terrified me.

I ran to the back of the house with the youngest child, Dusty, still sitting in the high chair. Cynthia eventually called me, saying, "It's time, Nadia," but I didn't respond.

All I could think of is, *Oh, great. Thanks, now he knows my name.*

She eventually found me seated in the kids' room. "What the heck is going on?" I mean, what the heck could I say? *Uh, lady, I was selling lemonade and, well, that man thought he could pay with his penis.* Instead, I mumbled something about him and the lemonade stand.

She must've remembered the news going around about

a flasher in town. The police arrived at the house while she was distracting him in conversation. One of the officers came back and talked to me. He was arrested. It was in the paper. It turned out he was the infamous town flasher. I just saw his dick close up in my face.

That same year, I went to a birthday party sleepover at my friend's house. The main bully girl was there and for some reason, I thought she was my friend. I guess this was a sign of my future to come. When we were lying in our sleeping bags, she whispered into my ear that she wanted to know if I had any pubic hair yet.

She didn't really give me a choice, shoved her hand down my pajama pants, and began doing things down there. I was a little shocked at first, but I had been trained before, so just froze. If I made a fuss, I'd have to start all over to get on her good side.

Don't move. Don't say a thing. Pretend this feels ok now, maybe it actually does. Oh no, you dirty little girl, my mind rang. But the house seemed less scary than the doctor's office, and she was my age, not forty years older. It was "ok," because it didn't cause me to feel nauseous.

Reality is, before I was eleven years old, I suppressed feelings of discomfort and violation in order to get through life, which instead created unhealthy levels of tolerance and survival responses. Decades later, in trauma therapy, I learned that these responses manifested themselves in specific behaviors or "parts" of me.

Dear Son,

I don't want to make you feel uncomfortable, so I will try to explain this like I wish someone had explained to me back then. The "sexual bullies" did things that exposed me to sexuality too early in life. One, big people should never touch young people in that way. Never. Ever. Whatsoever. Two, no one has a right to touch you without your permission, period, period. Three, you likely will discover you can touch yourself and it feels good. It's normal. But when a child does this alone when sad, scared, and confused, something bad likely happened and it is eating them up inside. I'm so sorry that I share here that I ended up doing this sometimes when I was young. It was worth being vulnerable and opening up about this, if it helps another person who may have gone through the same thing. I also hope it gives you a safe place in me to talk about such things.

Love, Mommy

***

My father's drinking apparently became a problem around this time. Strange as this is, I have no recollection of ever seeing my father drunk to the point of hostility or even stumbling. But most of my siblings say they did indeed. I was either lucky, absent, it never happened to me, or I blocked it out entirely. I don't know which. Maybe it's all of these. It doesn't matter. I believe them.

My recollection of this time was that my father became more absent, or completely absent. I rarely saw him anymore and just longed for my daddy. I missed our family dinners and him saying good night.

Sometimes I'd wait until I heard him come home, often

hoping he'd come in to say hello. But he always immediately went to the bathroom to brush his teeth. I could hear him gag when trying to get the smell of alcohol off his tongue. I didn't care. I just wanted a hug. It never came.

With all the financial stress of supporting several kids in college, owning a suburban home, working for his community causes, and running a law firm, there is no doubt he was under extreme stress. I think he was depressed too and felt unappreciated and misunderstood at home.

What a strange thing to have to accept. Overcoming so much and being in such privilege yet feeling so empty inside. Was it too much to ask for an hour of family church time together? No. Still, none of that means anything when your body craves alcohol for release from pain. "They'll never know how lucky they are, how easy they have it, what it's like to really struggle," he often said to my mom.

My father tried to drink away his depression, anxiety, and strife. He likely drank at work, after work at a reception or event, and then maybe more when he came home. I never understood everyone's criticism. This may or may not be healthy. I just always believed he deserved a break.

I liked to watch his routine. I enjoyed it when his eyes filled with joy taking that sip, carrying it to the piano, then playing a tune. A little gift to himself, a small thing. *Why can't he have it? It's not asking too much. What the hell is wrong with everyone? Get off his back,* I thought.

Trust me, today I know that it was never one drink. And I believe the others that too many led to bad times for them. Right before my eyes was the epitome of a "functioning" alcoholic, yet proof that if you drink because you are sad, it won't change a thing. In fact, it likely will create pain for those around you.

Daddy,

I get it. I do. I am like you. I do not know when my disease took hold. Do you? It just happens and we do not know. I did not drink much before you died. But when you did, I had to hide. The world was dark and gloomy outside. So I drank to drown the pain, just like you did. I drank to feel closer to you without understanding the disease. Oh how I wish you were still here. No words would be needed. As a fellow sufferer, you'd just get it, you see.
    Love, Nadia

It seemed that whenever my mom smelled alcohol on him after he came home in the evening, an argument ensued, although I didn't know this at the time. During the day, she would cry alone on the lawn chair in the backyard. I'd just watch her from afar, not understanding why. I wanted to go and comfort her. But I didn't know how.

Who taught her where to go when she was in pain?

How would I have learned what to do with the same?

Who taught her to remember our infinite home within?

How could I have learned how to do the same?

Dear Son,

I never wanted to burden you with my feelings and pain. But I know I did from afar and it wasn't fair. Keeping my mouth completely shut may have had that direct effect. I now know

*that being an authentic parent means I need to
share a little bit. Then to show you my solution
for not letting it control my life and head. I wish
I could've said then what I know now, dear Son.*

*"I am lonely and afraid, but it's ok to feel
this. There is no need to worry because our
home is within us. It is infinite love and light.
It is the truth of what we are. We are never
alone, and fears don't exist. Our mind merely
tries to separate and lead us into darkness. So
after I will share my feelings with another, I'll
remind myself of the truth held in that home
within me."*

*I know I will screw up and unload on you
without intent. I know that projecting is such
an easy habit to resume.*

*Please know that I'm trying to lighten the
burden placed on you.*

Love, Mommy

At some point, my mother abruptly left for Germany with
my two oldest sisters. It was rather shocking to be honest. I
don't remember being told anything about it, like a plan for
meals, laundry, and house care. I don't remember even talking
about it with my other siblings. All I remember is the feeling
in my gut the moment I walked in the door after school. My
mother strangely wasn't there. She always was. But this time,
she wasn't, and I had no clue why.

*Did they leave me? What is happening? Why was I left here
alone?* were the questions that I felt in my heart, whether they
were accurate or not.

Scenes with my father during those weeks will forever be

marked in my head. I experienced the sadness and loneliness inside him, alongside him. He'd sit on the floor with his back to the couch and a drink in hand. He'd turn on the television, gaze at it, but not really watch anything. I'd sometimes see his eyes well up, even if he tried to hide it. He knew that I saw, and I often brought a tissue.

I just sat there with him and felt his pain. And it helped me connect to mine. It was the most real thing I'd seen in the house for a very long time.

Hallelujah, I thought, someone actually is human.

The drink helped him through. He didn't know I'd later do the same. I have no idea if he ever tried to lessen the amount or stop entirely before then. My mother says he apparently reduced it significantly and eventually stopped. Cold turkey.

I was never angry at my father for his drinking. I admit, when anger arises, it is at others, not him. Where was the sympathy? When did he get a break? And why are we allowed to screw up and not him? Didn't they realize he had a screwed-up humiliating disease called alcoholism? *Would you have been more kind if he had had cancer and chemo caused irritability? Probably.*

But he's gone now, brothers and sisters.

And you can't redo the show.

***

Sometime between elementary and middle school, I honed the skill of shutting out uncomfortable feelings and bad memories again with high goals, roles, and lists of projects to save the world. It is not a bad thing. No, not at all. It works like magic and creates some happiness inside.

Helping others was and is my refuge, and salvation. Being a world warrior was so much better than seeing myself as a victim. That concept never once entered my mind. I felt blessed beyond blessed, and there was so much to do. Yes, I got sad. Yes, I got mad. Yes, I felt alone and so often abandoned.

But I always set my eyes on the good outweighing the bad. The darkness in the room was weaker than the light. I still didn't know that home within me. But I saw sparkles of love and hope in efforts outside me.

It worked this way over the next few years.

Soon enough, I appeared to be an independent, curious, outgoing, active, and fun girl throughout middle school. I even had real friendships with some very nice girls. They called me "Goofy" and honestly, it fit me to a "T." The others were Mickey, Minnie, and Donald, our little group of Disney.

I sometimes broke out in uncontrollable laughter for no reason in class, which caused the other students to do the same. The teacher would get pissed off and send me to the front office. A "Needs Improvement" or "Unacceptable" citizenship mark arrived thereafter. Still, I always got good grades and was successful in student government.

My tomboy ways led me to believe I could actually play sports despite my klutziness. Basketball, softball, track, flag football, volleyball, swimming—you name it, I did it. But I was never all that good.

They even called me "ET fingers" on the football team because my hands were so "alien" looking. I automatically, without thinking, used my hands expressively when speaking. Later in life, in an effort to fire me up, my staff even waved their hands side to side just before I approached the podium or a crowd to speak.

By the time I entered high school, I had mastered living life outside of myself. It worked so well, bad memories, fears, and low self-worth got buried deep down. As long as I could keep up, everything was ok in life.

***

Shortly after entering high school, my family split over religious differences and my best friend developed a serious eating disorder that became life threatening and she was sent away. There was a sudden massive void. No to-do list, goofy smile, or project helped.

We grew up Catholic. My parents took us to church on Sundays. Personally, I appreciate that they did this for a couple of reasons. While my spirituality today is not based on a religion, going to church taught me that there is something beyond me, period. It nurtured a curiosity to find out more. Most of all, it placed value on the need to have a sacred space and time to connect with "It," no matter where I am.

Anja and Marisa rebelled against Catholicism. I don't blame them. They converted to a non-denominational Christian church, one without sacraments, confessionals, and priests in between you and God.

My father was deeply hurt and angry, mainly because he took it personally. As a child, he went to mass regularly with Mama Candi to pray. Their God had rituals, traditions, and a gateway. But it was also a part of his heritage and culture, and thus ours. To carry the foundation of his life down to his children was all he asked for.

At the time, I didn't know anything about what was happening. I just remember snippets of brash arguing and yelling, then everyone disappearing into silence in their own space. It created an all-consuming heaviness in the house. Nothing was said or explained. My sisters were suddenly just gone.

My heart broke. I'd sit on the floor alone and cry, wondering, *What happened? Why? Where did they go? Are they coming home tonight?*

Every other sibling escaped in their own thing. It was just the way things were handled individually.

As the walls grew thicker, a strange existence was set in stone. The hustle and bustle of years before became numb and zoned out.

Will someone please say something? I wish I'd shouted.

What the hell is going on? Where did everyone go? I can't stand this silence. At least yell at each other. Give me something, anything, am I even here at all? But nothing came out of me. It wasn't even a thought. I did what little Nadia was used to and hid somewhere in a ball.

The sense of not having control over anything around me led to starving myself. Dwindling away numbed me from feeling the confusion and pain.

Every day, I consciously limited my intake to one 32-ounce Diet Coke and a can of green beans. I was so underweight and malnourished, my period stopped entirely. I didn't tell anyone.

I didn't like how I looked. It was beyond sick. Today, I see how what I saw in the mirror represented how I felt inside. My body was a billboard with flashing bright lights screaming, "I am dying here! Please help!"

But no one ever asked me about my heart inside. And if they ever did, they only said, "Go eat something. Stuff anything down your throat."

My sister Sabrina begged me to eat. I would try to change my clothes without her seeing my body, but one time, she walked in on me and started sobbing. My father yelled at me out of the blue: "What is wrong with you?" Wow, the attention! But I'm the one you don't have to worry about, remember?

My mother ended up taking me to a doctor. Nutrition drinks were prescribed. They thought that was the cure. I don't blame my parents, siblings, or anyone for that matter. This is not about that. This is merely demonstrating how life is often lived.

Life went on. Underweight and malnourished, I still had high hopes to save the world, high goals for my future, along with a master's degree in living life outside me.

Ironically, things "turned for the better" after I ended up winning two national modeling contests. The outside stamp of "you're ok" seemed to cure my struggles. When notified, they actually told me I should "gain a little weight." And so I did. I started to dream big, and take care of myself better.

I was one of only seven girls in the United States chosen in the Young Miss Magazine High School Covergirl Contest. It had required a long application and recommendations demonstrating a commitment to community service, as well as photos proving modeling potential. At the age of fifteen, I flew alone to the Big Apple and stayed a week at the Helmsley Palace. Covergirl Makeup and famous model Carol Alt were our hosts. Photos and wardrobe were in some fancy, real deal studio filled with various professionals in the field. I could see out above the New York landscape and thought about what was across the sea. The other girls appeared so groomed and ready to take on the world. It bolstered my confidence and opened my eyes.

My roommate was bulimic, and I listened to her throw up regularly from outside the bathroom. She was beautiful but had dark circles and yellow teeth. A part of her eyes couldn't hide the hole inside her heart. I found myself trying to convince her she was harming her body, that she should get help and talk to someone. Me? Really, Nadia? As though I knew any better, the one who had starved herself to skin and bones and hid in the closet.

A quote was selected from our applications and printed in the magazine with our photo. Mine was "I wouldn't feel successful in life unless my career benefitted society" while the others were something like, "I just want to shop all day and eat bonbons."

Would my life have been different had I focused on me?

Before returning home, I was offered a contract at a prestigious modeling agency. But I put it on the shelf and said I would "think about it." I wanted to save the world, remember. How would modeling help me do it?

That year began a series of projects and accomplishments focusing my attention away from the house to activities outside it. I basically became friends with everyone at school, navigating between the cheerleaders, quirky ones, jocks, and nerds. I was elected every year to student government, and eventually became ASB Vice President.

I organized canned food drives for the Food Bank and created a Super Spartan Award to encourage students' random acts of kindness. I established a student branch of Amnesty International with my AP history teacher. The school administration resisted so I advocated before the school board, demanding that it stay. We won. During lunch, students met and I'd share information about current human rights violation cases. Soon petitions for release from jail abroad were signed one by one.

I was on the swim and basketball teams, having improved my abilities significantly. I also had several jobs at various restaurants, record stores, and yogurt shops. I paid my oldest brother Mark to use his car over the summer while he was away in Europe for his music. I took off to Hollywood for trips and began modeling. I started saving money for college. I knew my father had enough on his plate.

And guess what? The "baa baa black sheep, dirty little brown girl," the quirky one nicknamed "Goofy," she was chosen to be the Basketball Homecoming Queen. But the best of it is the fact that my father walked me down the basketball court, arm in arm, with pride on his face. He was standing by my side when I was crowned.

It is so weird to think of that today. I wonder what he was thinking, what was going through his mind. Little did we know I'd never have a wedding, the kind in a beautiful white gown. You know those ones that every girl dreams about in her head. He died before I took a man's hand. And when I did, there was no wedding or gown offered.

***

My high school journals reflect an ongoing obsession with the well-being of others, almost an addiction to having to be a "good person." Seriously, we're talking daily journal entries written to God about it. Every daily entry includes the same reflections.

January 1987

Father, please help my friends to think of other things besides parties. Help them realize we can all have fun without alcohol. Help me in school and to be the best friend I can be to everyone. Help me be someone extra special to them, to be patient and easygoing, not boring or pushy. Give me strength and keep the mean girls away from me. Help them be kind and more sensitive. Help me to have inner peace and help everyone, especially my friends, to not screw up their lives. Please never leave me alone, Father. Help me be positive and please help me when I'm lonely and sad, with that weird feeling I get that makes me feel strange.

Help me know which area in life and school to concentrate on for my future. Help me stick up for what I believe and clearly know the difference between right and wrong. Help me to stop rumors hurting good people. Help me to

have common sense and judgment. Father, I'm
so sorry for this world and what it has turned
into.
   —Nadia

***

My first love, Joshua. I was indeed one lucky young woman to experience all of my firsts with him. He was a fraternal twin. Josh and Justin. They looked a lot alike but then they didn't. Their father, a veteran, had died young. Their mother was Japanese and a total sweetheart with a great sense of humor.

We loved crafting and would go to the craft store together. His mom would cook awesome meals and welcomed me in like a daughter. I began to frequently spend the night there. It was a safe haven and an escape from a house where everyone was distracted and disconnected in their own worlds. Together, we explored our bodies little by little over multiple months. Every single step happened at the perfect pace. I could laugh, talk openly, cry, everything and anything with him.

When it was time to apply for college, things changed. I decided I would try to maintain the relationship while in college and work as a waitress and model to support myself. Without my parents really knowing, I applied to all the local colleges because that would enable me to live at home.

But one day I spontaneously drove to UCLA alone. I wanted to see the law school and campus my father had gone to. Immediately, I began completing an application for undergraduate studies at UCLA, an entirely different process. I barely got mine in on time.

Sure enough, a few months later, I received an acceptance letter. At first, I hid it. I kept the joy and quandary of a decision inside. I didn't even tell Josh or my father. I was convinced it would be impossible to go and was not a realistic option. My father was already supporting several siblings in college.

But the dream held on to me. I thought about it constantly. My gut was calling. So at work one day, I sat down on break and began charting out costs for tuition, rent, and school supplies. I did the math and figured out how much I could contribute. Then I drafted a schedule that included school, work, and weekend visits with Josh.

On the evening before a response was due, I put the acceptance letter and financial plan in front of my father while he was sitting alone at the dinner table. "Daddy, um, I got accepted to UCLA, I really want to go, and here is how I think we can do it financially."

He was both shocked and overjoyed. After picking up the acceptance letter in his right hand, with a massive smile on his face, he looked down at my charts and quickly asked, "What's this?"

"It's my plan to reach my dream, like you did," I said.

Nothing else had to be said. We both knew about dreaming big. "We'll figure it out, Poobie. We'll figure it out."

Sure enough, I was the only child to "walk in his footsteps."

***

The four years I spent at the University of California Los Angeles were amazing and opened my world beyond expectations. I was going to make a difference and I knew UCLA would help me define and begin doing just that.

At first, I was very interested in documentary filmmaking. I wanted to expose the world's suffering in order to put a stop to it. But I would only get frustrated and want to jump right in and fix it. So I majored in Sociology with a specialization in Juvenile Justice.

I would go to class, study, and work during the week, then

drive back home on weekends to spend time with Josh and waitress at Polly's Pies. From being a hostess at various restaurants, a file clerk at a literary agency, and an on-campus ice-cream scooper, I took any job that worked with having classes in the day.

Eventually I found that work as a model was the quickest and easiest way to make the most money. I loved observing the phenomena of a production and meeting various people in the industry. I was in various commercials, music videos, and movie productions, and it was a fascinating experience. It is through this work that I met one of my longtime best friends, Maryann Tanedo, a producer now. She's one of those rare gems—an authentic, talented, family-focused, kick-ass kind of female professional and friend. She had barely survived cancer when we met.

But then something happened that changed everything. It sent the message loud and clear again, "You are just a body." I never processed it, nor told anyone until decades later. I can see now how much it affected me, how my behaviors changed, how I returned to that dissociated state, the same way I did as a child when bad things happened.

When I was eighteen and in my first year of college, I was violently raped. He tripped me with his foot, forced me to the floor, pinned down my wrists, held down my body, pulled it out, forced my legs apart, my dress up, underwear aside, and then shoved himself inside me. My whole body hurt. But most of all down there. He quickly ejaculated then remained lying on top, still inside and binding me to the ground.

I tried to break free from under him but couldn't. I remember clearly how he breathed heavily, having marked me forever as a mere body, imprinting another shitty video memory in my head that still enters now and then. He finally got up and walked out but I couldn't move. All I remember is shock.

I didn't understand a thing. Blinking, mind racing, I curled up in a ball and became someone else, something else. I stayed there stuck. I didn't hear a thing. Several minutes passed until I finally stumbled and ran out the door.

Between robotic and numb, tears rolling down my face, shaking, the drive back to the dorm was blanketed in numb confusion and panic. I drove in circles around the campus. I couldn't seem to park.

Eventually the physical pain broke me out of the trance and I just wanted to go in and hide. I didn't say a word to anyone, crawled into the dorm shower fully clothed, sat down, curled my head into my knees, shaking, crying, hoping no one would see. I could feel I was bleeding a bit and remember the shame it painted in my head, as though I had done something wrong. When I heard voices nearby, it was a painful reminder of reality outside. Once again, I was stuck back in those fucking four wicked walls I was in as a little girl. *Please leave me be, let me go,* I screamed in my head.

The only person I ever was with before that day was Joshua, my one true love. The man who raped me was a little older and a model I had met on a set who told me he could give me some advice. There were no warning signs. It began as soon as I walked in the door.

I was never the same. It solidified all that I had felt as a child into an internal mold. It was violent, it was bold, it was unexpected and cold. At least Dr. K. was calculated and contrived. At least I knew what to expect within his four walls.

My soul turned inward and off. I returned to life as just a body.

It was easier to live that way.

It was not a big deal, Nadia, I would tell myself.

You dirty little brown girl, just go wash your face and get up. You are just a body, but a body can be and do a lot. You

*can be safe, in control, know what to expect, that is, if you give
all they want to take. Your soul has no place anymore with sex.
Starve yourself and drink, it will help you play the part.*

I broke up with Josh shortly thereafter, not returning his
calls for days. I had no words to share with him what had happened. *It will break his heart if you haven't done so already,* I
thought. The day I ended it will forever be imprinted in my
mind and heart.

Dear Son,

> *That little girl, she has a voice now. I will do my
> best to remind you of yours too. Your mommy's
> voice is not silenced in starvation or drowned
> in booze. It is not muffled in fear or manipu-
> lated by shame.*
>
> *Nor does it always immediately point the
> finger at others, placing blame. She says, "No
> more, go away. I am not a body, but a soul with
> worth. I am me, whole, perfect and complete.
> So stop branding me, you cruel fools. I am not
> your label. I am not my shame. I am who I am,
> true self unchanged. There is a hurt child deep
> inside. Like you, I needed a safe place to cry.
> I once thought it was there, deep in the dark.
> But now I know there is light. There is a home
> within me, and one in you. It is there that we
> see the truth."*
> *Love, Mom*

Thankfully, I had a dorm roommate, and she broke the
isolation. When it was time to register for the following semester, she asked me what classes I was going to take. I had to

think about tomorrow. It got me out of a rut. Again I focused outward and walked on sheer hope. Soon enough, a semester passed while I was half-robot and half-myself.

It wasn't until I created independent studies with professors and found several internship placements that my outlook started to improve. I needed a change, and the change had to be helping people hands-on. I needed to see and do good in the world to get out of the one in my head.

***

My first internship was at the David Kenyon Juvenile Justice Center, a cutting-edge entity with co-located government and non-profit services easing the transition back into normal life for formerly incarcerated youth. I studied the challenges they faced and whether or not the model made a difference. I interviewed youth, social workers, and probation officers, observed court hearings during sentencing and progress reports. The experience further strengthened my conviction that there is a solution to every social problem in the world within three degrees of separation. Resources and skills needed are all out there. We just had to work better together. *God, bring me to that place and position where I can do my part,* I thought.

Thereafter, I was overjoyed to intern at the famed show *In Living Color.* My thesis was the study of whether or not racial stereotypes were promoted or dismantled through comedy. The Wayans brothers were just beginning to conquer the world, and I observed it all. Most of all, they treated me like I was part of the family.

Keenen asked me to head up a project to promote Black universities. I drafted letters on his behalf and sent them out all over the nation. I followed up with phone calls asking for their official college clothing so it could be worn by the entire cast at the end of the show during their famous group "See you next time" message. Naive, hopeful, and proud, I was thrilled they put my name once in the credits.

I saw Jennifer Lopez try out to be a Fly Girl, Jim Carrey goof-balling around the office with Damon, Shawn and Marlon cracking jokes while eating lunch, and Jamie Foxx speaking like his character Towanda at random downtimes just to make us laugh more.

I worked directly for the Clearance Supervisor, Gisele Sanchez-Hudson. She was truly a dear mentor I'll never forget. Her position was charged with preventing lawsuits in one way or another. Finding a proper picture of the presidential podium tweaked enough to forgo copyright violations or a prior source of similar character assault on someone famous in order to prevent libel and slander accusations was fun fodder for this prospective law student.

I also met my second love, Paul, here. We had a good relationship. A solid, healthy one. What I treasure the most is that he met my father. Paul approached the introduction as if my father was asking, "Are you honorable enough to be with and possibly marry my daughter?" He was right. Paul was, after all, seven years older than me, successful, tall, and handsome, with a gentlemanly, soft demeanor. A former professional football player, he had worked himself into a position of respect and future possibilities.

My father looked him in the eyes and extended his hand. They ended up embracing and conversing later. My dad liked Paul immediately. The fact he was also a minority was a plus. They could relate, whether directly said or not. That year, I met Paul's family too.

Paul said he didn't want to hold me back from my dreams and future studies. But I knew he felt behind the game in terms of starting a family. I felt a sense of him wanting more between us and it scared me. So I suggested we take a short break to think about our future. Days later, he showed up outside my apartment, got down on his knees, unloaded his heart, and proposed to me with a ring in hand, having clearly planned it out.

Looking back, how I wish I had accepted. But I did the exact opposite and ended the relationship. I walked away in an instant and left him there alone on his knees. Oh my God, I still can't believe I did that. To this day, he is the one and only man I actually could've built a life with, who actually met my father when I was an adult woman, and who proposed to me on his knees with respect.

But my mind was filled with illusions based on shame and fear.

How could his intentions be good? it surmised inside. *You aren't lovable anyways. He doesn't know you're damaged yet. Don't put yourself in harm's way by believing you deserve this.*

Interestingly, over the course of the next dozen years, before I met my ex-husband, a few other men asked me to marry them. They were good candidates to build a life with. But I always ended it and walked away. I didn't understand why then. It was automatic.

I met Carlos a year later when involved in the UCLA student hunger strike to prevent the closure of Native American, Chicano, and African American studies. He was handsome, passionate, and smart, yet struggled with depression, knowing his future higher education was uncertain as an undocumented student. He also carried a load of serious childhood trauma. We bonded over pain, conversation, cooking, social causes, and lying naked in bed.

I felt safer to love and save than to be loved and have safety.

I ended up sacrificing and placing myself in harm's way multiple times with him. His troubled mind caused angry episodes and the emotional toll started affecting my daily health and studies. When I tried to leave, he'd get suicidal or punch himself.

One time, he kicked me so hard in my side, I couldn't breathe. I went to a clinic and they discovered a broken rib. I never shared what was going on with anyone. I just began to believe true love meant a struggle. I had to work for and earn it constantly. I had to suffer for it to be authenticated.

My application to law school was at risk of being derailed as a result. At the same time, the *In Living Color* production staff called and offered me a position. Paul was still there, and it all seemed like a haven I could escape to.

Still, when I reached out to Gisele, she convinced me that I likely would feel limited and get bored. She encouraged me to follow my dream of going to law school. So I buckled down and got the applications done, despite trying to navigate an abusive relationship. I figured it would give me a chance to find escape from Carlos physically, mentally, and emotionally too.

Somewhere inside, that dream never let up.

I remember exactly where I was when I opened the acceptance letter. In a mostly unfurnished apartment I shared with my friend Alexandra, I gazed out of the family room window and immediately called my father at his office, which I had never done before. "Loyola Law School! That's great news!" he said, in a calm, excited kind of way. From my end of the line, his absolute bliss flowed out in trenches.

Daddy,

Do you remember that moment? I wonder what the look was like on your face. Did this bring you some joy that you so very much deserved? Did you run out and tell your secretary, law partners, who else? Did your hard work seem worth it? All the immense financial stress? Were you proud of me, your last child? How much? I'll never know exactly how you felt. I never took the time to ask you more things like that before you left. I never really told you how much all you overcame meant to me. I only hope it gave you joy and a sense of freedom.

Love, Nadia

CHAPTER 3

Dear Son,

this too shall pass.

The summer before I began law school, Oma's health began to fail. Opa had passed away a few years before that, and she was all alone. When my mother found out that Oma was placed in a hospital, she was deeply distraught. I needed to get away from Carlos and was blessed to go with her to Germany for over a month. By the time our plane landed, Oma had slipped into a state of little mental awareness and hope.

We went straight from the airport to the facility. But we had not prepared ourselves for what we would find. Up the hallway sat a now tiny, bent-over woman in a wheelchair, somber and trance-like. My mother walked closer, but the woman was looking down, still unrecognizable. Peering down to get a better look, my mom saw it was her mother.

"Muttie?" she said. Oma lifted her face slightly and pondered, as if she had heard a voice in her head. She opened her eyes wider, blank and emotionless. "Muttie?" my mother said again.

Oma blinked and then "woke up." She began shaking without saying a word. She broke down in sobs and soon it came out. "Meine Irmgard?" she asked in shock and confusion. My mother fell on her knees and dove her face in her lap. Oma's hands shaking, she held her daughter so close. The entire facility drowned with their piercing wails of emotion.

I'll never, ever forget that moment. I saw my mother as a daughter, a little girl who had a mother. I saw the child she was inside like all of us. I understood then that she did her best as a mother.

To me, she is my hero, an example to move toward.

Over the course of weeks, we navigated through various states of Oma's stability and awareness, often crying, often laughing, and often with a fresh cup of German coffee. Those days were spent talking, reminiscing and planning her future health care.

But she began to slip away again. Her diabetes and bleeding esophagus required more intensive hospitalization. She was transferred to a different facility, where we ended up sleeping in cots in her room. The staff brought us food and treated us like family.

Oma's roommate was the same age and must have felt quite overwhelmed by us. During the entire time we were there, not one single visitor came to see her. Her knee-high nylons never stayed up on her thinning shins and it bothered her. She would repeatedly pull them up after they immediately fell back down. Over and over again, she did this for hours. I figured having them in place made her feel better, so I began doing it for her.

"Meine angel," she would say, her hands motioning for me to come closer, and I would. I'd brush her hair and sing her songs as my mother and Oma sat and watched. Soon she began saying, "The whole world is going crazy" in German. It made us laugh while crying. And besides, she was probably right.

Oma took her last breath with us by her side. She was only seventy-eight. I can't imagine how alone she must have felt in those years prior. Did life, love, and family seem meaning-less without anyone there to comfort her? I am so grateful my mother had the opportunity to touch, talk, and say thank you to her mother before she went to heaven.

My father immediately booked a flight to join us in Germany upon hearing of Oma's death. I'm so grateful my mother had him by her side while processing the loss. There is a once-in-a-lifetime photo I took of them just after he arrived at the airport. Their embrace was so intense, you could feel their shared love yards away. They had made it through hard times and were closer than ever. The photo is of his face over her shoulder with the utmost joyful smile.

The three of us traveled around Germany in an attempt to heal my mother's heart. She shared Oma stories on the train and long walks. We laughed. We cried. We talked about the past. We talked about the future. We escaped in the pres-ent adventure. It was truly one of the most treasured times of my life.

I had my mother and my father to myself. I had no idea what such a concept would feel like. I picked their brains like I'd only have that one chance. I observed their friendship, ado-ration, and love for one another like a fly on the wall. I felt both sad and ecstatic. Like I had been missing out, yet had so much to look forward to. Like they had been strangers to me all this time, yet we were undeniably organically bonded.

My God, my parents are whole entire human beings too. With feelings, fears, joys, hopes, and regrets. With a past, pres-ent, and future. Why did we lose all those hours never talking? Why had life given a misguided way of rarely connecting?

"This too shall pass," my father reminded us.

"In times of despair, we must maintain hope, and in times of prosperity, remain humble," he said.

There are cemeteries in Germany filled with lush trees and flowers galore. They are not marked with a cement block and perfectly cut grass like ours. My grandmother was buried near a large, beautiful tree. It is now unmarked, but she is most definitely in everything flourishing green. Death is not an end, but rather a new beginning. Oma's spirit gave us a new set of eyes and a path ahead we may not have seen otherwise.

Upon returning from Germany, I decided to stay away from Carlos and began my studies at Loyola Law School. He quickly became the first stalker in my life. Unfortunately, my story includes many. I escaped into the well-gated campus and informed security guards about the situation.

I dove into my studies and quickly made friends. Priscilla, Angela, Veronica, Monica, Serena, Fahi, Alan, Mia, Matt, Tito, Brad, and more. We were a diverse gang, studied hard, and made time for a little fun.

Finally thriving, again in my element, I was active in the school's Public Interest Law Foundation and transcribed law books for a blind student named Ollie. I volunteered at the neighboring elementary school and was active in La Raza de Loyola, a group of Latino/Latina students supporting one another. I participated in corporate responsibility protests and organized a forum with friends about the proposition seeking to end the provision of health care, public education, and other services to the working undocumented. I did all right academically during my first year of law school. The few men I dated were healthy and are still my friends today.

In the summer of 1994 before my second year of law school, I studied Human Rights and Environmental Law abroad in Costa Rica and Panama. A group of friends from Loyola went together. We watched sea turtles lay their eggs in the dark, explored the jungles of Tortuguero, and contributed as best we could to two major international cases. It was absolutely fascinating.

In Costa Rica, we observed as the home sheds of Dole plantation workers, which were placed in the center of the fields where they worked, were sprayed with Dow Chemical pesticides. The result was years of sterilization of men, which went unrecognized until the incoming workforce began to dwindle. In Panama, maintenance and expansion of the canal required miles and miles of rainforest destruction in the middle of the Indigenous Kuna Yala homeland. We needed two translators for both Spanish and their native tongue in order to reach them on canoes and communicate once we arrived. They were so isolated and deep in the forest, their combined genes had created a few albino children. I remember taking out my contacts with a flashlight in one of their huts as the children watched. They thought I was taking out part of my eye and screamed.

Interestingly, the massive watershed produced by the trees was dwindling as a result of rainforest destruction yet was necessary for the functioning of the canal. Earth strangely had somewhat of an economic defense on her side. I saw directly how the law was applied in massive international litigations to make the world a better place.

It used to be very difficult for me to look at photos from this trip. I was totally in my element, innocent and free, ready to fly and face the whole world ahead of me. In every photo, my eyes are full of happiness and hope, reflecting an innate ability to truly live in the present moment.

My second year of law school began with limitless aspirations to change others' lives for the better and an intrinsic belief in the good that existed in the world. I had developed a logical, rational understanding of the ebb and flow of society, and faith that basic standards of humanity ultimately win.

If there was injustice, there was a map to seek justice. If there was a wrong, there was a way to make it right. If you made a mistake, there was a lesson to be learned and no need for shame. If you did the right thing, the world was a better place, and fears were quelled. If you contributed to the light and love in the world, darkness would always lose in the end.

***

One weekend, close to the end of my first quarter in the second year of law school, I drove home to visit my parents. While chatting with my mom in the kitchen, I suddenly saw my father peeking in through the sliding glass door. Dressed in his suit and tie, briefcase in hand, tall and handsome as usual, he looked so distinguished.

"My Poobie's home!" he exclaimed so loudly, we could hear him from inside. Unlocking and opening the door, we embraced. I'll never forget the feel of his large hand holding my head from behind as it pressed against his chest. *I am home. I am safe here,* I thought. My eyes closed, sensing a bond I can't put into words.

It was as if he said, "I get you. I know the excitement you're feeling inside about your dreams coming alive. I've been there too." Even more, "I got you, Nadia. It's almost time to spread your wings and fly. I'm right here. I'll always be there right by your side."

That was the last time I ever saw him alive.

***

It was like any other Saturday morning. My father told my mom they'd go out to breakfast after his regular weekend basketball at Morrison Park in Santa Ana. He played his first game. And then a second. Then sat down to wait on the sidelines for his third to start. Instead, the universe gave him a heart attack and he died.

He was gone forever, just like that. And along with him, everything else. My breath. My heart. My hope. My home.

Nothing made sense anymore.

Nothing was real after November 12, 1994.

There was no revival. No waiting in the emergency room.

No ifs, ands, or buts. There wasn't an ounce of opportunity given to anticipate or prepare for the concept of death, let alone his.

The only thing given was his cold, dead body.

Poof! Your hero's gone. Nothing can replace him. No one ever will. Oh, and you might want to know, young lady, there's a long, twisty, hilly road ahead without a dad, the universe mocked me.

In complete devastation and shock, my mother was totally incapacitated and unable to eat, drink, or sleep. It felt as though we were going to lose her too at one point. Sometimes the only thing I could do was drag her to the car and drive, drive, and drive for miles and miles without saying a word but crying the entire time, holding hands.

Our world completely stopped while others' seemed to continue. The sound of wheels turning, the passing scenery, and an innumerable number of moving vehicles and people. Just knowing something, anything was moving was both a comfort and a curse.

The immediate days following my father's death, the house was inundated with calls, visits, flowers, meals, cards, and inquiries from family friends, reporters, attorneys, judges, coworkers, community members, professors, neighbors, elected officials and more. It was overwhelming. People everywhere jump-started plans to honor and memorialize his legacy. But we were all in the twilight zone.

Someone had the wherewithal to organize the funeral and

burial services. Holy Family Church in Orange overflowed with patrons giving heartfelt words and acts of respect, love, and adoration. Stunning, beautiful dedications, music, poems, and more. Articles were written about his work and legacy across the state.

The pain and sorrow, heavy and intense, brought moments when words just couldn't come out. An undeniable light and warmth in the world was now gone. It was beyond tragic. It was purely inexplicable, unnecessary, unfair, irrational and maddening. When my brothers and sisters and I stood up and began to sing "Make Me a Channel of Your Peace," all anyone could do was cry, and cry some more.

The Juaneño Band of Mission Indians honored my father during the burial services at Holy Sepulcher Cemetery in the hills of Orange. A prayer was shared to all in the Acjachemen language. A beautiful plume of eagle feathers was placed on his chest in the shape of wings, and with them, he was returned back to the land of his Indigenous ancestors.

Daddy,

Just when I got my wings and could attempt
    to fly,
you left the nest without saying goodbye.
I did not yet know how to fly on my own.
I still needed you to teach me so much more.
I needed more time to listen, to all you could
    offer.
I had no guide to fly authentically with glee.
I flew too fast and then too slow.
I flew too high and then too low.
I had no clue how to find a steady way.
I tried my best, Daddy, I truly did.
I wish I knew then what I now know today.

Maybe I wouldn't have crashed and broken my
wings.
Love, your Poobie

The world doesn't stop when you lose your hero.

Just a few days after my father's funeral, I had final exams in law school. Every attorney knows that the first half of the second year is the most difficult. When you're numb and can't remember anything but how to open and close your eyes, the idea of taking and passing a law school test is crazy. And continuing law school? Totally out of the question . . . mentally, financially, and emotionally. My mother needed another person to live with her twenty-four seven.

I made an appointment with the Dean of Admissions to discuss my status immediately. My mind was made up. I was prepared to tell her I was dropping out. When I sat down in her office, I hadn't said a word before she began speaking. She said, in a serious, solemn, condescending voice, "Attorneys must set aside their emotions to be great practitioners of law."

"Excuse me?" I said respectfully, my decision to drop out flipping over in a millisecond after hearing her words. "I beg to differ. In fact, attorneys that set aside their emotions are the ones that give the profession a bad rap. They are the ones that bash down on a person or group unfairly just to make a quick buck. The best attorneys that ever existed do not set aside their emotions. They use them to dive into their genius intuition. They are the ones whose spoken and written word is so thought-provoking, it is inevitable there will be a better understanding of the law and its primary purpose. They are the ones who somehow evoke that 'ah ha' emotion in a judge, jury, or individual so as to sway them in their favor. They are the ones that use the law to make the world a better place. And ma'am, Ms. Dean, that's just what I'm going to do, whether you like it or not," I responded.

I didn't drop out and a few weeks later, just a week after burying my father, I showed up for finals. I didn't say a word to anyone. I knew I'd break down if I did. I just sat down at the desk, waiting. Then, one by one, my friends walked up in silence, each placing a feather before me on the desk as if to say, "You still have your wings and he is here." *Thank you so very much, dear friends.* They knew my father had been buried with the plume of eagle feathers . . . and they knew the depth of what this inspiration and life meant for me.

***

From there on out, I refused to say goodbye to my father. Denial helped me put one foot in front of the other in a world where light had vanished. The internal gears of inspiration that fueled me had diminished. Walking in a body was the best I could do.

It felt like my soul and all belief in good in this world were dying if not dead already. The thought of spreading my wings and taking flight was horrifying.

My mind said, *Why would I think of doing that here? All it would do is land me knocking my head against the glass like an aimless bird. The flicker of fire on the other side was a mere illusion anyways.*

So I turned to my own illusions that he'd hear me instead. I talked to him in my head. I talked to him out loud while driving. I talked to him through songs. My new commute from Santa Ana to downtown LA became a ritual of "conversations" while I played a few selected songs over and over again.

"Love's Recovery" by the Indigo Girls, "Pride" by U2, "Imagine" by John Lennon. But most of all, this song written by my oldest brother, Mark.

"Hollow"
You call it make believe
What you call rust I call silver
I'm just a fool to you
You call my stream, frozen river
I guess yours is the real world
This place where war is king
Where nights are cold and dark
And no one trusts a thing
But I am captured by a star
I know that I must follow
If mine is make believe
It licks your real world hollow
You call it make believe
Yeah, but yours is half gone
Mine's filled to the middle
I wasn't fooled by you
I found your record of truth
an unfounded riddle
Cause when a preacher screws a whore
You're there taking pictures of the scene
But when there's a hundred others filling
          hearts and mouths
You don't see a thing
And I agree the whole picture can be
a little too hard to swallow
If mine is make believe
It licks your real world hollow
Call it a fairy tale
You can call it fiction
Call it fake, call it unreal
You can call it lies
You can call it hypnotism
You can call it anything you feel.

Call it make believe
What you call rust
I'll call silver
I'll be a fool to you
When you call my stream a frozen river
And yours can be the real world
This place where war is king
Where nights are cold and dark
And no one trusts a thing
And I agree the whole picture can be
A little too hard to swallow
But I am captured by a star
I know that I must follow
If mine is make believe
If mine is make believe
It licks your real world hollow

Lyrics by Mark Phillip Davis, © 1994
    Inkling Music
(From the album *You Came Screaming* by
    Mark Davis)
Website: markdavisinklings.bandcamp
    .com

Decades after my father passed away, my mother told me that he had planned on practicing law with me in an office of our own. Undoubtedly, my life would be very different had that come true.

Recently, I found my journals from this time in life.

I didn't just talk to him through words, I wrote as though he were still living and could directly respond. Mourning his physical death was nothing. I never recognized that I also lost the experience of having a father as an adult woman, that I'd

never have his guidance when making huge career and relationship decisions.

What would he have suggested? Insisted upon?

What experiences would he have shared with me?

Would he have pointed his finger in a certain direction?

Or stepped in to protect me without even asking?

January 5, 1995

> *Daddy, A nightmare repeats over and over. I
> am running with all my might, screaming on
> the damp coast of a beach, as if it is to find
> sanity and peace, as if I'll find you there, some-
> where, to fall into your arms, to be injected
> with a sense of hope, answers, security, those
> which you always, always gave by simply being
> you. I run and run and run, because it not only
> leaves me swirling in circles, when I run and
> run, I don't have to live in the today. What is it
> anyways? Without all you gave and taught me,
> I would just run into the sea. There is nothing
> but darkness and despair now, there is no love
> and peace. What do I do now with all the evil
> I see?*
> *—Nadia*

Desperate to quell the pain and fill the hole inside, I mis-
takenly let Carlos back into my life. He convinced me things
would be better. One day, he admitted visiting prostitutes,
which floored me. He said he hated it and would never be
satisfied unless he was with me. "No, I can't do this," I said,
while driving on the freeway in my truck. He began punching

himself, so I pulled over and tried to stop him. His fists landed on me instead. One by one, he punched me in a complete trance. He had lost his mind entirely.

He opened his door, stepped out in the rain, and began tearing apart bags of belongings in the bed of the truck. Cars were speeding by within feet of him. I stepped outside and begged him to sit down. But he began rocking back and forth, as though he was going to take off into the lanes. He looked me straight in my eyes and said, "I love you," and began to take a step. I immediately waved my arms and walked straight into the traffic, thinking, *Maybe then he won't kill himself this way.*

As the cars slowed down and could see my battered face, a man stopped his car and tried to help me as I watched Carlos run away. For the first time in the relationship, I actually let him go. I didn't scream after him, "I love you too."

I just didn't have an ounce of will to try and love again.

***

After my father passed away, I did not know what love was nor where the one true source could be found. I believed true love was found through another human being. Some say it's love addiction, others say an attachment disorder from childhood. I don't know.

The internal work is more important today. There is no more making excuses. Perfect love can only be found within me, and yours in you. It took me too long to realize this, but at least I do today.

> *Please, dear Son, remember, it is right there in you too.*

Still, acts of true love came in so many forms from friends. My friends then are still my friends today. I will always feel like I received more than I ever gave to each of them.

After my father passed away, Priscilla was the shoulder I cried on. Sitting on the kitchen floor and sobbing, she would sit down with me and listen calmly and patiently for hours. Listen and nod, listen and hold my hand, listen and look me in my eyes, listen so intently that I actually started to believe she was convinced of the depth of my pain. She helped me smile while crying, to laugh in a self-deprecating "I'm a mess" kind of way.

Wine slowly became another best friend during this time. It led to getting involved in a few more unhealthy relationships, albeit short ones. The short escapes were only self-made setups for disappointment.

Priscilla just watched me sympathetically from the sidelines.

I managed to graduate from law school while helping my mom, never returning to really living again myself. When it was time to study for the bar exam, Priscilla offered to let me stay with her temporarily. And so I did. It was during this time that she wrote a song for me I will forever treasure and hold dear to my heart. It's called "The Legacy He Left This World Is You."

***

Thankfully, the vast community that adored my father kept his inspiration alive. They created pieces of hope I could see and hold on to. They took his life and inspiration and poured them into a scholarship, an award, and a school named in his honor. Perhaps one child would hear his story and remember to dream big. Perhaps one student would get the nod of confidence and financial support needed to carry on. By carrying on his legacy, they gave me no choice but to carry on. By being reminded of the fact he lived on in me, my purpose was restored.

The Hispanic Bar Association of Orange County, which my father helped to establish decades prior, created the Wallace R. Davis Memorial Scholarship Fund through the Hispanic Education Endowment Fund. The scholarship is awarded to young Latino law students who follow in his footsteps. It was my honor to be the first recipient and to thereafter present scholarships to deserving students at the HBA's annual dinner. These are some of the words I shared at other events honoring my father.

> *We must ask ourselves this. What is a true lifetime achievement? While success has often been associated with social status, money, and titles, a true lifetime achievement is far more untouchable, far more persevering. When people have given up on truth, morality, and compassion, there was always proof in Wally's example that having the courage to stand up and do the right thing was not only necessary, but also possible, no matter how difficult, challenging, or uncomfortable the situation might be. Whether it was through his smile and eyes, his insistence for honesty and kindness in a room full of dark intentions, fighting with passion for a cause on the streets or in a courtroom, giving words of love and encouragement to our youth, playing his saxophone, or shooting some hoops, he generated a warmth that people could not ignore, that we all long for. His warmth was more powerful in affecting people's actions, minds, and hearts than money and status ever will be. His integrity and hope for a better world was a*

breath of fresh air to those who did not know
him well, and a foundation of strength to those
that did.

In his old barrio, his story is rare and con-
sidered a miracle and he is remembered as
"Wallitas." In the legal world, he is best remem-
bered as the attorney whose successful lawsuit
against the Santa Ana Unified School District
abolished the practice of testing for aptitude
only in English, resulting in wrongful place-
ment of Spanish-speaking students in classes
for children with learning disabilities.

In his wife's heart, he is and always will
be her "schatz." In the hearts of his seven chil-
dren, he is and always will be Daddy. But to
each and every person who knew and are now
discovering him, he is also something invalu-
able, untouchable . . . undeniable proof that if
each one of us holds ourselves responsible to a
standard of integrity and selflessness, the world
could be a drastically kinder, warmer place for
all. Now that is a lifetime achievement.

The Santa Ana Unified School District founded the
Wallace R. Davis Elementary School in his honor. Hundreds
of poor Latino students have now learned his life story, that
he was just like them, and that if he can dream big and make a
difference in the world, so can they.

"Dream big . . . and once you have that dream, don't let
anyone take it away from you. You must have faith in tomorrow, and we must have faith in you." The school dedication
ceremony ended with the children waving paper doves while
everyone sang the song "I Believe I Can Fly."

Since then, I've often run into feathers along the path of life. I remember the plume of eagle feathers the tribe laid on his body before he returned to Mother Earth.

I rarely pass them by. I pick them up, carry them home, and put them with others in a beautiful glass tray on a shelf. Individually, each carries a story about a journey navigating through life. Maybe it's a parent's, sibling's, friend's, neighbor's, or stranger's. Maybe one of the stories is waiting for us.

Maybe we need to sit quietly and ask for them, listening more intently. Maybe together they can provide the insight and guidance needed to walk through life with our head held high.

This is what the community's words and stories about my father gave to me. I was convinced he lived on through stories that could inspire the young and old.

Gathering all the feathers together, I started seeing the shape of wings. I started believing that mine had returned. I started believing that I could finally fly again.

The Santa Ana community embraced me like their daughter.

I will forever be grateful for the support and heartfelt welcoming home. My father's presence was everywhere and throughout everyone. I was home, and it would be like this forever. So I jumped wholeheartedly into several local campaigns and community efforts.

It broke my heart that immigrant youths' dreams of a higher education were being stifled by general threats and a misunderstanding of the law. The political divides were ignoring the fact that these were children brought here by their parents at a very young age and who knew no other place as their home. This is where their lives and dreams were built. To be told they would have to pay non-state resident tuition rates in college smashed their dreams of receiving a higher education. "Don't let anyone take that dream away." Remember? How could I stand by and just watch this happen? So I did some research, found a loophole in the law, and independently wrote a handbook with simple directions for student applications. Soon I was conducting seminars throughout the state.

Then I was recruited to be Lou Correa's fundraiser for his bid to State Assembly, very much a grassroots effort supported by the Latino Caucus's desire to elect more Latinos to state-level positions. My commitment was mainly driven by the belief that government should reflect the electorate and youth should be encouraged to believe in it.

The campaign was filled with a group of awesome young professionals who became some of my closest friends, such as Alex Padilla, who became the California Secretary of State two decades later, and Kevin McCarty, who became an Assemblyman representing the Sacramento area. But what was the most rewarding was the recruiting and organizing of youth volunteers to walk precincts and encourage their own neighbors to vote. I then got to be a member of Congresswoman Loretta Sanchez's legal team, protecting the rights of new citizens against unfounded accusations of voter fraud.

Interestingly, less than ten years prior, six years before my father passed away, the GOP County Chairman decided to illegally station uniformed guards at twenty polling places, resulting in massive intimidation of U.S. citizens of Hispanic descent, preventing many from voting. In response, my father and other members of the OC Hispanic Bar Association created a Citizens Committee of Voting Registry to provide oversight and investigate the incidents. A lawsuit was filed by Latino voters against the Orange County Republican Party, who eventually paid $400,000 in 1992 to settle the case out of court two days before trial. The so-called Poll Guard Case triggered a civil rights probe by the U.S. Department of Justice and a revision of state election laws, making it a felony to interfere with a voter.

The same crap was still happening, and it wasn't right. So I decided to assist in the efforts of going door-to-door getting proof of citizenship from those wrongfully accused. A straightforward, factual way to prove the law was being complied with and voter intimidation was not acceptable. The effort became a massive community protest televised all over the state.

Thereafter I was recruited and hired as an independent contractor to create and organize a "Unity Dinner" for the Southwest Voter Registration and Education Project. The majority of Republicans in the County were aghast at what its local party leadership had ordered with the poll guards. And everyone, regardless of party affiliation, agreed that voter participation in general should be a priority. Thus, the Unity Dinner was a fundraiser to support nonpartisan voter registration throughout the County. I worked with the County's Chairmen of both major political parties and together we raised the funds, establishing one of the first politically unified efforts in Orange County.

Blessed to be asked, I gave speeches to youth about the importance of believing in justice. That laws and a judicial system were made to ensure it.

I witnessed firsthand people's actions to make the world a better place. My mind was more at peace because hope in the world had been restored. I finally started to believe that darkness and evil were not winning.

My father was right by my side and there was so much more work to do. With his spirit guiding me, I knew I'd be led to where I was needed most.

CHAPTER 4
———————

Dear Son,
justice is but an idea,
unless someone makes it real.

Several local leaders suggested I consider running for the
school board in Santa Ana. Seeking a position in public office
was nothing I had ever particularly planned for career-wise. I
needed to know there was a bigger purpose and potential to
help others behind it, so I did some research and discovered
that SAUSD had one of the highest dropout rates, teen pregnancy was at an all-time high, and it was the 5th largest and
one of the most overcrowded school districts in the state out of
nearly a thousand total.

"Ok, count me in, I hope to make a difference," I said.

My campaign was very much a grassroots effort. I knew
how to raise funds, recruit and organize volunteers, give
speeches, and do well at debates. I received the endorsement

of the teachers' union, firefighters, local community leaders, elected officials, and other trade unions.

But what I deeply enjoyed the most was walking door-to-door and directly meeting families and children. The face-to-face contact allowed me to personally introduce myself, listen to concerns about schools, and answer questions as best I could. It generated what I needed to stay motivated and committed, to see the needs and assess if and how I could help.

I honestly didn't care about "winning" just to win. It felt authentic and real once my passion was connected to the needs. But there was always another avenue, another way to contribute and make a difference in the community.

I met two of my best friends during the campaign, Bethzabe "Beth" Martinez and Armando De La Libertad. Both volunteered hours helping to get the word out. Our friendships have lasted for decades. Beth eventually created a local community group called Nuestro Pueblo, which still stands to this day.

Many of my father's closest friends stepped in to help: of course Al Stokke, but also Rick Aguirre, Ruben Smith, Wylie Aitken, Enriqueta Ramos, Rueben Martinez, Jess Araujo, Ed Munoz, Alfredo Amezcua, John Palacios, and more.

I was indeed elected to serve on the school board to represent the same district that had once placed my father in segregated classrooms as a child. If that isn't progress, then I don't know what is!

"Building on a Legacy," the Los Angeles Times article stated, "Nadia Davis Brings Father's Voice of Latino Activism to Santa Ana's School Board." "I feel he's made things happen for me," they quoted me saying. "I feel closer to him if I continue his vision." I was flying in my element, ready to bring more warmth and light into this world.

My friendships were real, fun, and immensely fulfilling.

We'd laugh, share stories, and open up about our day-to-day realities. It was absolutely wonderful. Looking back, I can see that I never had a sense of feeling alone or isolated. It wasn't even a concept to me then.

About a week or so after the election, Beth and I attended a community group meeting called Los Amigos of Orange County. I stood up to thank individuals for their support and offered to take any questions and hear any concerns regarding our local education system. Then I sat down.

Amin David, the founder and leader of Los Amigos, stood up and called on people raising their hands. A woman in the back stood up and began to speak in a desperate, emotional tone about her plight to "save" her son.

She said he was only sixteen years old and "innocent." That he was wrongfully convicted of several felonies and facing many years in prison. She said he had no prior criminal history and that there was no evidence linking him to the crimes besides a faulty identification received after police placed a hat on his head that wasn't his.

Someone interjected and shouted, "Nadia is an attorney now and she'll help you." The community knew me by then. I was a bleeding heart to the core. I thought, *Yeah, sure, count me in. I'll do my best to help you find an attorney.*

At least that was my initial plan. I had just received my license to practice law months prior and was well aware of my learning curve should I take up such an endeavor. And of course I believed in justice wholeheartedly, but I admittedly needed more evidence and information to believe he was actually innocent. I needed to see the records and files. I needed to meet him myself and look him in the eyes. I needed to know I would actually be fighting for the right thing.

Arthur Carmona was like any other child in the school district I was elected to serve. He came from a family like any other family in my constituency. He had an older brother who passed away when Arthur was only a year and a half. His younger sister Veronica was born when he was five and they shared a very close bond. They were raised in church and close to extended family.

His uncle Ray was like a brother to him and very much his role model. Arthur admired that he was going to college to become a police officer. He and his sister spent a lot of time hanging out at their grandparents', going to the movies, and doing chores or repairs on their house in Santa Ana.

Arthur was also close to his aunt Mona and her children. Mona was already a police officer in Santa Ana. Like other kids his age, when not with his sister, he hung out with his cousin Frankie and friends at the complex where he lived in Costa Mesa, going to the pool, arcades, or the basketball court.

During a normal school week, he went to school, headed straight home, had a snack, did his homework, then babysat his sister until his parents came home. He was a shy and average student with a slight learning disability.

On the weekends, he had a 10 p.m. curfew and Sundays were family day. He went to South Coast Martial Arts & Boxing and participated in many tournaments. His competitions became a family event, and they'd all celebrate afterwards with a BBQ.

Things changed at home when his father's drinking worsened. His father had an affair and became somewhat violent with his mother. Arthur found himself stepping in front of her so his father would not hit or push her. This went on for a year or so until one day his father never returned home. It was right before school let out in the summer of 1997.

Arthur's mother, Ronnie, sat him and his sister down and laid it out to them.

"Your father has some things to work out and I'm going to have to support you on my own now." She had just graduated from college and they had little money and food. On his own,

Arthur decided to help out and got a summer job through the J.T.P.A. Youth Program, a federally funded job training and services program for disadvantaged and at-risk youth, dislocated workers, and displaced homemakers.

During this transition, Arthur tried to stay in contact with his father, but his calls were rarely or never returned. He took it hard. The pain began to overwhelm Arthur and he began spending less time at home to escape it.

He could have turned in the wrong direction. But not Arthur Carmona. He turned to his church and his mother's side of the family for comfort instead. He also got close to Pastor Ken and the youth group at Seeker's Chapel. Pastor Ken would visit him at home just about every week. Arthur used part of the money he earned to attend the church's retreat where he made a deeper commitment to follow a spiritual way of life and never place himself in a position of compromise.

Eventually, Arthur, his sister, and his mother moved in with his aunt Mona. By the end of summer, Ronnie was working and able to get them an apartment in Costa Mesa. Arthur began his sophomore year of high school soon thereafter. When school was in session, he hung out a lot with his friend Paul, who was a good student and on the football team. He helped Arthur with school, and they worked out a lot in his garage gym.

That was the reality and truth of Arthur Carmona's life on February 12, 1998.

Tragically, Arthur's good spirit and intentions would be marred and derailed due to the bad, unjustifiable, and illegal acts of a long list of bad characters and selfish people—individuals who don't give a damn about a kid like him, who railroad innocent beings just trying to do their best in life with what was given to them, who spit on the rights of youth with dreams.

On the afternoon of February 12, 1998, a man named

"Walid" was working at a Juice Club in Irvine and noticed a young Hispanic man, maybe fifteen to eighteen years old, peering inside the store window. The man walked away. A little time passed, and he saw the man return and sit on the bench outside for a little while. But then he left again.

Around 3:30 p.m., Walid said the young Hispanic man returned again but this time entered the store. Standing at the cash register, Walid said he looked up at the man and gestured, *Can I help you?* Instead of responding, the Hispanic man walked over to a snack shelf, picked up a couple, then put them back. The entire time, the Hispanic man was holding a single dollar bill in his hand.

At one point, he opened his wallet and Walid saw it was empty. This caused Walid to get a gut feeling that something was off, so he removed all the twenty- and fifty-dollar bills from the register and locked them away in the back of the store.

Walid returned to the front of the store soon thereafter. The man was still there. Two female customers were now also waiting at the counter. Walid took the women's orders and began to make their smoothies. By this time, there were two additional Juice Club workers present in the front who were helping.

At that point, the young Hispanic man walked up to the counter, placed the dollar on top of the cash register, and said, "I need quarters." Walid opened the register. The man reached into his backpack, pulled out a gun, pushed it into the worker's chest, and said, "Put the money in the bag."

Another employee started to walk up, and the Hispanic man ordered that worker, "Get the fuck back." The coworker backed off and put up their hands. Walid quickly put all the money from the register into the bag, then showed the man that there was nothing more under the drawer.

"Everybody get down," the Hispanic man immediately

said, and they all did. They listened for him to walk out and when they heard the door close, they called 911.

That morning, Ronnie left home for work and Arthur woke up around 10 a.m. There was no school that day, so he slept in, stayed in bed, and watched cartoons. He got up to iron some clothes, clean his room, and listen to music, before returning to watch more television.

At around 1 p.m., Arthur said he got on the phone and talked off and on with different friends, including Edwin. They talked about possibly visiting a female friend later that day. After the call, he listened to music. Between his phone call chats with friends, at some point he turned the music up so loud, the neighbor above pounded his foot on the floor, insinuating the need to turn it down. Arthur turned it down.

Between 2 and 3 p.m., "Lisa" knocked on his front door to pick up his sister Veronica. Arthur opened the door and they talked for a minute or so before his sister left with her. At about 3 p.m., Arthur called his friend Paul and they talked for about five minutes. Paul eventually had to get off the phone because his brother was waiting for him outside.

About a half hour later, around 3:30 p.m. or so, Arthur left the apartment and took off on his bike without a helmet. He headed north on Harbor Boulevard toward Baker to visit his friend Roy. Roy lived with his family in Costa Mesa in a house just one street south of the 405 freeway, north of Baker, and west of Fairview. This is precisely where the 405 and 73 freeways merge and several interchanges are.

My handwritten notes:

We need all of this. Where is it? Did anyone look into these? Why didn't anyone testify? Challenge to timeline? 1) Cell phone records proving calls to friends between 10 a.m. and 3

p.m., Arthur's location; 2) Declaration and tes-
timony of Edwin regarding plans for later that
day; 3) Declaration and testimony of Lisa re-
garding Arthur's location between 2–3 p.m.; 4)
Declaration and testimony of sister, Veronica,
regarding Arthur's location same time; 5) Cell
phone record proving Arthur's location to
friend Paul; 6) Declaration and testimony of
Paul regarding call from Arthur; 7) Any apart-
ment neighbors, camera footage, workers in
stores on Harbor etc. that would prove Arthur's
bike route and his location at the time?

At this exact same time, the Juice Club in Irvine had just been robbed. It was located next to a video store, a flower shop, and a coffee shop. In addition, a Texaco gas station was across the street. A man named "Cashion," an Irvine resident, no-ticed an older-model pickup truck painted a primer gray color beside the station. He saw a man inside sitting in the driver's seat as though he was waiting for someone.

When Cashion finished filling his tank, he then saw a young Hispanic man running across the street toward the gray pickup, wearing a black coat with white stripes and carrying a black bag. For a moment, Cashion lost sight of the man, but then he saw the gray pickup pulling out onto the street. The driver was turned and leaning toward his right as though he were talking to a passenger.

Cashion had a gut instinct and decided to write down the li-cense plate number. Soon thereafter, he heard sirens on the way.

My handwritten notes continued:

8) What about video footage of any store, park-
ing lot at or around the Juice Club stores, gas

station, intersection that day? 9) Any finger-
prints taken from the store or off snacks robber
held? Bench? 10) Declarations and testimony of
main worker, two employees, two female cus-
tomers, and gas station man can use to chal-
lenge timeline Arthur couldn't possibly be there;
11) Declaration and testimony of Cashion re:
time he was at gas station and saw men in car;
12) Exact time of 911 call? Arthur could not
have been there at that time!

Irvine police arrived at the Juice Club moments after the 911 call. They received a statement from the main worker, Walid, and got descriptions of the robber from all three employees (Walid, "Joseph," "Samuel") and the two female customers (Janet and "Stephanie"). Between the five of them, the descriptions varied considerably.

- Employee Walid's description: maybe 15–18 yrs. old, thin mustache, dark, very short hair, wearing blue jeans, sweat jacket with a white stripe, bright-white tennis shoes, a black Lakers cap on his head, black backpack.
- Employee Joseph's description: male Hispanic, 6' tall, 165 lbs., slim face and body, wore a baseball cap and black pants.
- Employee Samuel's description: 5'9" tall, 150 lbs., wore a black baseball cap.
- Two female customers' description: 5'4" tall, 110 lbs.
- Gas station customer Cashion's description: Hispanic man, black coat with white stripes and black backpack.

The police were puzzled. But then the man at the gas station, Cashion, ran up and told the officers what he saw and gave them the license plate number. Officers ran the plate and found it was connected to a thirty-three-year-old Hawaiian named "Kawaii" with an address of 1000 South Coast Drive in Costa Mesa.

Around 4 p.m., police officers from both Irvine and Costa Mesa headed toward this location; 1000 South Coast Drive in Costa Mesa is located immediately north of the 405 and 73 freeways, west of the South Coast Plaza. There are several routes one can take from the Juice Club in Irvine to 1000 South Coast Drive in Costa Mesa.

A woman named "Hoffman" lived in the same neighborhood as Roy, which is on the opposite side of the two merging freeways. Hoffman's house was on Cheyenne Street, immediately next to the 73 freeway sound wall. The sound wall was in her backyard at the top of a rising slope covered with grass and trees.

Around the same time police were heading toward Kawaii's apartment, Hoffman was lying on her sofa watching TV when she saw a young Hispanic man appear at the top of the wall, coming from the freeway side, then jump down to the slope into her backyard. She said the man was wearing a dark cap and a dark-colored T-shirt with a long-sleeved white shirt underneath. She said the Hispanic man started running south through the yards and shrubbery directly along the sound wall. She called the police.

Just before or around 4 p.m., Arthur was still on his way to Roy's house. After going north up Harbor, he headed east going right on Baker toward Fairview. After he crossed Fairview, he noticed police around.

Arthur did not know why a police helicopter was hovering above. The police presence made him nervous. Why? Because he didn't have a helmet on and had received a ticket for not wearing one before. He thought it would be a good idea to drop off his bike first at his friend Frank's house before going to Roy's.

Frank lived nearby on Mendoza Drive, south of Baker. When Arthur knocked on the door, Frank was vacuuming the carpet. He stopped vacuuming and opened the door. Arthur explained there were police around and that he didn't have a helmet, then asked if he could leave his bike there. Frank said ok.

A little after 4 p.m., after dropping off his bike, Arthur made a quick phone call to his friend Paul as he headed on foot to Roy's.

My handwritten notes:

What time did Hoffman call the police? 13) Proof Arthur went to Frank's and dropped off bike? (Yes, bike remained there for months) 14) Declaration and testimony of Frank stating time he saw Arthur physically? 15) Arthur and Paul's cell phone records showing location and time of call? 16) Declaration and testimony of Paul re: Arthur's call at this time?

A little after 4 p.m., both Irvine and Costa Mesa police officers arrived at 1000 South Coast Drive, Costa Mesa. They saw the truck with the license plate and asked the apartment manager to call Kawaii and tell him his truck was about to be towed.

Kawaii walked out a few moments later. He was detained and told the police that he had been at a gas station, a guy got in his car, had a gun, and told him "to take him down the freeway and drop him off, that if I told anything to anybody, he'd kill me."

The police found a Lakers cap in the truck. They searched his apartment and found walkie-talkies, a black backpack, a Juice Club cup, and a 9mm pistol that was reported stolen five years prior in Meridian, Mississippi.

As Arthur was walking north into Roy's neighborhood, police were on patrol in the entire area south of the 405 and 73 freeways. The description of the Juice Club robber broadcasted over police radios was "young Hispanic male, wearing a baseball hat and a dark jacket, carrying a backpack."

The police helicopter above directed Costa Mesa Police Officer "Sanders" toward a "possible suspect" walking along the sidewalk near the intersection of Pierce and Concord Street, smack in the middle of the neighborhood where Roy lived, and Arthur was walking.

Officer Sanders pulled up alongside the "young Hispanic man" in his police car. He told him to stop. Arthur stopped, confused and bewildered. Within seconds, Officer Sanders pulled out his gun, aimed it at Arthur, and asked him his name.

"Arthur Carmona," he said.

Do you think a guilty person would stop, let alone respond truthfully to a question like that? No. But an innocent kid does. An innocent kid doesn't run to escape like the guy hopping the fence did.

"What are you doing? . . . Where are you going? . . . Where have you been?" Officer Sanders asked, back-to-back, interrupting Arthur as he tried to speak in a state of shock. All the while, helicopter propellers sounded above and more squad cars arrived and blanketed the entire street like a swarm.

While all this was happening, Arthur did his best to calmly answer Officer Sanders's questions. But the officer determined Arthur's answers were vague, that he was "hesitant" and thus "suspicious." He was also unaware Arthur had a slight learning disability.

Arthur's 16th birthday was a week before that day,

February 5, 1998. The only illegal things he had ever done in those sixteen years were to ride a bike without a helmet and carry a small bat to school in his bag.

He had never committed a crime and had no criminal record.

At the time, Arthur had an average build and was 5'10" tall, about 165 pounds, and wore his black hair shaved pretty close to his head. He also had a goatee and bad acne. When he was stopped, he was not carrying a backpack, nor wearing a hat or dark jacket.

Tragically, he lost his youth and freedom just because he was walking in the wrong neighborhood at the wrong time to do what any youth would do on a day off from school, hang out with friends.

Why did police zero in on and stop Arthur?

Police later admitted the description fit a number of people in the area at the time. Actually, it probably fit thousands within a mile radius. Fact is, police already had a burning desire to catch someone, anyone, even an innocent kid, for what had been a string of Juice Club and other robberies in the County before February 12, 1998. The pressure was on.

Just catch "him" . . . the "young Hispanic man with a dark jacket."

That is what Arthur became to them, and nothing more.

A proud "we got 'em now" sort of thing.

To them, he had no soul, future, or hopes. He was branded guilty in a flash. And from there on out, his entire identity was replaced with a big fat lie.

***

The police theorized that the robber ran away from Kawaii's apartment on the other side of the freeway, somehow ran across the entirety of two different freeway junctures, climbed the sound wall in Hoffman's backyard, ran away going south in the dirt and bushes along the wall, but then suddenly changed his mind, turned around and walked straight into the neighborhood of patrolling police cars.

Um, does this make sense? I don't know, but at least a jury should have been asked this question.

Arthur was not out of breath.

Arthur's clothes and shoes were clean, free of dirt and shrubbery.

Does this matter? Um, I don't know. Would a jury want to know Arthur's complete physical state and appearance at the time he was stopped? Maybe. Should they have been given this information to consider for themselves? Yes.

What happened after he was stopped is an unbelievable tragedy.

The proof of Arthur's innocence was destroyed. How?

Witnesses from the Juice Club were brought to where Arthur was being held. "Take a look, is that the young Hispanic man?"

None of the witnesses could identify him completely. There was no "yes, without a doubt" or "that's him" straight shots.

Walid, the Juice Club worker at the cash register and closest to the robber, said he was maybe 80 percent sure. But the police needed more.

Hoffman was brought to the scene. While she was sitting in a police car about a house length away from where Arthur was, in the rain and at dusk, she was asked if he was the man she saw in her backyard. She wasn't sure either.

But then she asked if Arthur had been wearing a hat.

The police should have said no, right? Well, they didn't.

There is a concept called evidence integrity. Any information that derives from the examination of physical evidence depends entirely on the level of care and protection it is given in order to prevent contamination. All police officers know that physical evidence is supposed to stay in what is called a "chain of custody." This means limiting the number of individuals handling evidence, confirming that all names, identification numbers, and dates are listed on the chain-of-custody documents, and ensuring that all evidence packaging is properly sealed and marked prior to submission for testing.

But instead of ending their attempt to receive an identification and preserving the evidence found in Kawaii's vehicle, officers did something extremely unethical and unusual. Consult any expert law enforcement witness and they will undoubtedly tell you what happened next was a flagrant, flat-out disregard of evidentiary integrity, let alone planting of evidence.

Remember, they found a Lakers cap in Kawaii's truck parked at his apartment. It was on the other side of two freeways in a parking space nowhere close to Arthur. That infamous hat contained the golden key to his freedom: DNA . . . sweat, hair, and skin residue. Tests can reveal the identity of the person who wore it and exclude anyone that never did. It should've been sealed and sent away as is.

What happened instead?

Police transported the hat to Arthur rather than a DNA lab.

One of the officers placed the hat on Arthur's head.

DNA of the guilty was tainted.

DNA of the innocent falsely planted.

Worse, Walid and Hoffman were now convinced Arthur was the guy. It went something like, "The face alone, I can't do it. But I recognize the hat."

Arthur was immediately handcuffed, detained, and put into the police car.

He watched in tears as the cops all gave each other high fives. He watched them walk away moments after his freedom was lost.

My handwritten notes:

17) DNA tainted on cap when placed on Arthur!!! What the hell! Any follicle hair found and tested? 18) Any camera footage at Kawaii's apartment structure, all main streets around 405 and 73 junctures, on and off ramps, gas station footage to track truck's possible route? 19) Any fingerprints taken off pistol? (reported stolen in 1993, Meridian, Mississippi. Arthur was 11 years old. Proof of where he was at the time? State, city, school?) 20) Any fingerprints taken off juice club cup? 21) Any fingerprints taken off car doors, seat, belt? items in car? 22) Any evidence of such from other robberies Kawaii connected with and same MO? Additional guns, jackets, backpacks, scanners, hats found; 23) Did his defense attorney make any Motions to suppress???

But there was not only overwhelming reason to challenge the timeline, faulty identification, and lack of physical evidence, there was also a load of compelling physical evidence that police and prosecutors were never able to link to Arthur.

Remember, they found a couple of walkie-talkies, a used Juice Club cup, and a 9mm pistol at Kawaii's apartment. The robber opened the door of the truck, sat inside it, and thus probably also touched items in it. According to all the witnesses, he was not wearing gloves. Were any of these tested for prints? Not really.

This is the deal. There apparently was a fingerprint found on a CD in the car that did not match Arthur's. Even more exculpatory, Arthur's fingerprints weren't found anywhere, on anything, in the car or Kawaii's apartment. The police even gave a detective dog the scent from Arthur's T-shirt, but the dog was unable to identify the scent in the gray pickup.

***

Later that evening, Arthur was interrogated by two Irvine police officers, "Cain" and "Montgomery."

"Would you like to talk to us about what happened today?" Officer Cain asked.

"Yeah," Arthur said.

"Yeah? That was yes?"

"Yes."

"Ok. Basically, it's our understanding that the Juice Club was robbed by somebody with a gun matching your description. We had several people go over to where you were stopped in Costa Mesa and they said you were the guy who did it," Officer Cain said, then went on. "Now, we have a lot of questions. We think there might have been somebody else involved. We're not sure. We'd like to hear what your side of the story is on this. Why don't you go ahead and tell us what went down, what we need to know about it?"

"I don't know anything about that," Arthur said.

"You know, we want nothing from you but the truth," Officer Cain said. "We don't want you to be trying to shine us on. We've got a lot of people. We got people that identified you."

"I'm telling you the truth straight up," Arthur said.

> *Officer Cain, let me tell you something. The jury and the public wanted the truth too. Did you ever talk to Arthur's friends? Did you ever look at his cell phone? Did you ever even try to verify anything he said at all? No, you didn't.*

*Why not? 'Cuz you didn't care about the fact
you were destroying an innocent kid's life in
order to get a ribbon!*

After not getting what they wanted out of Arthur's mouth, the investigators changed the tone of their line of questioning.

"Let me tell you something," Officer Montgomery said, now chiming in. "You can lie to us if you want. We'll put all that information down, and we'll go to the judge."

"I'm not lying," Arthur insisted.

"We can absolutely, positively prove that you were in the truck," the officer continued, obviously lying, thinking the "young Hispanic man" in front of him would cave in.

"We can absolutely, positively prove that you were there and committed the robbery. You won't talk to us. I understand that. And you'll lie to us, and we'll just put that information down, let the judge make the decision once they get all the info, 'cuz we can prove that you were there, and we've got video showing you at the gas station running into the truck. We've already looked at the video, and it's you, and it's him," Officer Montgomery continued.

But Arthur didn't let up and continued insisting he was telling them the truth. Even so, the interrogation continued in the same pattern over and over again for hours. Threats, lies, more threats, more lies.

But they couldn't break Arthur. He repeatedly insisted he was telling them the truth. That he had nothing to do with the robbery. That he did not know Kawaii. That he was just on his way to see a friend. That he made some phone calls before leaving home.

Then he tried to describe the route he took on his bike but couldn't remember the names of streets in the exact order or Roy's specific address. What kid knows their friends' addresses by heart? Don't most just walk or ride their bikes there?

So the police determined his answers were "suspicious." Arthur was charged with multiple felonies, placed in a holding cell, and thereafter, transferred to jail.

> *Remember all the cell phone calls he made? Records could have shown his location. Remember all the conversations he had with friends about plans for the day to hang out? Interviews could have substantiated his words. Remember the people who directly interacted with him? They could have said where he was and at what time. Remember he dropped off his bike at a friend's minutes before he was stopped? That friend could have said what time he saw him and verified the bike was still there, etc. etc. Did the jury hear any of this evidence in his defense? No. And I get more and more pissed off as I write this decades later!*

As a mother, you can feel and see connection with your child through their eyes. Children don't need a lot of words when their eyes are looking straight into yours. When there is a shift inside them, you just instinctively know. It is called deep attunement. Whether it be love, glee, fear, or anger, a mother can read their eyes and tell in a split second. Even more, if there is a deeper change in character, a mother sees it happening way before any outward display.

Arthur's mother, Ronnie, was called by police at 6:30 p.m. that same evening. When she heard the officer's words, "Your son Arthur was arrested for armed robbery," the shock hit her like a dagger in the heart. She knew her son had no capacity in any part of his being to do such a thing. Her son's eyes held an innocence and hope for the future. Shy and timid, her son's eyes looked upon others respectfully. Her son's eyes had dreams and innocence and love.

How could this be? she thought over and over. Nothing made any sense.

She immediately paged her sister Mona, the Santa Ana police officer. Mona called the Costa Mesa Police Department, and said she was a fellow officer and also Arthur's aunt. She ended up speaking with the supervisor, who seemed uncertain and confused, like he wondered why Arthur had been arrested. He asked her many questions. Did she know Kawaii? Did the family know him in any way? Did Arthur have access to her weapons? "No, no, and absolutely not," she said over and over.

Ronnie and Mona talked most of the night. Over and over again, they repeated to themselves, "This doesn't make sense. It's impossible. How could this be?" They questioned themselves as mothers and aunts. They analyzed their own past mistakes. They had worked hard and enabled progress and stability for the family.

With Arthur, due to his father's absence, they paid particular attention to teach him good values and steer him away from drugs, gangs, and bad influences. They had evidence their efforts paid off when they saw how he respected the law and police. In fact, Arthur defended the police and their fairness when his friends complained they couldn't be trusted, proudly telling them that his aunt was a police officer, and she was fair and trustworthy. He respected his 10 p.m. curfew and looked out for his sister.

They immediately went into first gear to fight for Arthur's freedom, bringing a former Santa Ana police officer turned private investigator, "Marshal," on board.

***

First things first. Solidifying Arthur's alibis.

Marshal contacted several people Arthur spoke to or was

in contact with, and confirmed the interactions. All probably could and would have testified or provided a statement. Even more shocking was the fact Marshal discovered police were trying to connect Arthur to a string of other similar robberies, but he had the best alibi ever . . . school records proving he was in class at the time they occurred. And of course, there was absolutely no physical evidence connecting Arthur to the slew of other robberies they were attempting to lay on him.

Did the jury hear Marshal testify about this? No. Did Arthur's defense attorney call these alibis to testify? No. Did he question police if they were aware that Arthur was in school at the time of the other incidents? No.

Second, the veracity and lack of eyewitness identifications.

Upon interviewing the in-field eyewitnesses the day of Arthur's arrest, Marshal discovered both Walid and Hoffman were not certain they had identified the right "young Hispanic man." Even more striking is the fact that Officer Cain subsequently contacted the two female customers in the Juice Club the day of the robbery; neither could identify Arthur.

Did the jury ever hear Marshal testify about this? No. Did Arthur's defense attorney call Marshal, the in-field witnesses, and the Juice Club customers to testify about this? No. To express their uncertainty that Arthur was the robber? No. That they couldn't identify him based on his face alone? No. That they only recognized the hat? No. Did Arthur's defense attorney present any example of what a solid witness identification would look like? Any expert on the matter? No.

Third, the lack of any link between Arthur and "Kawaii."

Three different investigators were unable to find any evidence of any prior existing contact or relationship between the two. Investigator Marshal could attest from experience that similar age and ethnic groups showed a pattern of committing crimes together. Kawaii, thirty-three years old; Arthur, sixteen. Kawaii, Hawaiian; Arthur, Hispanic. To Marshal, it was a highly unlikely duo.

Still, Mona vigorously asked his friends and her children if they had ever seen or heard any slight indication from Arthur that he had an older friend. Was he in contact with someone Hawaiian? Had he done something bad? Was he planning something serious? No. Nope. And no.

"Mom," they told her. "Art just hung out with kids."

Irvine police investigator Cain's attempts to find any connection between the two were also unsuccessful. When he first questioned Kawaii, he said he was carjacked by a robber. This crazy claim was smashed, of course, when the gun, backpack, walkie-talkies, and Juice Club cup were found in his apartment.

It was also noted that there was little if any acknowledgment of each other, nor exchange of words between Kawaii and Arthur when they were put together in the back of the police car. In normal police practice, this is apparently highly unusual.

Officer Cain then tried to track down Kawaii's ex-girlfriend but to no avail and noted in the report he couldn't even remember her name. Did Officer Cain speak to Kawaii's mother, with whom he lived at the time of the robbery? Strange that the reports do not show if he did. We don't know. However, sure enough, a different private investigator named "Rowell" later did. When Kawaii's mother was shown a picture of Arthur and asked if she had ever seen him at her residence, she responded, while looking at the photo, "He doesn't look familiar," nor did she recognize the name Arthur Carmona.

And Kawaii? What did he have to say about Arthur? Tragically, with minimum effort and reflection, he quickly signed a three-sentence statement naming Arthur as the robber in exchange for a short term of two years in jail. However, when visited in jail by Investigator Rowell, Kawaii said he did not know Arthur prior to the arrest, that the first time he ever saw Arthur was when he was asked to identify him the day of arrest, and when they were both placed in the back seat of the police car.

Kawaii then said Arthur "didn't have anything to do with it. And I know he wasn't involved in it." Then he even had the audacity to tell Arthur he had said that, obviously somewhat remorseful. *What an absolutely incredibly sick jerk.*

Did the jury hear that there was no proof of any existing relationship between Arthur and Kawaii? No. Did they receive any data information about age and ethnic patterns of crimes from Marshal or elsewhere? No. That there was no interaction between the two in the police car and this was highly unusual? No. That Kawaii's mother said she never saw nor recognized Arthur? No. That police forgot Kawaii's ex-girlfriend's name thus couldn't track her down? No. That Kawaii later stated he did not know Arthur prior to the arrest? And Arthur didn't have anything to do with it? Was not involved? No, no, and no.

Did Arthur's defense attorney call Mona, Arthur's friends, cousins to testify about this? Did he call Kawaii, the officers, or any one of the private investigators to testify about any of this? No.

Four, the robbers' getaway route and clothing.

The witnesses said the robber was wearing different clothes than Arthur. So Officers Cain and Montgomery looked for discarded clothing by walking the journey from Kawaii's apartment, across the 73 freeway, over the sound wall into Hoffman's backyard on Cheyenne Street, up to the spot on Pierce Avenue where Arthur was stopped. They found nothing.

> *Did the jury hear that the witnesses' description of clothing worn by the robber differed from Arthur's? That officers found no discarded clothing? Did Arthur's defense attorney question the officers about this on the stand? No.*

No one, not one single person close to Arthur, expected they'd actually keep the charges. Still, Arthur was charged with the Juice Club robbery and, shockingly, a completely separate Costa Mesa Denny's robbery. He faced a dozen years in prison.

Eight months passed not knowing the future of anything before Arthur came to trial, October 13–21, 1998.

When you look at the photos of Arthur prior to his arrest, it is heartbreaking knowing what I saw in his eyes after months of wrongful incarceration. The cost of injustice on an innocent child oozed like blood out of his eyes, stature, and entire demeanor. Everything about the before and after is beyond tragic and undeniable.

> *Dear Son,*
>
> *Today, as I write this, you are the same age Arthur was the day of his arrest and loss of freedom. Just sixteen years old, with your entire*

life ahead of you. When I imagine this happening to you, I lose my mind. Tragically, there are thousands upon thousands of innocent sons and daughters—youth and adult men and women—held wrongfully, unjustifiably behind bars today . . . How and why can we as a society accept this? Exoneration is possible through DNA testing and reforms must continue throughout the criminal justice system to prevent further injustice. Your generation can and will continue the fight, no doubt. In the meantime, I'll strive to do all I can to raise awareness and seek justice. (www.innocenceproject.org) (www.californiainnocenceproject.org)

    Love, Mom

CHAPTER 5

Dear Son,

the truth is the truth

and it must win.

Brace yourself, the Arthur Carmona trial was quite a painful, tragic, and unbelievable set of scenes.

Arthur was given a court-appointed attorney in lieu of a public defender. His name was Kenneth Reed, an experienced criminal lawyer who had tried more than eighty jury cases. He was aware the state's case depended entirely on unreliable eyewitness identifications that were dependent on the wrongful placement of the Lakers cap on Arthur's head. Still, he made no effort prior to trial to exclude them. If he had done so, the prosecutor would have had nothing to present to the jury. Instead, Deputy District Attorney Hoffman focused like a laser on them.

In court, Joseph, an employee at the Juice Club, said he just wasn't sure the robber was Arthur and could only identify him after police put the Lakers hat on his head. He also said the robber held the gun in his right hand. Arthur is left-handed.

Samuel, the other employee, could not identify Arthur in court.

Cashion, the gas station customer, testified that the only thing he could say to police was that "his body shape was the right size," and nothing more.

Hoffman (no relation to prosecutor) testified that it was only the Lakers hat that "concreted in my mind that it was him."

George, a witness at the Denny's robbery, testified that when he was shown a photo lineup, Arthur's picture was merely the "closest" to the robber. He also said the robber held the gun in his right hand, but remember, Arthur is left-handed.

Casey, another witness at Denny's, said she made her identification of Arthur based on his eyes.

On cross-examination, Reed made some headway. He indeed was able to question the witnesses enough to suggest that identifications weren't solid and mostly depended on the Lakers cap.

Some hope for Arthur, you'd think.

Now it was time to win the case. To give the jury something to weigh against any possible lingering false belief in the tainted identifications.

What happened?

Reed failed to call an expert witness to the stand to challenge anything related to the hat or eyewitness identifications, including the tainting of physical evidence, the actual robber's DNA, the breach in chain of custody, the difficulties of identifications across ethnic lines, and more.

Reed failed to call to the stand Arthur's many alibis who either saw him that day, spoke with him on the phone, or both. Reed failed to call to the stand any of Arthur's character witnesses, including his pastor or teachers.

He didn't even call Arthur to testify. He gave the jury no set of eyes, tone of voice, nor shy demeanor to remember as they deliberated.

The only defense witnesses he presented were his mother, Ronnie, and his younger sister, Veronica.

When the prosecutor, Hoffman, gave her closing argument, she stood up, clearly knowing no exculpatory evidence or defense had really been presented. She actually had the guts to argue that the blunders of the police didn't matter because Arthur had been "positively identified by eyewitnesses."

This was not true, we all know.

You see, the truth didn't matter to her.

A kid's entire life didn't even vaguely enter her mind when she said this, knowing the placement of the hat on Arthur's head was a disgrace. All she cared about was "winning." *And for what, Ms. Hoffman? To get a high mark on your file?*

Worse, in the immediate moments after, Reed just sat there, without any slight shift in his body or minuscule effort to challenge such a fraudulent, unjust, and horrific statement.

In fact, shockingly and to the utter devastation of Arthur and his family, these were Mr. Reed's last words to the jury on behalf of Arthur Carmona prior to their determination of his fate.

"Ladies and gentlemen, there is a constant in the criminal law. It's the same from Bangor, Maine, down to the Florida Keys. No different from Alaska than San Isidro at the foot of the state . . . That constant is that no state, no federal prosecutor . . . may take the life, liberty of the individual, of a person, without first proving that the person is guilty beyond a reasonable doubt." A passionate beginning, yes. However, from there on out, he made no sense, was unfocused and rambling, quickly losing the attention of the jury.

Further exacerbating the punch of even a pitiful closing summation was the fact that the judge interrupted him for a short recess. Why? One of the deputy marshals responsible for watching Arthur was actually nodding off as Reed spoke.

When court resumed, Reed continued, then concluded, quite painfully and desperately, with this: "I've been up here today almost fifty minutes but been up here for the better part of an hour, and my voice is getting dry, and I am tired, and I am missing things," he said. "I write these notes, and I get wound up and forget what I am saying, so I will stop . . . We go to law school, got to give us a chance to talk to you. Part of the rules. We need to be able to talk and say what we feel. We need to argue. I made arguments or said things, objected, argumentative. This is the time for me to argue to you . . . So when I sit down, I know I have forgotten something because I've forgotten something every time I've done this." It tragically continued like this, until he finally wound down and he stopped speaking altogether, having actually said nothing at all.

Any dedicated attorney realizing they perhaps held an entire child's future in their final words would prepare a focused, succinct, logical presentation clearly outlining evidence sufficing to create reasonable doubt, right? Easy peasy in a case with lists of exculpatory evidence.

All he had to do was read a list of alibis, holes in the case, and say something simple for them to hold on to, anything for them to hold on to: "Members of the jury, when you go into deliberation, please remember these three things: the hat wasn't his, no one could identify him without it, and it is impossible he could've been at the scene of the robbery."

It is maddening, indescribably painful to read the transcript.

I can't even fathom what it must have been like for Arthur and his mother to be forced to sit there in the courtroom and listen.

Now that, Your Honor, should be a crime.

The jurors deliberated.

Arthur was found guilty.

Now he faced up to thirty years in prison.

***

When I think of the pain Ronnie Carmona went through in this moment, my heart breaks tenfold. It is impossible to fathom and excruciating to imagine.

What can a mother possibly say or do to give their innocent imprisoned child hope? Where does a mother place that vigorous yearning to do something, anything to comfort their child when walls, bars, steel, guards, and miles separate you from the very flesh that grew in your womb?

When I first met Ronnie, I was not yet a mother. Nor did I know the excruciating pain of being separated from your child. But I would someday, and Ronnie's example of impenetrable strength helped me through.

The tiger mama instinct is impossible to quell. And Arthur had a mother that was never going to give up. Ever. And neither did I.

***

It was shortly after the trial that I first met Ronnie Carmona at the Los Amigos meeting. We set up a time to meet alone. She brought boxes of files with her. She told me years later that she thought I was just a kid and was concerned.

Indeed, a handful of other local elected officials told me to "be careful" or "watch your back," that it would negatively affect my "career" and relationship with law enforcement. Frankly, that motivated me more, their status quo and representation a disgrace in my eyes.

I spent several days late at the office reading over files, taking notes, doing general research. The pile of yellow pad pages is enormous. Questions, questions, and more questions. They were endless. There were hundreds of holes and unanswered questions. A ton of exculpatory evidence no one ever cared to obtain or present to the jury. It was almost as though Arthur was a piece of chattel in a traveling cage, going from one professional handler to another without any consideration that he was a human being.

> *Oh, and Mr. Reed, yes, I admit, I hadn't a clue where to start. But time was running out. Oh, and where the hell were you the last year, knowing the kid was railroaded and still in jail? I just don't understand. Will someone please explain it to me? How do you live that way?*

From the police, to the jail guards, to the court-appointed attorney, prosecutor, jury, and onwards, he traveled on a systematic factory belt without a single professional stopping and saying, "Hey, uh, something doesn't look right here. Oh, and by the way, there's a kid's life on the line."

I went to get advice from the best person I knew to get it from, Al Stokke, my father's former law partner and best friend. It felt like a homecoming. It felt surreal, but then so normal at the same time. I told him the facts. I said I couldn't ignore the injustice.

He said, "Nadia, I heard about this case, and, yes, the kid was railroaded. But I can't take it. You do it. You can do it," he said.

Ok, I thought. *At least I can get the fight for Arthur's freedom off and running. After that, we'll see where we go from there.*

I thought, *How the hell can I turn my back on this kid and his mother when here I was asking hundreds, thousands of families to vote for me? Children and their parents that fit the exact same profile? A "young Hispanic man and his loving mother"? What was the worth in being an elected representative of the people if I just stood by while this injustice continued?*

The first time I went to the Santa Ana jail, I was on the preferred side of the glass, in a suit, and free. The guards looked at me with respect.

I sat down and waited. Arthur walked in several minutes later. He was shy yet surprised, solid yet fragile. He had already been in jail for nearly a year, and it showed.

"Hi, my name is Nadia Davis. I met your mom, and we talked a lot. I'm going to try and help you," I said. "There are people out here that believe in you and your truth." He looked up, then looked down and shook his head. "Arthur, the truth matters, and I will do everything in my power to see that it wins," I continued.

He looked up immediately and gazed straight into my eyes like a small child. Innocence was written all over his face. It oozed from inside out as he said, "Thank you." But it seemed my words had stabbed him in the heart.

The kid was trying to separate his soul from his body in order to survive. No kid should be forced to do that. It is murder inside. The state was killing a kid. Didn't they realize that?

Arthur,

> *Today, I know what it feels like to have your truth denied. I do not know as a kid how you managed to survive inside. Thoughts enter the mind like, "My truth is my truth; the truth is the truth, period. But no one in power will ever acknowledge it. The truth is inconvenient and easily thrown away. I might as well give up all hope and stay numb instead." I know you understood exactly how this feels. And I know*

you were just a kid who had to bear it all alone
locked up. Did you begin to let your mind win?
How did you maintain hope? You are my hero,
dear Arthur, you saved me you know.
    Nadia

The kid is really innocent, Nadia! I thought as I walked out
the doors to freedom while he was being walked back to his
tiny cell. *Oh my God, there is no turning back now. You gotta*
free this kid. You gotta figure it out.

Looking back now, I should have put my energy into raising funds to bail him out. Sadly, it had been set at a range for
a three striker, $250,000. Astonishing, considering he had
absolutely no prior record. I still could've done it. Just never
thought of that then. Hindsight is a bitch. I would've bailed
him out, looked him in the eyes, and said, "Get the hell out of
here, kid," with a map to Canada and my car keys.

God, I wish I had done this for so many reasons. You'll see.

The next court hearing was around the corner, February
5, 1999.

I was literally sworn into public office two weeks before and
in the trenches of closing down campaign practicalities and
the filings required. I also was inundated with binders from
the Superintendent's office providing an overview of the district, the sixth largest in the state. Board meetings began and I
took the role very seriously, reading page after page of weekly
dockets with proposed policy changes and legal matters.

But for Arthur, time was of the essence.

In other words, I was in over my head.

It's clear I approached Arthur's cause more as a community advocate and organizer than an experienced attorney
from the get-go. My legal learning curve was high. But my
commitment to justice was unbreakable.

I have piles of yellow pad notes I can't count. To-do lists out the wazoo, as though I had an entire outreach team and legal staff. Varying factual and legal questions, phone numbers, faxes for attorneys, investigators, community leaders, elected officials, teachers, and more.

My best friend Bethzabe Martinez helped me as best she could while I quickly drafted a Retainer Agreement, Substitution of Attorney, and Motion for Continuance of Sentencing and New Trial. Without any experience in such matters, I literally taught myself and typed at the same time.

This was around the time of the four-year anniversary of my father's death and the holidays. I was beyond grateful to be distracted from the pain in the trenches of Arthur's case while mourning.

Get it done, Nadia, just get it done now! I said to myself, in my element and feeling close to my dad with a legal book and pleading in front of me.

Arthur, you helped me in so many ways. Thank you, dear Arthur, thank you so much.

Who the hell decides to try and free a wrongfully convicted kid? Let alone when it is their first case as an attorney? Who the heck believes that someone, somewhere in power, will do something, anything to right a wrong? Or even take a second look that one didn't happen? Well, I did. I do. I think it's always been from a naive place in me. But if naivety leads to justice and truth, then who gives a damn what they say.

The more I read, the more my heart and soul ached for this child. I had no choice but to help set him free. What was the worth of becoming an attorney otherwise? What was the purpose of the law for that matter? What would Daddy have done? How could an hour, day, weeks of time given be put anywhere else more important?

These unethical jerks in uniform and court had to see justice at work and real. The bad guys had to know they cannot get away with denying the truth. The truth is the truth and it had to win!

If you call that having guts, so be it.

But it wasn't. It was having a heart.

It didn't surprise me that the first thing out of Arthur's prior attorney's mouth to the press was, "I don't mind being second-guessed, but not by somebody who has never tried a criminal case. She's been a lawyer for less than eighteen months."

Well, Mr. Reed, you at least were right on that one.

Ronnie entrusted me with her son's freedom and future, perhaps even his life. As a mother today, thinking of what happened to her son happening to any one of mine terrifies me. No wonder she couldn't sleep and cried at night. No wonder she couldn't sit still and had to be doing something every day for him in some way.

I filed a Substitution of Attorney on November 28, 1998, "in the interests of justice to accord defendant his right to make a motion for new trial based on ineffective assistance of counsel." Then I filed a Motion for Continuance of Sentencing and New Trial "for counsel to become familiar with the case," stating a denial of the opportunity would "fail to accord the accused his right of counsel in any substantial sense."

On December 5, 1998, Judge Everett Dickey granted the continuance before a room full of Arthur's community supporters. Looking back, it was likely a rare scene in all of Orange County's courtroom history up until that time.

Who knows what thoughts were going through Judge Dickey's head? He knew Al Stokke was helping me. He knew my father was Wally Davis. But I was a "clueless," "female," "bleeding heart," and "naive" new attorney.

Plus, there was a group of diverse, casually dressed individuals with a look of protest in their eyes sitting behind me, all looking at him in his high and mighty seat of power, letting him know this one was not going to slip through the cracks.

I'm sure a bunch of thoughts like *What a naive bunch of people ran through his head. They have no idea what the hell they are doing and are wasting their time.* Or maybe not, perhaps it was, *You have a hell of a long road ahead.*

From that point on, I knew we needed help.

You see, we expected that our request for a Motion for New Trial would be denied. One can only make arguments that are based on the record. It was merely a procedural hurdle we had to jump over to get to a real appeal. It doesn't allow for submitting evidence not already presented at trial, including everything Arthur's prior defense attorney failed to present to the jury.

To do that, we would need to file an Appeal and Habeas Corpus Petition in a higher court, and that was by no means a task for a new, individual attorney without the meat, credibility, and bang of a big, well-respected law firm.

The feelers and spreading of the word went out across legal and community lines. Who would help us free Arthur Carmona, donate, or invest hundreds of thousands of dollars in legal work?

At that point, it seemed impossible.

Not only did Arthur need a strong legal team, we needed to increase community awareness of his plight, to advocate for his care, education, and assigned placements in jail, to raise significant funds to pay for legal fees and investigators.

I knew I could buy time by substituting in another attorney. So I found a local attorney, Mark Devore, through Al Stokke, but he had a small price tag. I also found a private investigator, Robert Navarro, who also had a small price tag.

The Arthur Carmona Legal Defense Fund was born, and the fundraising began out of my house. I sent out hundreds of emails and letters while Ronnie and I made pleas for donations at multiple community meetings.

Then, something miraculous happened. Ronnie and Mona called a man named Dana Parsons, a columnist for the *Los Angeles Times*. After an overview of the case, he got stuck on a couple of facts that he couldn't budge from his brain . . . the Lakers cap and the lack of link and big age difference between Kawaii and Arthur. At this point, he wasn't sure of Arthur's innocence, but he was convinced that the trial was unfair.

> *Dear Son,*
>
> *The press can be a lighthouse to the truth or an artist of scandal. A reporter can be an angel of light or a thief of hope. Sometimes facts are sought out and uncovered. Sometimes they are ignored and marred. Thankfully, Arthur got an angel in Dana Parsons. If I had one of those later in life, instead of the scandal maker, re-turning to my truth and home within wouldn't have been so hard. Where are the Dana Parsons of the world? I know they're out there. I know they are. For you, dear Son, I now make the call for them to come out.*
> *Love, Mom*

Over the course of a month, Dana Parsons literally began his own investigation of the case. He read the entire seven-hundred-page trial transcript, interviewed witnesses, police officers, investigators, attorneys, experts in eyewitness testimony, and tried to talk to Attorney Reed and Prosecutor Hoffman.

Then he wrote a series of columns back-to-back over the

course of a month, questioning varying aspects of the case and shedding light on the truth to the public. Unlike the jury, the public was finally getting the opportunity to weigh all the evidence and determine whether Arthur was guilty "beyond a reasonable doubt."

"Can Justice Be Blinded by Eyewitnesses?" May 7, 1999. "In Question of Accused Teen, There Are No Easy Answers," May 9, 1999. "Sometimes a Stacked Deck Is Really a House of Cards," May 12, 1999.

Within the course of a few weeks, a key witness to the Denny's case, Casey, contacted Dana Parsons and stated she was plagued with doubt. Still, newly elected District Attorney Tony Rackauckas said through a spokeswoman that he had reviewed the Arthur Carmona case and had "complete confidence in Deputy District Attorney Jana Hoffman," who prosecuted Arthur.

Soon thereafter, a juror stepped forward and stated he shouldn't have voted to find Arthur guilty. On May 14, Arthur's sentencing was delayed when that juror actually contacted Judge Everett Dickey.

But it didn't stop there. Various news sources, including the *OC Register, Los Angeles Times, Orange County Weekly*, and more, continued to cover the matter. Most of all, Parson's articles were relentless . . .

> "Reexamining Prosecutor's Eyewitnesses," May 16, 1999.
> "One Man's Word Could Clear Young Convict," May 21, 1999.
> "Things Now Look Different to Witness," May 26, 1999.
> "Calling D.A. to Stand in Carmona Case," May 30, 1999.
> "A Guilty Plea to Obsession with Injustice," June 6, 1999.

"Vote to Convict Haunts Carmona Juror," June 9, 1999.

On June 10, we went back to court. With the courthouse packed with supporters, the judge heard our arguments in support of the Motion for New Trial. Our main argument was ineffective assistance of counsel.

We also included a declaration from Casey.

She explained that before she testified, the Deputy District Attorney told her that "Arthur Carmona's case was an 'open and shut case,' and that they had 'his gun, his backpack, and his hat' and that 'he was seen in the truck.'" Astonishing.

We asked multiple individuals to speak on Arthur's behalf regarding his character. Pastor Ken Wilson, from Seeker's Chapel in Fullerton, was one of them. Arthur actually attended a church retreat the weekend before his arrest. Pastor Ken said that on the retreat Arthur expressed his desire to get more involved in church activities, and that afterward he saw that Arthur was genuinely moved by having attended. Since the time of his arrest, Pastor Ken visited Arthur in jail three to four times a month. "It's impossible for me to believe that this is the type of kid who could stick a gun in someone's face and demand money."

Then, two of Arthur's teachers from the Santa Ana jail, where Arthur had been incarcerated for nearly fifteen months, testified. Neither teacher had ever testified for another defendant.

Teacher Julie Bauer emphasized that she was testifying because "I do believe he is innocent." She said his "whole demeanor and personality is unusual. He is unlike any other inmate I ever taught in the past five years. He is very quiet and shy, but when you get to know him, he is very personable. He is very nice and loving, and he is a caring guy. I have nothing but positive things to say about him." Teacher Stephanie Harrigan said Arthur is "the only one that I have faith in . . . if people really got to know him, he is not this criminal that everybody thinks he is."

Thank you, truth tellers. Thank you!

We still lost.

Arthur was denied a new trial without an evidentiary hearing and sentenced to twelve years in prison.

Judge Dickey said, "No trial is perfect," as Arthur sank his head in his prayer-positioned hands. There was nothing I could do to bring comfort sitting there next to him. My hand on his back, he tried to hold in the tears, find whatever dignity he could muster. I just said, "It's not over, Arthur, the fight is not over."

Arthur, the truth matters. And so do you. Someday, in my darkest hour, you'll be the one reminding me of this too.

Dear Son,

The truth does not come and go, nor shift or change. A Course in Miracles (CIM Lesson 107) teaches that it can't evade being captured, nor does it hide. But that it stands always right there in the open light. That if we seek it, we cannot fail, no matter what anyone in this world might say or do, even when it comes to a court, or the press denying it. If we give truth its respect within ourselves, it will give us ours out there. So we do not have to suffer, thinking it is lost. Our Creator will correct the rest. Truth always remains. No matter what happens, it wins in the end.

Love, Mommy

A week later, Arthur received a letter from witness Casey saying she'd "been crying since I found out you were sentenced . . . I believe there is a very strong possibility I made a very horrible mistake . . . I don't expect you or your family to ever forgive me. I don't know that I can forgive myself."

Then, a second juror came forward, publicly questioning Arthur's conviction. Sandra Dinardo said she was haunted by the thought that she may have sent an innocent young man to prison. Even more, she said other jurors pressured her outside the jury room to vote guilty when she had reservations about the evidence. They wore her down, and she changed her vote ("2nd Carmona Juror Says She Felt Pressured," *Los Angeles Times*, OC Edition, Friday, June 18, 1999). Jurors are admonished by the judge to not talk about the trial anytime or anywhere outside the jury room.

With possible jury misconduct, there were stronger grounds for a new trial. But it is very hard to prove, and an appeals court can only rule on procedural mistakes made during the initial trial, excluding any consideration of Casey's statements.

Arthur wrote a two-page handwritten letter to Dana Parsons after he was sentenced, thanking him for his advocacy.

> *I'll never forget what you did for me. I'm angry, but who should I be angry at? Am I angry at my lawyer or the DA or the judge? I'm not angry at them. They were just doing their job. Maybe I'm angry at the fact I told them the truth but still got found guilty and got twelve years . . . I'm not going to let this get the best of me. I'm still going to do all the positive things I've been doing.*

***

Angels were watching, and a few came down to stand by Arthur's side. Within three degrees of separation is the answer to most things. The desired skill. The needed resource. The mind, ability, and power to solve anything.

A fellow church parishioner of Seeker's Chapel had a sister who happened to be an attorney, Debra Muns-Park. Debra worked at an extremely prestigious and respected law firm, Sidley & Austin.

On June 18, 1999, Sidley & Austin announced they would represent Arthur on appeal at no cost. To this day, I still can't believe it. It is an extremely rare and exceedingly generous donation and commitment for any law firm to do something like this, let alone one with the caliber of Sidley & Austin, an international law firm specializing in representing businesses with a thousand attorneys operating on three different continents.

"Hang in there, Arthur. It's not over yet," Dana Parsons wrote in a *Los Angeles Times* article.

> *To Nadia—*
>
> *I just wanted to thank you for the many things you have done and the things to come. I told my mom to buy you a flower that will last a lifetime. I hope you appreciate my thanks, which I know you will, so Thank You.*
> *Very sincerely,*
> *Arthur Carmona*

I now know that God, and my father's spirit, intervened at the perfect time.

You see, dear Son, . . . twelve days later, I died.

CHAPTER 6

Dear Son,
always wear your seat belt.

My father's spirit and inspiration gave me the guts to begin what became a larger-than-life fight to free Arthur Carmona. That little bright-eyed brown girl who simply wanted to save the world but sometimes hid in the closet was now a thriving, passionate attorney and school board member standing front and center.

Branded an up-and-comer, the buzz of a professional and political future grew loud and clear. But I didn't pay much attention to what people were saying about my life then. I just wanted a normal one. You know, the kind where you wake up in the morning, give thanks, kiss and hug the loved ones around you, make pancakes and cuddle on the couch on weekend mornings, maybe peek out the kitchen window at the trees and flowers and think, *Today is going to be a good day.* The kind of life where work is meaningful and makes a difference in the world. The kind of life where on bad days, you pick up the phone and call a friend and together give a sigh of relief, knowing it will pass. Then you wake up the next day, give thanks, and continue the fight for justice.

That very well could have been my life.

That is, before July 5, 1999.

It was like any other normal evening. I had a work meeting. A dear friend and confidant of mine and I talked outside, said our goodbyes, and I went about my way with a smile on my face.

As I waited at the light to enter the freeway, I noticed a big, beautiful building high up on the hill next to me, Edelman's Children's Court. I had never been inside. Little did I know, two decades later, I'd look down at that freeway from the third floor.

I entered the on-ramp and merged onto the freeway with the intention of going home. That's the last thing I remember.

They say my car was hit by a big rig, thrown into the guardrail, flipped three times, and landed off the freeway in the embankment completely out of sight. Someone called 911. No one knows who or if they were involved. I wasn't breathing when they found me. No one knows for how long. Proof shows no alcohol was involved. But some will always wonder anyways.

Dear Son,

You were there that night I died, long before any human idea of you ever came to be. Beautiful you, whole, perfect, and complete in your true self. My dear daddy's soul embraced you in a warm, glowing circle of light. "It" was a magnetic, undeniable force drawing me in until "I" myself was part of the inexplicable. No choice in the matter, it just was. Infinite life, everything made sense. Past, present, future all merged into one. No fear, doubt, judgment, sorrow, worry, or pain. It was home, warm, safe, and free.

I very well might've stayed, dear Son, but a directive came my way . . . "Now is not the time." Another's breath was forced inside me, and a thump of my heart was heard again. My soul returned to a body that would struggle to survive.

But now I know the reason it did. It was to carry your life.

Love, Mommy

I would be dead but for the grace of several people.

My niece Miquela, because she always reminded me to fasten my seat belt. Without it on, I would have flown out the window.

The person who hit me or witnessed the accident and called for help. Without that call, no one would have come to rescue me.

The police officer who ran down the embankment and breathed for me until the ambulance came.

The EMT worker who chose to quickly cut my side and insert a tube into my lung, draining it of fluid so I would not suffocate.

I could go on and on.

Thank you, angels on earth, indeed there are some.

I was brought to the USC ICU, a renowned emergency health care facility. I was immediately put on life support, a breathing machine, blood transfusions, and hundreds of tubes and contraptions, they say. Questions were raised about measures to take. My brain was hemorrhaging and swelling. Punching holes in my skull would possibly be next.

I had twenty-two broken bones, some of which pierced a lung that was thus suffocating in body fluid. Install a trachea or not?

Internal bleeding. Surgery or not?

But no one was there all night and through early morning. Hospital staff apparently looked up my address through the internet and called my roommate Sylvia, who then called Ruben Smith.

Ruben was like an uncle, an attorney and longtime family friend who knew my father well. He had to make the difficult call to my mother and hide the truth of my uncertain condition and future.

He knew she had received a similar call before, when my father died abruptly. "Nadia was in a bad car accident last night and is in the ER. We must go now," he said.

"What happened? Is she ok?" my mom asked.

"I cannot say. I'm on my way to pick you up and take you."

My mom tells me she hates that day with all her might. *No! Not my Nadia too. I can't do this again, oh Lord, I won't make it through,* she thought.

When you're in a coma, it's like you're dead. I don't remember anything. I have no idea what it looked like as I lay there all tubed up and tied, a body kept alive by a machine. My chest going up and down to the sound of a suction cup's routine. Beeps all around. A bruised face, shattered body.

Dear Son, if that were you, I'd lose it too.

And they did. One by one.

Looking back, I wish I'd seen myself in that state. Perhaps I would've expected less of every part of me for the rest of my life, body, mind, and soul. Perhaps I would've listened better to the crying voices inside, the physical pain, begging me, *Stop, just stop! Will you just stop? Nadia!* Or the humming moments of dismay when my memory is lost. *Wake up, Nadia, your brain is not all right. You need to take it easy, you need help.*

Perhaps I could've ignored the messages in my mind saying, *Ache after ache, you'll always be just a body, Nadia, and this one here will keep you tied down.* Perhaps I would've better expressed how I felt, instead of hiding it from everyone all day, faking it with a stupid, "I'm ok." Perhaps I wouldn't have reached for that drink to get by, holding the pain inside, numbing it away.

***

I was in the ICU for several days. Stabilization meant breathing on my own, no increased brain swelling, and cessation of all internal bleeding. Because of the angels, amazing medical help, and lots of drugs later, I was eventually transferred to a Kaiser Hospital in Orange County. I do not have a single memory of the transfer, nor the first weeks there.

What is my first memory after the concussion? They are not specific, but general. There are not many, but they are significant.

I vaguely remember my hand held something, and someone placed their finger on my thumb and pressed it down, now and then, regularly. Maybe the nurse giving me my dose for the morning, evening, both? I don't know.

But eventually I knew I could press it too. "Tap, tap, tap." Pushing the button seemed to be the only thing I could do for that matter. What I didn't know was that it was an IV line to morphine that'd be feeding the addiction genes in my brain for over a month.

I vaguely remember a repeated distinct, harsh, sudden

pain on the left side of my chest. Now I know it was the hospital staff regularly ripping off the dressing over the chest tube wound because it was not stitched up but had to heal from the inside out.

I vaguely remember my feet being touched. Much later I found out my dear sister Marisa lovingly, regularly put lotion on my feet.

I vaguely remember a low tone "haleakalaaaa" in a singing voice. Much later I found out someone brought in a boom box and played music, probably to help stir my consciousness back. Well, it helped. It did. *Thank you to whoever did that.*

I remember most that I never felt alone. It was like me and something untouchable, undefinable, in total peace, witnessing and watching my body from above. That, or I was in a mere morphine high for weeks.

They say my sister Marisa was the guard. She worked like a hawk protecting my privacy, recovery, and room from being bombarded by the community and press. She fielded calls and inquiries about everything and restricted anyone and anything from entering my room besides my direct family.

Marisa,

> *Thank you. I needed that. And I wish so badly I had asked you for help to do the same later in my life. I wish I had remembered how you made it important to have privacy and my life unadvertised for everyone to know about. I wish I had followed your example before naively moving into an even more public life.*
> *Love, Nadia*

After a couple of months, I was transferred to Orange

Hills Rehabilitation, an inpatient hospice and skilled nursing facility. Yeah. Seriously, as in, people prepare to die there. I had two different roommates during my stay. Both died. All the patients were elderly.

My only sustenance for over a month had been IV hydration and morphine. I was an eighty-five-pound, five-foot-nine bag of mending bones and muscular atrophy.

My memories are clearer here but limited to key events.

There wasn't an "Ah-ha!" waking-up moment. That's not how it was for me. It started with an internal instinct I was lying in a bed. There was no thought, as in, *Oh, I'm waking up.* Rather, I had no thoughts at all.

I remember there was no fear, nor even a tad bit of curiosity at first. It wasn't a complicated "What happened?" or "Where am I?" It was basic. More of the immediate thing happening to me or in front of me. Nothing about the past or future.

I remember counting the repetition of the leg wraps, eyes closed. Placed on my legs to encourage circulation, the rhythmic movement and sound of the machine were all there was in my small little wakening "world."

I remember a sense I was not alone physically in the room. I recall hearing a voice moaning and groaning over a period of time, then chitter chatter, hustle and bustle. I later learned an elderly roommate was basically dying and eventually did.

I remember the "inside" body pains. The broken bones, a full-body migraine, the crinkle cramps and jabs in my left lung, the left shoulder pulling strings down my arm, around my neck, and up my head. It was all-consuming.

I remember brief hazy gazing before actually opening my eyes. No one was there. I just lay there, opening and closing them.

I remember I had an instinct to "get up" after time passed, thinking it'd be like any other normal morning rise. You know, when we simply decide it's time to set our feet on the ground and start a new day? Yeah, that's the kind I thought it'd be.

I tried to move, in the normal way we do as human beings. You know, we just move a limb. Mine didn't. My legs and feet wouldn't budge. I had no sensation or feeling in my entire lower body. *Please let me go,* I thought. *Please let me go.* I remember that desperation began.

The next attempt to move was more like an exerted effort.

As in, I spoke to myself. *Move foot.* Still, it didn't. I tried the other side. Nothing. *Focus, Nadia, focus.* I tried again and again. Nothing.

Moments like these repeated themselves over and over.

Fear, panic, fear, panic, fear, panic . . . *This is not my home* thoughts began. *Where am I? I'm going to die here, aren't I?*

A fight instinct arrived, and I discovered I could move my arms.

So I tried to scoot my body closer to the edge of the bed. Slowly but surely, I got my torso close, the effort needed with each centimeter demanding. After a while, I tried to use my arms to move my legs over, but then began sensing I was going to fall completely off the bed and onto the floor.

Fear, panic, fear, panic, fear, panic . . . *Someone help me, please, anyone!* I thought, and wanted to say, but I didn't speak. I hadn't yet. It seemed to go on like this forever, until suddenly my mother walked in. Tears rolling down my face, my eyes in sheer terror, "Oh Nadia . . . my Nadia . . . finally."

In shock, numb, and blank-eyed. *Mommy?* I thought but did not say.

She pulled me securely back into bed. Tears rolled down our faces. It was the first real human connection I can remember after the accident. *My mommy, dear Mom, you caught me just in time.*

***

Several weeks passed without much change to my mobility. I was not all there for quite some time. But I remember when I finally noticed all the posters and flowers covering the walls, filling the room up. There were well wishes, messages of love and support from community members, family, and friends. Groups of children from various schools throughout the district I represented made signs with words like "Licenciada Davis, please get well. We love you."

I also heard vague talk from visitors that people in the community were gossiping, apparently those who once saw me as a threat. "She'll never be the same." "She's a goner." "She's out of the way now." I look back today and think, *How selfish and cruel. I nearly died.*

Weeks passed with the same hospital routine. I don't remember much more than lying in bed, using the bedpan, eating, and sleeping.

But then I noticed something next to the tray of food on the moving table. There, in the corner, was a little golden-brown Beanie Baby bear. I picked it up and looked at the tag. It was named "Hope." Arthur had sent it to me from jail.

That did it. Somewhere in me, the will to fight my condition woke up. My brain said, *Change this. Do more. Try to get up and walk. Get out. You have a purpose in this life. Forget what those people are saying. Get back on your feet again! Just like Daddy did when he was thrown into that pile of trash.*

Arthur was still in jail.

I didn't remember the accident or how I landed unable to move in a hospital bed, but I clearly remembered Arthur, his courage, and my father's spirit.

I have to get out of this place. I have to figure out a way, I thought. *For Arthur, for them, and for all the other people out there.*

The first sessions of physical therapy were in my hospital

bed. Task number one? Wiggle my toes. Two? Move my foot back and forth. Both took a while. It was hard mental and physical work every time and a big deal if it happened.

I was then given a "reacher," which I could put under my foot to lift and move my entire leg. Then I was taught how to use a "sliding board," a little wooden board put between two spots and mainly used to get from the bed to the wheelchair. If I could use my arms to get my butt on the board, I could slide down it, then use the reacher to move my legs down.

Once they took the IV line and catheter out, I was free to try a normal diet. We started simple. A poached egg every day. I had no appetite. Nor did I have a craving for anything or even remember what it was to taste something. The solution? Tabasco sauce.

My sister Marisa brought a bottle and put a few drops on the egg. She put a small bite in my mouth, and *Bam! There we go,* my brain went. I could actually taste that. And it felt like childhood.

Why? My siblings would tickle me, or they'd topple playfully on top. When I couldn't break free, I'd panic and bite someone. As punishment, my father would put a yellow chili on my tongue. But I grew to like it and anything spicy for that matter. The nurses ended up putting a super tiny single-serving Tabasco bottle on my tray at every meal from there on out.

Trying to use the toilet with the commode like a normal person was a big ordeal and an overwhelmingly exhausting feat. Call the nurse, use the reacher, move the feet, get the board, position the board, position my butt, slide down, slide my legs off the bed, position them on the wheelchair footsteps, then do it all again to get on the commode.

By the time we got my butt on the commode over the toilet, I was spent. Plus, I could only tinkle. My digestive system had been knocked around and bled. Unused for a long time, it shut down. My intestines filled with crap, nothing seemed to help find release. Medicine, massage, and more.

It became the daily repeated question, "Did you go?" When you're in this state, to eat is to cause more belly pain. So when it was bad, I wouldn't. A crappy catch-22, no pun intended.

I remember the agonizing ambulance trips from the rehabilitation place to Kaiser for regular, what seemed like daily, x-rays, CT scans, or whatever. Every damn time they had to move me from the gurney to the shitty metal table, it was absolutely excruciating. Like a rag doll on a bed of needles, every inch of me hurt. Skin and bones, it was like a dental drill on fifty rocks and nerves inside me at the same time. But unlike an electric chair, I had to survive and live after every time.

It took all the energy of the day to get through the whole process.

I remember gazing out the window to an atrium on my right. My mind would often wander to Arthur in the silence of sundown. He in his cell, another day in hell.

I'd stare out the window, my mind made blank by pain and exhaustion. I remember my body trying to cry, but it was numbed by quiet tears of confusion, a sense of doom, and the feeling of permanency in that place. *I'm never going to get out of here, am I?*

But there beside me was a Beanie Baby named "Hope." Arthur visited me in dreams. *"Don't give up, Nadia. Please don't give up."*

All the while, my heart sank for what he must be going through behind bars with an impending transfer to adult prison.

Would his heart get hardened more? Of course. To survive in adult prison, he would have to change. It was inevitable. Would his hopes begin to dim because they were just too damn painful to hold on to? Most definitely. There isn't much one can do to prevent permanent damage after that point.

Time was ticking. The legal team could focus on the court documents and filings. *I could still try to keep him safe inside. I could try to raise the public's support. I could try to keep his dreams alive in the meantime,* I thought.

I asked Ronnie to bring files to my hospital room. *Let me figure out this transfer thing. Where is the best place for him to go? Let me figure out his education, his high school degree, before he leaves. Let me figure it out.*

***

When I started going out of my room to the big physical therapy area, it was a huge deal. I wasn't "paralyzed," but along with severe muscular atrophy and frozen bones, my brain needed synapse retraining and recovery to properly direct physical movement.

I remember the light coming in from the windows hurt my eyes, but I had to keep them open. It reminded me there was a life and a world out there I was missing. I wanted to walk in the light again. I wanted to get better.

I had to work to a minimum "weight-bearing status." That meant transferring from the wheelchair to another seat using pressure on one foot and leg, not just the sliding board.

The therapist would lift me up so I could put my hands on two bars. Once up, they would hold me so I could try to stand and move my legs as though walking.

Did I stand? No, at least not on my own. Did I walk? No. Drag, yes. But only with the support of bars and another human being.

I couldn't feel my feet and legs entirely. I could feel a pen dragged over my skin, but it's entirely different to feel a secure foundation underneath you. To trust your own limbs. Falling down was inevitable if I let go.

To this day, I sometimes have to hold on to something and stall before walking after standing up. My leg gets weak as though it's fallen asleep, and if I take one step, I trip and fall. That or a sudden jab in my hip stops me in my tracks. Sometimes people wonder what I am doing, thinking I'm a klutz, or perhaps even drunk.

Dear Son,

Our ego mind in self-will can indeed help us to get up again when we are knocked down and broken, when we are bullied or have a personal hardship to walk through with courage, when others need our help to make things right.

It comes from a survival instinct we need to thrive. This was indeed a time when that strong-willed little girl in me, the "I can do it all by myself and not cry," was needed. But there is a harmful level of that same self-will too, and we must be cautious of it.

That ego mind can get so strong that we begin to forget who we really are inside. It wants you to feel separate from the infinite, to abandon that home of truth, love, and light. It will create thoughts that convince you to believe your worth is derived from outside things. Appearance, belongings, titles, degrees. Successes defined by society. Love and approval from others, even when unsafe.

Fact is, dear Son, I should've stopped and taken much more time to heal.

I could've still helped Arthur and not gone

back into the public eye. I could've been honest about my physical pain and mental delay. Said it hurt to wake, walk, drive, do anything. Been honest about words scrambling into a big blank empty space. That what was said would disappear within seconds in my head. That I had no former inkling of insight or guide to get me back to where I once was.

I do not know why I chose to hide it all inside.

I do not know why I failed to stop to rest and heal.

I am so sorry I didn't because we both ended up paying the price.

Love, Mom

Several weeks passed by. I remember feeling impatient and frustrated. I remember my progress seemed too slow. *If only I could practice more,* I thought. Maybe it was the detox from the morphine, or the pain meds they were giving me. Maybe it was just that my brain was still healing from the concussion.

I just remember feeling extremely low and defeated again, but this time it poured down and utterly began to defeat me.

My mind had taken control.

You're a goner, a loser, a failure, forgotten. You'll never walk again. Face the truth of what you are. A dirty little brown girl, now broken and disabled.

I remember once quietly crying like I often did, alone, and a male nurse came in. He noticed. He was the same one who always helped me with the bedpan. "I don't understand. There must be a mistake. I don't belong in this place. I have to go. Help me," I said, probably in a jumbled order.

"I'm so sorry you're feeling that way," he said. "I heard

all about your work in the community and understand why." *Huh?* I thought. But then he leaned over and attempted to kiss me. Pressing down, I tried to turn my head. He went to my neck. I tried to push him away. My voice mumbled a "stop" and he finally walked away.

I was numb. I felt like stone inside. There was no way to get up and hide. No closet to run to. When my sister Sabrina arrived later, she could tell something was off. I must've briefly shared about it. Many months later, I found out she let management know and he was let go. Why did I feel guilty? Because my mind said I should.

I was sent home shortly thereafter in a wheelchair and merely given a walker and commode to get by. Sometimes I think they did so much earlier than they should've because of that incident.

It was late September. The physical pain began intensifying more and more as I was weaned off the strong stuff. At some point, it was just too unbearable and I lay in bed crying all day, broken and depressed.

I just wanted to be "normal" again. I just wanted my life back. I was tired of having to sit, wait, and be useless. I forgot that my self-worth was inside me. I needed my purpose back. But my ability to do anything depended on several things. A wheelchair, someone to drive me, a reacher, a sliding board, a commode, a shower chair. Oh, and maybe a functioning brain and memory.

Regular visits to outpatient physical therapy began. It was terribly difficult and kind of a mess. I felt pitiful and ashamed I couldn't do more every time. Then there were biweekly visits to the orthopedic doctor for x-rays and bone growth monitoring. Every time I lay on the table, it just reminded me I was broken and deformed.

No one knew I was having headaches and pains I could not explain. That I struggled to process, remember anything, and never felt "all there." It felt like living in a body and being alive but not being able to actually live. Like I was being mocked by something and told, "You are stuck like this now."

A friend took me out in public for the first time. We got a pedicure. I hated the way people looked sadly and pitifully at me—not because I didn't appreciate their sympathy but because it reminded me of how powerless I was, or felt. I couldn't fake I was "ok" to anyone while sitting in a wheelchair.

Still, despite the reality of my physical condition, deep struggles inside, and need for a significant period of time more to recover, I rolled right back into the public eye and school board meetings in my wheelchair and still unable to walk.

Looking back, I so badly wish my father had been alive then. He would've insisted I give myself sufficient time to heal. He would've put his foot down after having seen me on life support. He would've told me it was ok to take additional time and that my purpose would still be there after, that he'd protect it and keep it safe. But he wasn't. And it hurts. I needed my father. Oh how badly I needed him then.

***

By this time, Arthur's plight for freedom had quieted down into a solemn community sadness. He had now been wrongfully imprisoned for nearly two years.

All the while, an angel was busy working in a quiet space of her own. Debra Muns-Park patiently and diligently drafted an Appeal and Habeas Corpus Petition on Arthur's behalf. This is no easy feat but her commitment never swayed. Under the guidance of her boss Jim Harris, Arthur was being given one last chance.

Arthur, my hero, kept going. He kept his education and dreams alive. While in jail, he worked hard in school, looked into college, read books, worked out, and drew. His efforts to try and stay hopeful were unwavering, drawing strength from the visits of friends and family. *I wish I could have been there more for him then.*

"I've been keeping up with my schoolwork. I would like to go to college. My dream is to become a chef, to own a restaurant," he said to a reporter behind the thick glass ("The Kid Is Innocent," by Bob Embers, *OC Weekly*, September 17, 1999). He told the reporter his dreams. He told him he dreamed. He still dreamed.

Months passed and from the wheelchair to a walker to walking on my own, I was soon appearing like a "normal" person.

In addition to school board meetings, I began working on a few key efforts on Arthur's behalf as best I could. Ronnie, Beth, and some local activists, including Selinda, Randy, Larry, and others gave supportive helping hands.

Fundraising. We needed money to pay past attorneys and investigators that had billed us prior to Sidley & Austin taking over. We made bumper stickers with "Free Arthur Carmona Now" and the Arthur Carmona Legal Defense Fund information printed on the bottom. I sent out multiple large donation requests once more. We went from meeting to meeting, asking for help again.

People from across the county and beyond sent small donations and tokens of encouragement. From the grandmothers in South County who sent little angel cards for Arthur to high school students that held car washes in multiple locations, his struggle caught the attention and compassion of thousands all over.

We organized and held a benefit concert on Arthur's behalf in partnership with the *OC Weekly*, Rage Against the Machine, and actor Esai Morales (*La Bamba, Mi Familia, CSI: NY*), whom I met by three degrees of separation through my longtime friend Veronica. After I expressed a few words to Esai on Arthur's behalf, he was in.

Another focus was Arthur's education and dream of receiving a high school diploma from his alma mater, Costa Mesa High School. You know, to feel like the normal graduating teenager that he was. *Maybe part of his dream could be saved,* I thought. *Maybe he'll be free before graduation or he can receive his high school diploma from his alma mater.* While imprisoned, Arthur completed sixty-six class credits toward his high school diploma.

Thereafter, it was time to lobby Sacramento directly. I know many in public office probably thought I was nuts. I didn't care. Separate from formal procedural legal documents, I figured we could try to raise an official's conscience, or better yet, eat away at it. This wasn't a legal strategy, but a moral "this is a kid's life destroyed" one.

I drafted a petition to then Governor of California Gray Davis, Congress members, senators, assemblymen, and other state-wide elected officials. We began collecting signatures everywhere with the help of local community groups.

Funny side note is that my handwritten notes include a phone number to then Attorney General Bill Lockyer with his name misspelled as "Lockyear." When I saw it years later, it made me chuckle because little did I know his name would soon become my married name.

> *Governor Gray Davis,*
>
> *I am often asked to speak to students. I encourage them to stay in school, work hard, and dream big. Yet today, I have to ask myself, "Who am I to ask them to dream big when we have allowed something like this to happen to*

*a young man who was doing just that?" Arthur
had dreams of becoming a culinary artist and
going to college. At the time of his arrest he was
doing fine in school, working to help his family,
participating in church activities . . . and yes,
he was dreaming.*

*I became an attorney on the inspiration of
my father, Wallace R. Davis, who was former
Governor Jerry Brown's campaign chairman for
Orange County at the time you worked for him.
Basically, I met you at my house when I was
a little girl. I recently had a minute to speak
with you at the Democratic Convention and
mentioned my father to you. You immediately
remembered him and that he had passed away.
I greatly appreciated your words of encouragement. He taught me to fight for and never give
up on fighting for one thing . . . justice.*

*For Arthur and in the memory of my father,
I ask you for your assistance in and prompt attention to this matter. A boy's future depends
on it.*

Sincerely, Nadia Davis

We had a semi-victory with one hundred percent crap
encapsulating it. Yes, Arthur was going to be transferred to
adult state prison, but they would send him to one in Southern
California, closer to family. Any consolation? Not really. Did
knowing his family would be able to regularly visit help?
Ronnie thought so.

Silly me, I thought bringing Esai Morales along to tell
Arthur the semi-good news might make it better. Maybe it
would give him a glimmer of light for the dark, ugly passageway

into adult prison hell ahead. When I asked Esai to accompany me on the trip up north, he surprisingly agreed.

Arthur entered the visiting room and was understandably numb and puzzled. He looked at me, then Esai, then back at me, then Esai and said, "Chucho?" It was his character's name in the film *Mi Familia*.

I just gave a brief smile, introduced them, then left the room. *Let them talk man to man,* I thought. Outside the guards were chatting. "Is that Esai Morales?" they asked. I just nodded, smiled, and said, "The kid is innocent." They let them chat longer than permitted. At the end, the guard walked in as I gave Arthur the news that he would be transferred to an adult facility, but at least in Southern California, closer to family.

Arthur broke down in tears. The officer didn't rush him.

I guess it was worth the effort after all.

A little light in the darkness for a kid behind bars so long.

But after the transfer, Arthur's vigilant hope and internal grounding suffered greatly. Threats, humiliation, and beatings were the norm. All that Ronnie could say to her son was, "Do what you have to do to survive, until I bring you home." She said, "He just felt like giving up at times." He told himself, *Forget it, you're not getting out. Your life is over.*

He knew he had countless supporters, but that didn't help him with the inevitable dark hardness behind bars breaking his spirit down. It didn't help with the fact that he was there while everyone he loved was out here. He said he worried about his family and how they needed him. His sister was only twelve by then and had to stay home by herself when his mom was at work. "It broke my heart," he said. "I wouldn't be able to forgive myself for not being able to be there if something happened to my little sister."

At one point, things inside got so bad he told his mom, "Don't visit me anymore, Ma, don't come anymore."

Arthur didn't understand that she was in prison with him.

She said later, "I had no freedom. They took my freedom too. They took my life. I was losing my will to fight. And the only way I had to reinforce that fighting was to see Arthur, to hear his voice, those visits." She told herself, *This is why I'm doing this. You can't stop. If you stop, he stays. How can you live with yourself? If I stop fighting for him, I have everything to lose, everything, everything.*

In the meantime, those in power who could so easily do something acted like heartless robots. More and more, certain people in positions of influence or power began to admonish me and warn me of repercussions. My boss at the time even got on me, and with blatant chauvinism and a shameless sexist flair.

One day, he asked me to be at a meeting and then made introductions, saying, "I'm bringing Nadia in on this. You've heard of her. I mean, look at her," moving his hand up and down and pointing at me. With only men in the room, I just smiled, thinking, *Incredible! Cruel, idiotic pigs.*

Worse, days later my boss got so nervous about my activism outside the office, he called me into his office and questioned me. It seems he wanted to use my looks and public image only if it helped him make money, but not if I was actually to do the right thing.

***

Finally, in January 2000, an appeal was filed on Arthur's behalf. It was highly critical of Arthur's court-appointed lawyer: it alleged he failed to interview witnesses who could have supported Arthur's alibi and to suppress questionable evidence, including the officers' placement of the hat on Arthur's head and the resulting identifications.

Dana Parsons wrote, "Now, after spending all night reading Sidley & Austin's mammoth brief, I think I can offer Carmona something other than false hope: Hang in there, Arthur. It's not over yet" ("Hang in There, Arthur, It's Not Over Yet," Dana Parsons, *Los Angeles Times*, January 12, 2000).

A few months later, in early March, the 4th District Court of Appeal in Santa Ana issued an order requiring the original trial judge Everett Dickey to consider new evidence in the case. They ruled that prosecutors must show why the writ of habeas corpus seeking Arthur's release should not be issued.

"This is very unusual," Jim Harris of Sidley & Austin said. "The great majority of these cases get dismissed offhand." A senior assistant attorney general who was reviewing the case on behalf of the appeals court agreed the order was uncommon. "We did not expect it," he said.

After the appellate court nearly forced his hand, Judge Dickey set August 21, 2000, to hear new evidence and arguments and ultimately decide whether to grant Arthur a new trial. Considering what had been revealed since Arthur's first trial, it was nearly impossible to imagine that the DA would attempt to take Arthur's case to trial again. Essentially, there was no evidence for them to present and they admitted that if a new trial was granted, they'd be unlikely to win.

So the DA made a last-minute offer instead.

Arthur would be released, and his convictions would be vacated, if he agreed. But if he agreed to what?

Arthur had to sign a document stating that the arrest was made upon probable cause, and that it was not the result of police officer misconduct. Clearly, the DA preyed on Arthur's agony and desperation. Worse, if Arthur signed it, he would only be exonerated, not found factually innocent, which makes a significant difference when it comes to rebuilding one's life.

If he refused, he would go back to prison and wait for an undetermined amount of time for a new trial, a new offer, or the higher court to grant his habeas petition. In my opinion, at that point, all three were very likely. And he would possibly be declared "factually innocent" and be able to sue for damages and relief.

I wanted to insist Arthur and Ronnie refuse the DA's offer.

I wanted to scream it at the top of my lungs to the world.

But I was no longer the attorney of record.

Nor was I the one suffering behind bars.

Ronnie sat down next to me after hearing the advice of others.

Distraught, hesitant, and in pain, the words in the offer cut her like a knife. "Was that justice?" No. "Would it make things right?" No. But Arthur's suffering behind bars could all stop within hours. I gave her my opinion, explained the options, then said it was ultimately a decision only a mother and son could make.

> *The Orange County District Attorney's office offered me a deal, and after three years of suffering beatings, threats, and degradation in a series of juvenile and state prisons . . . I accepted it.*
> —*Arthur Carmona*

It wasn't until the following day while waiting in front of Theo Lacy Jail Facility that Ronnie heard someone say, "Mrs. Carmona, there is your son."

They fell into each other's arms.

"I don't want to let go," Arthur said. "I don't want to let go, Mom."

"Dear Son," Ronnie said. "Take my hand, and don't look back."

When Arthur realized he was actually going home, he began to sob.

"Don't look back, don't look back. You're never going back there again," she said.

Arthur couldn't believe it until he actually walked out into the air. "Get me away from here, take me home, please take me home," he said.

A crowd of reporters swarmed, but Arthur fell into his mother's sheltering embrace as she led him immediately to her car.

Arthur showed an incredible amount of dignity and grace.

Days later, he expressed heartfelt gratitude for the support of the many who toiled to overturn his conviction. "What I want to say to anyone who supported me in any way—by praying or any kind of law work or just telling me it was going to be all right—thank you very much." Then he paused. "That's a deep, sincere thank you, right there."

He did not wish to vilify police or prosecutors. "I was raised to turn the other cheek, look the other direction," he said. "There's no real reason for me to sink to their level. I'm out. That's all that matters."

He continued to express respect for law enforcement and actually wanted to be a probation officer someday ("Carmona Freed from Prison: 'Take me home,'" Dana Parsons, *Los Angeles Times*, Wed., August 23, 2000). The article further quoted Arthur and his mother:

> *My mom's my hero . . . an incredible person. I'd probably still be in there if I didn't have a loving mom like her. My mom showed me what a mother's love truly is.*
> *—Arthur Carmona*
>
> *If I had anything to say to other mothers going through what I've gone through, I would say*

fight. Don't give up. Find others that will stand with you. And fight together. Do anything and everything you have to do.
—*Ronnie Carmona*

CHAPTER 7

Dear Son,
any time you ask for help,
you deserve an award.

Exactly a year before Arthur walked out of jail, I was physically incapable of putting my own two feet on the ground. It was his strength that inspired me to get up and walk again. His inspiration fed my perseverance to push through physical, mental, and emotional pain that is simply inexplicable. He helped me see beyond the suffering both inside and around me. He is the reason I didn't give up and melt away. He is the reason I just kept pushing forward in search of the light.

Yes, the accolades, awards, and ribbons all came.

Yes, I was beyond grateful, happy, and proud indeed.

But it truly was a community effort, and without Sidley & Austin coming on board before my car was hit by a big rig, Arthur's freedom would've never been obtained. It is Ronnie, Debra Muns-Park, and Dana Parsons that deserved the awards.

I merely wanted to do the right thing, and I am happy I did by getting the ball of justice rolling.

Articles were published with titles like "Lawyer Inherits Legacy of Public Service" (*OC Register*, September 2, 2000), and added "Activist's daughter Nadia Davis faces a bright political future if she wants one." They quoted Ronnie Carmona saying I was "the first one to stick her neck out on behalf of a convicted robber who insisted he was innocent," and more. They pointed out that I was frequently asked if I was going to run for higher office, but also noted the truth: "She's motivated more by helping others and making a difference," said Ruben Smith. "I think her personal life is her public life. She gets a lot of satisfaction out of that."

Then it was the John F. Kennedy Jr. Award for public service, California State Democratic Party, 1999; Orange County Hispanic Woman Recognition Award, 1999; Annual Suffrage Day Award, Women for Orange County, August 1999; Orange County Human Relations Commission Outstanding Service Award 2000; Woman of the Year, National Woman's Political Caucus; and others.

I am grateful, I truly am.

I am proud of all I accomplished and did.

But, dear Son, the fact is that I was also deeply struggling inside. I wish someone had told me that I'd get an award if I had asked for help.

You see, I solidified a survival mode that began as a child.

Be the image of outside perfection while thoroughly masking the inside pain, whether physical, emotional, or mental, they are all part of the game. It was my entire approach to living for the next two decades.

And boy, did I do it well. It actually worked for a very long time—that is, as long as I had something to ease the torture.

And what was that? Too often something unhealthy and outside me. A drink and the comforting arms of a keenly selected man.

I failed to recognize what happened to me, that I had actually died. That I was living in a broken body, run by a bruised brain, that was now addicted or highly susceptible to addiction after being connected through an IV to morphine for over a month. That all of those things could become grave challenges to living spiritually connected to my true self and home within me.

Still, I would've chosen a gazillion more car accidents and their effects instead of the loss of my father if I had been given the choice, if it meant the joy of seeing him meet his grandsons and showing him that I could follow in his footsteps.

Maybe everything would've been ok if he had lived and the accident happened. Maybe everything would've been ok if he had died and the accident never happened.

But both? I was ill-equipped to handle it. I was a mess inside.

What is it like to live with a broken body?

Ask Frida Kahlo. She knows.

It is a curse, inside and out. You can never again really be yourself. Living with pain is a sentence of depression, irritability, lack of sleep, mood fluctuations, personality changes, difficulty concentrating, and crazy making. The stress, stigma, and feelings of hopelessness can be overwhelming, sometimes leading one to feel that life is not worth living.

Hearing "hope you feel better" or "have you tried this" often makes it even worse. Anyone who really has it has tried everything already. Doctors and nurses out there, please don't ask me what my pain level is "on a scale from one to ten." Would you even believe me if I said it is a thousand-fold? And don't give me your pain medication unless you're willing to admit that it made me a full-blown addict.

If x-rays show my deformed body, well, I've done a good job of hiding it. A shattered shoulder blade that is now placed very funny. A fully broken clavicle mended incorrectly, literally two bones lying on top of one another, cutting a few inches off the length God intended and thus smashing my once torn tendons and ligaments together. Six flailed fractured ribs that made an indentation. A broken hip that is now a mound in my lower back. A broken pelvic bone now the form of a unique triangle. Two chest tube incision marks on the left of my breast.

And the markings on my brain? "Unusual brain loss," a doctor said later in life. And what is it like to live with a brain that bruised and bled? That computer in my head once deprived of oxygen? Trying to take in anything often turns into headaches and detachment. Forgetfulness and scattered thinking became my two best friends.

My memory bank was robbed of many meaningful moments.

So very often it seems that all that's left there are the bad ones.

Sometimes I cry for the brain I once had.

That mind that once thrived unmarked and unbashed.

That mind that never was flown against the broken glass.

The mind that never had a hand around its neck.

That normal brain that so very many easily take for granted.

I'd do anything to have it again, the one I feel was stolen.

But life doesn't stop when you sometimes need it to in order to catch up. In fact, it went on quickly as I still served on the school board, did my best to earn an income through the practice of law, and stayed active in the community. All the while, I was living with conditions I was too overwhelmed to recognize, let alone know what to do about, or where to start.

***

Several months after Arthur Carmona was freed, I got a call from my best friend Priscilla. "I need you, please come," she said.

Dearest Priscilla, my longtime best friend from law school, the one with whom I mourned the loss of my father, the one who patiently listened to my pain sitting on the kitchen floor, the one who sang to and with me, the one who I could laugh with, be myself with, be free. The one who wrote me a love song. I didn't know it was about me until it was too late.

She had lost her period for months but didn't think anything of it until the day she found out she had stage four ovarian cancer. That same day, she called me. She asked if I would do her the favor of informing her family in Chicago and stay with her for surgery the following day. Tragically, the cancer had spread vehemently to all her nearby organs. They removed as much as possible.

But she never came back. Her body yellowed with jaundice as I just sat there in shock, gently stroking her hair, quietly singing songs in her ear, and whispering, "I love you." Soon the room was filled with loved ones and we just waited. I was by her side holding her hand as I watched her take her last breath. I just buried my face into her heart, out of breath myself, barely alive and broken. I could've, would've, leaped bounds and fallen alongside her into the hole she sank in.

Later, our mutual friend Veronica told me that Priscilla not only loved me, she was apparently in love with me all along. I had been blind to it when she patiently listened to me cry after my father died. I loved her too. Had I told her enough? Been there for her enough? Listened to and fulfilled her needs?

Priscilla died on November 12, 2001, the exact same day my father passed away seven years prior and two years after the car accident.

***

By this time in life, I could've just melted away. I drowned my sorrow and physical pain in tears and alcohol. Drunk, I could remove the mask, unplug the battery of body aches.

I didn't know a better way then, dear Son, I just didn't know where to put the pain.

I carried on through life as a brokenhearted, highly functional alcoholic in a shattered body. I played the roles well and accomplished a lot, always ending the day feeling like I was taking my last breath.

Thankfully, I had my friend Beth. A Bolivian immigrant, she'd left her abusive alcoholic husband and was supporting herself and two sons on her own. She went from having nothing to being a human resources manager for a major company, founding a local non-profit encouraging cultural awareness and education, having a business for temporary work placement, and becoming an accountant and realtor.

She watched patiently from the audience as I worked in the public eye, always knowing she was there as I lived my own lie. Looking back, she was waiting for me to tell her I couldn't sit and pretend it was all ok anymore. She saw my head hurt, the wandering thoughts and eyes. She knew when the pain threshold was reached, then helped me limp out alone, away from everyone's sight.

Eventually, I began to indulge in energy drinks, heavy doses of ibuprofen, and long workdays, never forgetting I'd be able to get some relief with a drink or two in the evenings. This became the routine for months.

I dove into trying to increase our college attendance rate, improve communications with the City Council, and lower the teen pregnancy rate.

I ended up serving as a board member at Planned Parenthood Orange County. One of the school board members had people protest and block my entrance to school board meetings. But I persisted. It's funny that some think sex education and pregnancy prevention are somehow teaching abortion.

The district worked tirelessly to successfully pass a local school bond that provided funds to build much-needed schools in our extremely overcrowded district.

At this same time, I was School Board President and the Tustin Marine Base was closing. A major reuse plan was in process. The base was to be divided between all localities within its boundaries, including Tustin, Irvine, Santa Ana, and the community college districts. Santa Ana Unified was given an equal share when the federal government was in charge. But the law changed, and the City of Tustin was given all the power. They cut out Santa Ana Unified entirely and gave everyone else a piece.

Why? They wanted to build a Walmart instead of schools. Some said it was because they didn't want the poor brown kids filtering into their border. The fight for the kids was on.

I began to lobby with the Superintendent. We convinced Senator Joe Dunn to write a piece of legislation that prioritized educational use over commercial. It was drafted narrowly enough to basically only apply to the immediate situation. It took an entire year of directly lobbying local and state representatives to support it. Once passed in the Legislature, we then had to convince Governor Davis to sign it into law. Once the Governor signed it, the City of Tustin sued.

The State Attorney General, Bill Lockyer, had to defend it.

Yep, that's how we met.

Bill Lockyer was being honored at a local Democratic Party event. His friend, Frank Barbaro, was the County Chairman at the time. Despite the crowd hovering around vying for his ear, I walked straight through them and up to Bill, looked him in the eyes, and said point-blank, "We need your support to prioritize children's education over a shopping day at Walmart. Do we have your support? You'll defend it, right?"

Bill looked at Frank standing next to him; they smirked and smiled and looked back at me, up and down.

"I'll take that as a yes? Yes," I said, then walked away.

"Who is that woman?" Bill asked.

"Oh, no, no, no, Bill, we've all tried that one. No chance," Frank said. This is Bill's version, not mine, by the way.

Frank cleverly scheduled a breakfast meeting for all three of us the following morning. Bill's time was minimal and our need for his support imperative.

When I arrived, I said, "Thank you for your time on this important matter," as they looked at me from head to toe again. I just smiled back, knowing the high level of brains and IQ that still remained in me.

I jumped right in and made another plea for prioritizing children's education over shopping, then asked if there were any questions. "No, thank you," Bill said.

"I have to get to work. Have a nice day," I responded then stood up.

"You're so thin, Nadia," Frank commented.

"I like it," Bill made clear.

Now I see how that was a very subtle, yet powerful, body image message. Little did they know how deeply I was hurting inside and often had a hard time eating, or merely chose not to.

Thereafter, Mr. Lockyer was relentless. He got my cell phone number from his friend, called, and left messages. I did not respond to any. Then he upped the ante, found out where I worked, and called my office.

"Ms. Davis, Attorney General Bill Lockyer is on the line," the receptionist announced. The entire office stopped. I shrugged my shoulders, said, "Ok," and shut the door. Several associates and their bosses wondered why. I worked for a prestigious law firm in the Public Law department, which represented local governments, some of which Bill had sued.

Bill threw me off. Like, a lot. I was not attracted to him nor did I have an interest in becoming romantic. After he'd called me multiple times, I eventually agreed to have dinner with him. It was very nice. We talked and talked, mainly about policy and politics. I liked that.

But it wasn't until he walked me out to the valet for my car that he made his intentions clear. Handing me a rose, he kissed me on my hand, then closed my door, and said, "I will talk to you very soon." Here I did get giddy.

I admit the novelty of his intelligence and power certainly drew me in. He appeared to be a man I could actually debate with, talk issues with, run ideas by. I was bored with the men I'd dated. And the one I loved wasn't quite available to build something real. But there was something more. It was hard to put my finger on way back then. Still, it was enough to agree to have dinner with him again.

One evening Bill left a key at the hotel's front desk and asked me to go to the room first. I thought, *No harm, no foul.* When I walked in, there were champagne, roses, and chocolate-covered strawberries on a cart. I sat down, he poured a couple glasses of bubbly, and we began chatting. At some point, I got up to use the restroom.

When I reached down for the toilet paper, I saw a plate of pre-made lines hidden a bit on a little shelf.

Was it his? I don't know. It doesn't matter anymore.

A physical craving kicked in like a bomb.

It was deep in my bones before I ever touched the plate.

Oh God, a drug, a drug! Who cares what the hell it is.

Give me the IV please and put that button back in my hand.

No one knew I'd become an addict and it would destroy my life.

Still, it's fair to say intentions weren't all that good.

Call it what you think it is and divvy up the blame.

I had to stop pointing the finger and I'm sorry I ever did.

Holding myself accountable brought back power and home within.

My clothes came off because I was high. I know they would not have otherwise.

***

Thereafter, Bill made a concerted effort to see me at least once a week. We got into a rhythm and way of connecting. One night, out of the blue, he told me he loved me. I wanted to believe it then, but I knew it was more lust.

Whether or not it was love, he seemed so happy when we were together, like a young man in a new playground of life. I enjoyed giving and being that for him. He made me feel special, worthy, and safe, and I needed that so much at the time. Sure enough, we got pregnant very quickly.

Dear Son,

Now I know, almost two decades later, that your father represented a "home" to me. His strength, intellect, commitment, and unabashed self-confidence made me feel safe and worthy, and still often do today. I have worked hard to understand that this belief is most often unhealthy and unfair. No one but me can truly love, protect, and take care of myself. No one but you can do the same for you.

Love, Mom

I was alone at home when I took the pregnancy test. As soon as I saw the positive result, an intense instinct filled my gut. I sensed my father's presence right then and there and thought, *A soul is coming into this world and it was always meant to be.*

Of course I was a bit panicked. But I wasn't afraid. I'd never had a more certain conviction that my child was meant to be than anything else in my life.

It was as though my consciousness was reignited and I was finally really living again. The blood was flowing, hearts were beating, and together, my baby and I were reborn. I decided to focus entirely on the safekeeping of the life in me.

How can I create a peaceful pregnancy? How can I protect Bill's reputation?

There were rumors floating around about us already, so I decided to tell Bill that I was pregnant before the election. But when I did, he said something that cut like a knife, that I'd find hard to forget for years to come. He said I should end the pregnancy "before it's too late."

Today I know his statement was due to fear of his personal life being exposed. But back then, his words broke my heart in an instant. I needed him to be the partner I thought he was at the time. I had hoped he would respond with care and concern for me and our child, not what came off like a dictate.

I wished he had said, "I'm sorry I can't be there for you," or "Let's walk through this together." I made the mistake of holding on to his words somewhere deep in my heart.

After hanging up the phone, I cried and cried, thinking, *Does he have any idea how much this child is meant to be? How organically, spiritually right this feels inside? Does he even love me like he said? In fact, does he even care about me or our child at all?* I prayed and connected with my father's spirit. I knew what I had to do.

Tiger Mama is here now, little one, I thought. *I don't need Bill's approval for anything. I can raise this child perfectly fine on my own.*

I met with Beth and we made a plan. A really good one.

I'd save money for a month or so then ask the law firm for pregnancy leave. When I started to show, I'd go to Bolivia, where Beth's parents had a home. I'd stay there until giving birth. Everything here would have subsided by then.

I stopped campaigning. Political daggers were sent my way. And to no surprise of mine, I lost re-election by a hair.

Bill easily won re-election as Attorney General and celebrated in Sacramento without me. Soon thereafter, while pregnant, I attended my last school board meeting.

Santa Ana Unified School District Board Meeting Minutes, November 26, 2002 Farewell Comments and Presentation to Nadia Maria Davis:

School Superintendent Dr. Mijares spoke. The following is a summary:

Nadia has served as a Board Member for four years, as Board President from 1999–2001 and Vice President from 2001–2002. Ms. Davis is an intelligent and hard-working individual who has a great love for people. St. Paul, several hundred years ago, uttered the following: "Though I speak with tongues of man and of angels, and have not charity, I have become as a sounding brass or as a clanging cymbal." The word charity comes from the Latin word "carritas," which means for love of humanity and benevolent good will. Nadia is like those who are linked emotionally with their followers and those are the people that one admires in all society. Looking back at the great leaders of our time, they are characterized with that love. One can have all of the great skills, but if one does not have love, they are nothing more than sounding brass or clanging cymbals. It is not lasting.

Nadia left an indelible mark on people. This characterizes Nadia Maria Davis. People don't care how much an individual knows until they know how much you care.

After the Superintendent spoke, I asked a young lady named Lyndsey to join me at the podium. She was a junior at Santa Ana High School, the lead saxophone for both the concert band and wind ensemble, and planned on becoming a music teacher in Santa Ana. Her mother, nephew, and band director were also present.

With gratitude in my heart, I took a deep breath in my final goodbye to the district, then handed her my father's saxophone. It was a final gesture of service to the school district that held his legacy.

A month or so passed without a word from Bill. I focused entirely on the pregnancy and my work as an associate at a well-known law firm. I had a great salary and benefits that would support me and my child just fine.

Unfortunately, my plan was unhinged when my boss called me into his office one day and, in one way or another, said that past suspicions of a relationship between Bill and I had been confirmed and I had to resign immediately.

I explained my confusion and that we were not involved anymore, but was only given a load of unsatisfying explanations. My already broken heart crumbled onto the ground. I was devastated, to say the least. In a bit of shock, I packed my things and left, dismayed and distraught.

There I was, four plus months pregnant, alone, and without a job. Full panic set in. Without an income for the time being, I had no clue how I was going to pay the next month's rent and bills. So I asked my mother and sister, who was a single mom, if we could all move in together to reduce costs. They thankfully agreed. I told them that I was pregnant and that the father was a lawyer, nothing more.

> *Nadia,*
>
> *I have no doubt you'll make a wonderful mother—I see it in the great love you give Miquela who is not even your own child. Even you give me advice that is correct and wise—I cannot wait until I get to love your little Poobies and Poobitos!*
>
> *I thank you for all your help and "mothering" of Miquela—and for your sometimes "mothering" and guiding me. You are so loved and appreciated.*
>
> *Love, Sabrina & Miq*

I had no idea how to manage the fact that I was pregnant while seeking employment. I was beginning to show and soon would be unable to hide it. *Who is going to hire me?* I thought. I put the word out to various attorneys that I was available for independent contractor work and filed for unemployment benefits at the same time. I got a couple of jobs doing depositions and special appearances, but it wasn't enough, and soon I was struggling financially.

This time was a mixed set of emotions. I was full of joy about the child growing in me, but felt alone, abandoned, and betrayed. I didn't want a husband. I knew I had made a choice.

I wanted my child's father present, or checking in. At checkups and ultrasounds, I wished I could hold Bill's hand or call him to share the joy. But it was just me alone every time, so I told myself, *Get used to this.*

I tried always to focus on gratitude. But I admit that when I observed couples with a pregnant partner holding hands, talking gleefully, then imagined them falling asleep at night touching a growing belly together, it was hard. I'd see photos of my law school friends and their children playing with the dad by their side. They were teams. I thought, *Why aren't I and my child worthy of the same?*

At times, I spoke to my baby and my father's spirit until I fell asleep.

Dear Son,

You kept speaking to me from inside my belly. I deeply treasure those moments when it was just you and me. The conversations I had with you, all by our very selves. The songs sang, stories told, things I showed you about my father and childhood. Photos of places traveled, my family, Priscilla, and Arthur. Poems I'd written, necklaces made, awards received, and music played. No interruptions, opinions, or judgments. Just you and I, in celebration of life. You kept a fire burning in me, knowing it was all meant to be!
Love, Mommy

When I was about five plus months pregnant, Bill tracked me down and apologized. I believed he meant it. I don't know why. Perhaps he called because I had been out in public and was showing. Gossip was alive. Perhaps it was based on self-preservation of his public image. Perhaps it was based on genuine care. I will never know what it was back then.

It's ok, I told myself. *Give him the benefit of the doubt.*

He invited me to visit him in San Diego the following week. I decided to go in order to update him on my plans to raise my child alone as well as show him an ultrasound picture and share the joy, hopefully. I'll never forget that he said our baby looked like "a salamander."

> *Dear Son, that indeed was your first of many nicknames.*

I started going out even more in public, happy and proud of my growing belly and baby. Soon enough, Bill called and insisted I do something for him. He said since he was so much older, we should ensure the baby's neurological health with an amniocentesis. "Sure," I said, naively.

If I had known his true intentions, I would not have done it. I was almost seven months pregnant and an amnio presents significant risks to the fetus because the embryonic sack is punctured. Only Bill, his Chief of Staff, scheduler, and unknown girlfriend knew the real intentions.

"Is he really the father? Do you have to marry her?" I'm sure they questioned at the time. This cut like a knife when I found out later.

Like pawns or pieces of property, my son and I were put through a clearance process to determine if we'd be part of Bill's life or not. Worse, an orchestrated marriage and public announcement were being prepared as damage control, unbeknownst to me.

During the amnio, I honestly believed it was for the health of our child. When asked if I wanted to know my baby's gender,

I said yes and asked the nurse to write it down on a piece of paper and place it in a sealed envelope.

That night, Bill grabbed it from me and opened it. "Do you want to know what it is?" he asked. "Yes!" I said. "I'm not going to tell you!" he said jokingly. But I already knew in my gut, which was further confirmed by the look on his face, that it was a boy.

Bill Lockyer was going to have a son! He couldn't hide his joy because deep down, he knew the baby was his.

The happiness in my naive heart was immeasurable.

A little Wally, I thought, then cried happy tears.

All I wanted was my son and a warm, safe, loving home.

All I hoped for was a normal, quiet life with peace and calm.

A few days later, Bill called and immediately after I answered said, very unexpectedly, "It's mine. Will you marry me?" No brief prologue, sweetness, or tiny preparation for what was one of the most important decisions of my life. Just a flat-out request for my hand in marriage over the phone.

It's not his fault that I should have said, "Let me think about it," because honestly, looking back, it kind of felt like an ambush. Instead I said, "Um, yes, I guess," having no real clue regarding the actual lifestyle and intimate partner I had just made a lifelong commitment to.

I wish my father had been alive at this monumental time in my life, just like when I returned prematurely to the public eye after the car accident. What would he have said? "Nadia, dear, have you really thought this through? You are not merely committing to fidelity, you're committing to public life on the road with a man thirty years older than you. Why not give it some time?"

Oh I wish I had experienced that father-daughter discussion. I may or may not have made the same decision. But I

certainly would've prepared myself a bit more mentally and
emotionally for the monumentally different life ahead.

***

Sure enough, my life changed dramatically overnight on a
rapid train with an unknown destination. I "had" to fly up
north within a week and be married in a court. I went on autopilot, informed my family, and told my best friends. My family
was unable to go on such short notice, even my mother, but a
couple of treasured friends made it, thankfully. Bill invited no
one, only his security guard was present, and we were married
on April 18, 2003, just two months before our son was born, in
the early morning hours of an entirely empty courthouse.

We briefly had lunch with my friends, but Bill was understandably restless the whole time, awaiting an important press conference scheduled immediately after, a block
away, to announce a DNA match in the Laci Peterson murder
investigation.

Within two hours of marrying, I entered heightened public life in the realms of a huge conference room filled to the
max with reporters. My new husband walked ten feet ahead of
me, continued walking, and I was lost.

I stood there, not knowing where to go or sit, a complete
fish out of water, and very pregnant in a white suit. People
looked at me with what appeared to be sympathy, even his security guard. Inside, my heart sank in shame and hurt rather
than soared in pride and glee.

I don't mean to sound and certainly wasn't ungrateful, but
looking back, it felt like being in the twilight zone on a con-
veyor belt, not a meaningful celebration of a bond shared and
being committed to. It felt transactional and orchestrated, like
our child and I were commodities rather than human beings.

Obviously, I don't believe this was necessarily intentional

on Bill's part. I think he thought he was doing the right thing while preserving his public image.

Still, I let it dig a hole of hurt in my heart and carried that into the marriage. Coupled with my own personal hardships and challenges, complete naivete, and lack of support for the rigor of publicly being Bill Lockyer's wife, our foundation was fragile from the start.

It was my first marriage. It was Bill's third.

I was thirty-two in three days, he was sixty-two in a few weeks.

Thank you, Bill, for trying to do the right thing and giving our child a present father.

When I first moved into Bill's Hayward house, it felt like our child and I were merely guests for a long time. This is not Bill's fault. He had lived there for nearly two decades prior after all. I think I packed only three bags for both of us. I had no idea what to expect in our home life with such little time.

The spare room was filled with shelves of books, a dresser, and a full bed. At first, I did not know if or where I could set up a nursery. So I decided to make things as comfortable as I could for our baby without moving a thing, and put a portable crib at the end of the full bed and a take-along bag of baby supplies. I figured I'd merely gauge what he was comfortable with little by little.

But then I saw that the closet, medicine cabinet, and nightstand were filled with female things. Face cream, shampoo, books, and even a lipstick-stained glass.

My heart broke in an instant for the hopes and dreams of the future I held in my head. Parts of me collided in what would become a chaotic set of thoughts and feelings I tried to manage alone for years. Clearly, a recipe for a surge of fear and resentment was made.

The deep hurt and a sense of worthlessness made me think, *Maybe I should double-check if it's ok to sit here, or open that door. Can I touch this, or use that? No, you better not, it might upset him. Are my baby and I just guests? Should I make a backup plan again? Are we intruding on Bill's life rather than giving him so much? Was pity merely granted, disaster merely prevented? Does he even love me, us? I am unworthy, unwanted, and a nuisance to him. I want to go hide in the closet and cry away the pain, just like I did as a child back then.*

It just seemed I had to walk this new way of life alone as a robot. I could have stood up for myself and said I was not comfortable with the current arrangements. But I stayed silent and didn't say a thing. I was unaware of my true worth inside, that I had a voice and didn't have to hide.

Is it Bill's fault I did not know back then? No. Should he have treated me better? Definitely. Should he have known his actions were a bit predatory? Yes.

***

Still, today I ask perhaps an even more important question. Where did he learn it's ok to treat women like that? Where do they all learn it? Did it come from his own upbringing? Was he hurt as a child too?

I am not excusing his actions, but some will say that's what I did. I don't give a damn if they do, because we ultimately have to get to the truth. Accountability is just the first step. We must and can do more. We must ask the men that do this, "Why do you think you do?" We must ask all sons the question, "What is your story behind it all?"

Did someone hurt you back then too? Did someone make you feel like just a thing? Did they tell you to hide your tears and to never show the pain? Did you learn that all you can do with it is to objectify women? Were sons out there ever taught there is another way?

**

I wish I had insisted Bill stop in his tracks, sit down, and give me five minutes of his full attention. To look me in the eye and be honest. To tell me he loved me or didn't. But what could he have said? "Yes, I love you, but I had to save my ass and marry you," or "No, I don't love you, but I had to save my ass and marry you."

Still, something like an "I was scared to death and didn't know what else to do," or "I just tried to do the right thing for you and our child," and "I'm sorry I didn't handle things well" would've helped. That kind of vulnerability always can get to the truth and healing.

But like I said before, hindsight is a bitch.

> *But it doesn't have to be that way for you,*
> *dear Son.*

Over the next month, I continued to go with the flow of Bill's life, home, and work. I believed with my whole heart it was my obligation and privilege to be grateful and give it my all in every way possible. And let's face it, I stuffed my feelings down.

The sheer joy of the future birth of our son filled my days with planning, reading, and preparing myself to be the best mother I could be. My family had a baby shower down south and surrounded us with love. The absolute miracle and blessing that the youngest child in the family was having a son were celebrated and cherished.

Life up north in the Hayward house settled into a routine. I planned and cooked dinners for Bill and appreciated giving him a source of stress relief and relaxation at the end of a long workday. Thankfully, we found our way back to that little but powerful light of a bond we shared before Diego was born.

As we lay in bed one night, I placed my head on his chest. He placed his hand on my shoulder, drew me close, and said, "Thank you. I'm sorry." I knew in my heart what he meant.

I kissed his cheek then we turned our bodies into cuddled spoons. With one hand on my belly and the other on my breast, he said, "Good night, I love you. I can't wait to meet our son."

And there it was . . . a sense of having a home in Bill's arms.

It was all I'd ever wanted since my father had passed.

It would take much longer to find it within myself.

CHAPTER 8

Dear Son,
you are the best thing
that ever happened to me.

Diego Wallace Lockyer was born on June 20, 2003.

Well, silly Bill and I, both rebels and advocates for the underdog type, also added "Spartacus Tacumseh" as middle names. Let me be clear. Diego is utterly beyond uniquely special in every way. Since the day he was born, I've been in absolute awe of him. He's the most intelligent, kind, and graceful human being I know.

Marrying Bill brought blessings beyond imagination in many ways. Diego was given the opportunity to directly and regularly receive his father's love, guidance, and care from the moment he was born. The first time Bill held Diego in his arms, he whispered, "I will never leave you. I will always take care of you. I will always love your mom."

He stayed true to his word indeed. No matter how much I

allowed my head to doubt his good intentions, Bill's dedication to us has never wavered. I see that in all its truth today because my head no longer runs the show.

Bill said we gave him the home and family he longed for. In Diego, he saw himself. He found his true self.

Through Diego, I truly got to witness and know the real man inside. With Diego, our love flourished and the house became a home.

Slowly but surely, I started adding my touch here and there. From little things like hanging photos of us on the walls, to big things like completely reorganizing the pantry and kitchen cabinets. I potted flowers and built a play area for Diego. I made a garden box with sunflowers. I bought a real crib for Diego and moved out the full bed. I added glow-in-the-dark stars on his ceiling and baskets of toys in the family room. I even had my father's baby grand piano shipped up north so Diego and I could place our hands on it.

Dear Son,

You were always in my arms or the baby carrier attached to my body before you could walk, like a baby kangaroo in its mama's pocket. I rarely put you down, nor would you let me. You were a "taquito boy" wrapped in a blanket all snug. Looking into your huge brown eyes as you sat perched on my knees was pure bliss. From sunrise to sunset, we remained inseparable.

I'd gently sway you back and forth while softly singing in your ears. We'd gaze out to the bay together from the family room or deck. I'd reach a hand out into the fresh air and thank our Creator for the beauty all around us.

*Daddy sometimes flopped into the hammock
and I'd lay you on his chest. In those moments, I
felt deep gratitude for the bond so clearly there.*

*I felt closer to my own father with you and
through you. He is so very much in you, dear
Son. Through your eyes, he shines. Through
your smile, he glows. In your unending curiosity, intelligence, and kindness, he thrives.*

*I love you more than you could ever know,
always and forever, dear Son.*

Love, Mommy

At bedtime, I sang a particular song I'd made up.

"Close your eyes, rest your head, feel the peace, my baby.
Mommy loves you so so much, and I always will. Dream big
dreams, stay safe tonight. Remember that I love you. Close
your eyes, rest your head, precious baby boy." It is in the same
rhythm and notes as a song in German handed down from
my mother. I am forever grateful that Diego remembers it to
this day.

Diego only fell asleep on my shoulder, lying next to me, or
on a drive. Every time I tried to put him down, he'd wake up
immediately and cry. I'd pick him back up and linger longer in
the love. This would go on for hours. Sometimes I'd fall asleep
in the rocking chair holding him.

Bill didn't seem to like the zapping of my time away from
him, so I tried the whole sleep training thing, but to no avail.
As Diego cried in his crib, saying, "Mama, Mama, Mama," I
cried on the other side of the door. I just couldn't do it.

So eventually there we were, like three love bugs snuggled
next to each other in the same bed. Who cares if it is a no-no.
It worked for us and was pure heaven.

Dear Diego,

On this day of your baptism, January 20, 2005, at All Saints Episcopal Church in San Leandro, California, the Bishop described God as light, as the power of the Universe we have yet to completely discover, may never fully know, or understand beyond earth and our galaxy . . . but it is light that created life. The Sun that gives us the ability to live—when he described God scientifically and through nature, it was exactly the way we hope you know the Creator and learn to live life with a constant connection to "God" and nature, "It."

His words also reminded me of the many ways you already know and connect to light. One, by following and being amazed by your own shadow. Two, by saying "hah, hah, hah" for something you sense is hot. Three, your awe with lights and how you point at them and say, "Te Te."

Most of all, when I go on the balcony, hold you in my arms, and together we look at the beautiful view, the trees, the waters of the bay, the Golden Gate Bridge afar on a clear day. I say, "Thank you, Creator," and you say, "Doooooo," in your sweet attempt to say the same. Your intentions need no clarity in speech. You know what you mean, what you feel, what you are grateful for.

We love you dearly, little one. Today was one of the most special days of our lives. After being a little restless, your spirit and body completely calmed at the time of your baptism. The

*water poured on your head and you were to-
tally at peace, dear one.*

*I love you more than all the stars, comets,
planets, everything out there in the universal
light, always and forever unconditionally.*

Mommy

When Diego started walking, he ran nearly simultane-
ously. One of Bill's security staff nicknamed him "Speed"
because he took off like a rocket. Putting him down on the
ground in certain settings was rarely an option. We had fun
with it along the way.

He was fascinated with windmills and saw the hills filled
with them on our regular drives back and forth to Sacramento
or Southern California. "Wini," he'd say, pointing his finger in
awe. Silly me, I ended up building one of those eight-foot-tall
metal ones in our backyard. Bill just chuckled when he saw it.

Diego also adored dolphins. We'd snuggle on the master
bed, watching calming documentaries capturing their beauty
with sweet Native American music. He could make a perfect
dolphin squeaking sound. We'd laugh and smile every time.
Bill came home one evening to find me painting an entire dolphin ocean scene on our backyard wall with Diego playing
nearby. I was like, "Uhmmm, I hope it's ok." "Cool," he said.

Diego loved lighthouses too. During our many travels,
we'd always find one on the map and make the long trek out
for an exploratory adventure. Diego probably set foot on at
least two dozen along the coast of California and around the
world. I ended up putting a large map in his room and placed a
star on every single one we were lucky enough to visit.

With Diego, I could escape the world outside our four
walls and be myself. He fed my heart and soul no matter
where we were or what we did. At home, I'd often escape in

our backyard and family room playing with him. Out in the public, he was like a shield when someone recognized our last name. Their eyes were nicer and more welcoming then, at least it seemed to me.

Together, we'd fly into life's most dazzling moments and discoveries. Every day was an opportunity to do something new and explore undiscovered terrain.

The list of journeys and creations is innumerable. Parks, beaches, trails, play places, bookstores, museums—you name it, we were there. Hand painting, pretend cooking, sticker crafting, clay molding—you name it, we made it.

I'd plop him in his car seat and say, "We're on a mission!" like the characters in the cartoon *Little Einsteins*. When Bill came home from work, he'd ask, "So what was your mission today?" always anticipating that he'd hear about a new location or creation. I'd tape Diego's art on the kitchen wall where he made our morning cappuccinos and he'd say, "Wow, Diego, you made that?" with a smile.

Days, hours, weeks, months, years passed this way.

Many of my most treasured moments in life are here.

Bill and I also made a great traveling team with our dear son in tow. Our combined Taurus stubbornness was more than enough to get us through any frustration, wait, or terrain. He was the planner and timekeeper. I was the navigator and photographer. In addition to required weekly trips from Northern to Southern California for Bill's work, we traveled out of state nearly every month.

Bill's scheduler sent his weekly itinerary home and I planned everything in Diego's and my life around it. Looking back, I don't know if that was a good or bad thing as a general matter.

Sometimes I should've put my foot down and insisted Diego and I get a solid, calm, normal week in one place. The lack of it most definitely contributed to the sense of difficulty

making friendships, establishing healthy daily habits and rou-
tines, and managing heightened anxieties.

At the time, however, my number-one priority was being
together as a family as much as possible. Bill loved that about
me and appreciated all the effort. So I focused on all the positive things about it and practicing gratitude, pretty much unaware of any possible negative impact as life went on.

From Oakland Airport to LAX or John Wayne in Orange
County, we were well-known regulars. The Omni Hotel in
downtown LA and Best Western in OC were our homes away
from home.

On top of that, we saw every part of California and the nation, from the mountains to the seas. We explored the nooks
and crannies of faraway countries we likely never would've
seen.

In fact, Bill and I likely made traveling with a child look
misleadingly easy. We had it down like a clockwork drill.
Breaking down the stroller with one hand while holding Diego
on my hip with the other was my job while Bill loaded luggage
on the belt and handed over tickets. He didn't want any special
treatment to bypass public lines. We did the whole deal like
everyone else is required to in airports and frequently up to
four times a week, albeit often with a security detail in tow.

As soon as we arrived at our hotel, I also immediately
transformed it into a kid-friendly zone as best I could. Plastic
coverings went on outlets and square tables in corners. The
sofa seat went directly next to my side of the bed for Diego
to sleep in if we were lucky. A portable playpen went near the
bathroom for use when a shower or toilet trip was needed and
Bill was working.

Most importantly, a space was somehow made for Diego and
his toys. I always packed a bag filled with his favorites and every
other practical child necessity, plus a suit and gala dress if I ever
had to switch from mommy mode to public wife on a dime.

Dear Son,

When Daddy worked during the day, you and I would play in the room and take walks around the hotel and nearby city. You'd run down every hallway. We'd go up and down the elevator. We'd visit the guest store and get a new toy. We'd pick the flowers in lobbies and stick our hands in the pool. We'd explore any local park or museum if possible. When it was time for a nap, I'd hold you close and walk in circles in our room. We'd cuddle together on the bed and fall asleep in each other's embrace.

Daddy had dinners and events in the evenings and always preferred I attend with him. Sometimes, we used a local sitter, but you cried, and I hated having to leave you with a different stranger every time. I tried to use the same one, but it never worked. If we were in Orange County, I was thrilled if my sister Anja was available to help, which she loved to do.

So I did my best. I pulled out a new toy to distract you as we walked out the hotel room, all the while we could hear you wailing as we entered the elevator. More often than not, I could sense your calling in deep attuned listening. I'd try to be a good Lockyer wife, but often went back to comfort you in the room before Daddy was done. I couldn't help myself when the sense that you were unhappy was strong.

Love, Mom

When we were lucky, we turned a work trip into a family

getaway for a few days or week after. We loved the redwoods and Sea Ranch north of the Bay Area.

Diego ran through coastal trails framed with beautiful yellow flowers as we searched for seals below. If it was the right season, babies nestled with their mothers on the hot rocks. Together we would sit and watch in awe. Diego would always find a little cave in the coastal mountain wall. He'd give it a name and make up a story, always leaving a gentle mark of "hello" for the next human being who might find it.

In Hawaii, Diego went with Bill on an inner tube in the pool's lazy river. When it was time for the water slide, he went with me. On the beach, it was all about castle building for hours, and I mean hours. It was as though Diego was building castles he once stepped foot on. He got lost in the joy of digging and forming trenches and walls, always creating an elaborate moat.

On a trip to New York, the detachable part of the car seat became known as the "bucket." During the flight, a snowstorm had hit the city. Totally unprepared, we walked from the airplane to the subway and then to our hotel with luggage, a baby in a bucket, and slippery shoes. It was concerning but comical, and undoubtedly a sight to behold for New Yorkers accustomed to snow in the city.

Then there was the parasailing experience at Coeur d'Alene in Idaho. Diego wanted to fly, so I took him with me in a double seater directly attached to my chest. They strapped us in securely and slowly raised us higher and higher along with the smooth flow of the boat. Extending my arms out, Diego did the same. We were in complete peace, fearless, and free flying like a mama eagle and her baby.

In Maine, Bill found us a sweet bed-and-breakfast surrounded by greenery. When he was at conference meetings, Diego and I explored the grounds and made "statues" with various pieces of nature. We found a butterfly garden and happily got lost in winding lush trails. Everything was quenched and colorful. The entire area felt homey, as though we were in a fairy-tale book.

Diego's adoration of lighthouses was born in Maine. He literally took off running toward one, standing in majestic beauty at the very end of a long stone-piled walkway. At first, I panicked. Then I gasped. Then I finally caught up with him. Like a ninja on a mission, every step he made was with a precision I could not match. Upon arrival, we just sat and gazed upon the surrounding beauty in pure awe. We finished the day with Diego holding the wheel of a very large sailboat, sitting stoic as ever, like a pro. The photos from this trip are stunning.

In Florida, we landed during a strong, humid storm. When we arrived at the hotel, we ran out to the balcony into the damp wind. Diego whirled in circles of powerful, vast, pure air. The smile on his face in this photo is priceless. We explored another lighthouse and butterfly garden in this state, just miles apart from one another.

There are so many more treasured memories from Denali in Alaska, Zion in Utah during the solar eclipse, Crater Lake in Oregon, Lake Michigan in Illinois, Ontario in Canada, as well as others—too many to all put down here.

Trips abroad were also frequent and a huge blessing. I had tricks to ease the long plane rides for Diego that Bill always found amusing. Little surprises from the dollar store would each be wrapped and put in a bag. Small magnets, cars, silly putty, and puzzles worked nicely. Every half hour or so, I'd pull one out to surprise Diego and keep him occupied. When all else failed, the portable DVD player was a godsend.

When Diego was just five, we flew all the way to Beijing. While Bill was at meetings, I took off with Diego alone to explore the Summer Palace and other sights. We happily got lost in the colors and corridors. All three of us ended up at the Great Wall later for a grand gathering under lights.

Tensions around the world were high that year regarding Beijing hosting the Olympics. On a visit to the Forbidden City, Diego sat on a step playing with a tiny rock. A local boy gazed upon him nearby, then edged closer and closer to his side. Diego smiled, stood up, and extended his hand out with a second rock. The symbolism and beauty in the photo of this moment is stunning, the Chinese boy leaning closer to get a good look. They ended up playing together without knowing each other's native tongue. My father was shining down saying, "My most joyful moments were playing with rocks and a friend, no matter what was going on outside La Colonia."

In England, "Captain Dickory" was born. After exploring the park surrounding Buckingham Palace, Diego wanted a flag. So I got a little one, placed him in the stroller, handed it to him, and we took off with a map of London in hand. I must've walked over twenty miles that day as we went from one sight to another.

Our first stop was Trafalgar Square. Diego climbed up the steps, held out his flag, and announced, "My name is Captain Dickory." I bowed then bestowed upon him the honor of knighthood. Captain Dickory and I were on a quest to save the world from its misery. From Big Ben to the London Eye, and up and down the river, Diego and I spent the entire day exploring multiple sites. He was about four or five years old.

Outside London, it was all about castles. Bill stopped at every one along the way to Stonehenge. As soon as Diego was within feet of the castle, he became Captain Dickory.

On a second trip to England, we went north to a farm town called Buxton. We stayed in a bed-and-breakfast and journeyed up the surrounding green hills. A herd of wild horses encircled us in glory. I was worried at first and held Diego in my arms. But we just stood there engulfed in their beauty, gazing into their eyes framed by long beautiful manes. I set Diego down. Immediately he won the trust of a stallion and placed his hand gently on its side. The photo that captured this moment is stunning.

In France, we walked all the way up Mont Saint Michel's pristine layers. In Paris, we gazed up at the Eiffel Tower after exploring various museums and churches. In Italy, we got lost in tiny street corridors, explored multiple magnificent sights, and ate the best meals ever followed by long walks at sundown.

The depth of gratitude inside my heart that I carry for Bill and the fact that he gave us all these beautiful memories is immeasurable. I could go on and on. Our traveling adventures hold some of our most treasured moments as a family.

I was happily obsessed with being the documentarian and photographer on all these adventures, hoping to translate somewhere the love shared between us and Diego's unending curiosity. Every moment felt magical and rare. There was a sense of sacredness and fragility present, as if it could all be snatched away in an instant. A photo or video was proof to me it actually had happened and might be repeated.

There are many printed photos of these adventures on our walls and a gazillion more stored elsewhere. My hope is that it will bring our dear son joy to share them with his own love and children one day. A "look where I went, what I got to explore" type of sheer glee. That would be so beautiful to see!

As Diego grew older, our home activities together evolved.

The living room became the location of a new "territory" every week. Every possible ingredient was used. Blocks, magnets, boxes, Legos. Boats, trains, planes, and automobiles. Pirates, soldiers, astronauts, farm and sea animals. We started with wooden train tracks, sprawling them out in every direction. Then we went to huge baskets of blocks and magnets in every shape and color. They would turn into large structures and each given a purpose. I made the farms and houses while he made the Eiffel Towers and port entries. Using every last piece, Diego's attention to detail was fascinating to watch. Classical music was always playing in the background.

At some point, usually after a couple days, Diego would suddenly stand up and announce, "Ok, Mommy, it's done," and give it a name. That meant it was time for his ship to set sail and for me to play the Enya song "Ebudae." He'd start in his room and work his way slowly in accord with the song's nomadic beat, sometimes even laying his head on the ground in an imaginative and observant kind of way. By the time the song ended, the ship had arrived. This beautiful ritual repeated every week or so.

Bill would come home and ask how the "territory" was doing.

If a new one had started, it was a big deal.

Then there were the "waterways."

Diego dragged the hose across the grass and placed it at the base of some large green bushes. I'd turn it on lightly, like a serene dripping waterfall. We watched as natural "waterways" chiseled the dirt. Soon he'd dive his hands in and the story began. Trucks and dinosaurs careened, taking sips of the Niagara jewel. If the supply of vehicles or animals ran low, I had backup stock within reach so his concentration and imagination wouldn't be interrupted. White lilies swayed in gratitude for the quenching. The mud was filled with wonder.

Summertimes filled our house with children from throughout the neighborhood. Running in the sprinklers and fighting with water guns were the norm. Often a tent would be put on the deck or grass. They'd take breaks playing with Legos and games inside.

One day, the fire abatement goats took over. Diego came to the kitchen and said, "Uh, Mom, there are goats in our backyard."

"Ok," I responded, thinking nothing of it.

But when I looked out, I could see nothing except white goats covering the entire backyard. It was like a scene from a movie. We laughed and laughed. Diego, his friends, and I attempted to direct them back down the hill, each of us with a broom in hand. It didn't work, so I ended up calling 911. Within a minute, our entire house was surrounded by police cars. Unbeknownst to me, Bill Lockyer's house was on an immediate reply list.

"It's just goats, it's just goats," I said, over and over, smiling, five boys chuckling behind me with brooms held high. The officers didn't know what to think until they saw goats breaking through our front gate and approaching them. They ended up calling the herd owner.

This memory makes Diego and me laugh in an instant to this day.

Dear Son,

Do you remember the waterways as much as I do? I always wondered if you knew exactly what you wanted to create before you began, or if your idea evolved over time. When I think about it, this is how life is too.

Sometimes we know where we want to go, what we want in our life and then take action to get there. Other times we don't and just go with the flow. Repeated over and over and over again, a chiseled pattern and routine are set in stone. Going with the flow without conscious choice is most often not a safe or healthy way to go.

Please think ahead and remember your hopes, desires, and needs.

Where do you want the water to bring you?

What type of flow is best? Where will your true self shine the most? The answer is within you. Listen to the "this doesn't feel right in my gut" instincts. Because habits are chiseled in our bones and become difficult to change. If we listen in deep attunement to the signs along the way, we'll chisel our way into living authentically.

Love, Mom

CHAPTER 9

Dear Son,

please make self-care your best friend.

Bill is indeed thirty years older than me. His childhood began in the forties, mine in the seventies. Our upbringings were obviously dramatically different in terms of cultural history. He also grew up in Northern California, me in Southern. He was an only child most of his youth until his parents adopted a girl when he was a teenager. Me? The youngest of seven. To say that we are different is an understatement.

Bill said his mother, Hazel, was a fun and outgoing woman, and he often told me I reminded him of her in those ways. His father was present, but a workaholic and alcoholic. They planted roots in Oakland before Bill was born and remained there throughout his life until their passing decades before we met.

Like many of us, Bill witnessed unhealthy ways of dealing with life's pains. He told me about a time when his mother fell into a depression and entered suicidal ideation. Tragically, he walked into the garage to find her standing on a chair with a noose around her neck, crying. His father, he said, was likely drunk at the nearby bar.

This memory is probably symbolic of a basic imprint set on Bill's brain regarding human connection, attachment, love, and how pain is dealt with. Did he learn how to reach out for help or ask for support when needed? Did he learn how to offer help to a partner or give support when they needed it? I doubt either of those things happened. And, without a doubt, I am sure his parents did the best they could with what they knew at the time too.

By the time Bill and I met, he had held office for three entire decades, including as President of the California Senate and State Attorney General. After we met, he added another four years as Attorney General and eight years as State Treasurer.

He had a positive impact through every committed endeavor. His acumen and skillful problem-solving across party lines engendered accolades from vast sectors and rare alliances. There truly has never been another leader comparable to Bill Lockyer when it comes to political and policy-making skills and accomplishments in the state.

He was and still is one of the most highly respected and adored elected officials around, even after retirement from public office. On top of that, his closest personal friendships have remained over a lifetime.

How I ended up having the honor to become his wife and that our marriage lasted nearly two decades still eludes me.

Fact is, I wasn't prepared.

I did the best with what I knew at the time indeed.

I just never could adequately adjust.

It never felt quite right in my gut. No matter how much love and gratitude I carried in my heart for him, and still do to this day, those couldn't quell the reality of our core differences.

As our first years of marriage passed quickly, I started

cracking a bit. It became more and more difficult to manage weekly travel demands while also attempting to give Diego a consistent routine. On top of that, my own physical and mental health needs were going unacknowledged and unmet.

It just seemed impossible to do either while traveling so much.

Chronic pain flare-ups started hitting me hard. I had no idea at the time what to do about it. My shoulder and neck aches would rise up into my head like a hammer on automatic before I reached for an ibuprofen. Worse, sharp strikes of hip pain forced me to literally stop in my tracks, hold on to something, or sit, sometimes even causing me to trip or fall. I'd just say "ouch" to myself and try to move on. I had no clue how physical pain affects us psychologically, emotionally, and mentally, nor how to reach out for help. I began to fall into a deep depression and further isolate.

When alone at the house or in the car running errands, strong longings for my father and his voice of comfort and guidance returned. He would've listened patiently and insisted his daughter get the medical help she needed. I tried to turn to Bill for support during this time, but he simply didn't or couldn't respond in the way needed from a spouse. Sometimes he even appeared agitated or angry with me for saying anything about the struggles.

It seemed there were no moments of "I hear you and am here for you," or "What can I do to help?" I only remember feeling like I was speaking to his back and being met with a shrug of his shoulders as in a "What's the big deal?" kind of way. I'd try again when it seemed he was more relaxed after intimate moments before sleep, but the conversation always appeared to be a burden to him—it was shut down or dismissed.

I also didn't know what, or how to ask for what, was needed in him as a spouse with specificity, clarity, and grit. I saw and knew other couples communicated and lived differently, truly supporting one another. I could've just said, "I need to be in one place for a week or more. My body is aching and I'm feeling really down. Please hold me in your arms like you did back then." Instead, my mind ordered, *Just stuff all your feelings down until you don't feel or recognize a thing. Just freeze there, shut up, and stay in your place.* It wasn't a choice, that mind in control thing. It was automatic. I didn't know any better then. Sadly, an extremely impersonal, disconnected mode of married life set in stone.

There is no fault or blame here. I chose to marry Bill and stay married at the time. With his own emotional awareness and ability to communicate interpersonally limited, how could he have done any better? Today I can see that. Back then, he simply evoked being a cold, distant, and disinterested partner.

Even worse, I truly believe living in the public eye added a hefty layer of challenges. For some, they may have been fine. For me, it became very stressful. On the outside, I was a master of social chitchat and looking pretty. Yet on the inside, it was grueling work. Princess Nadia, I played the part well.

Little Nadia was chiseled to feel loved only through the approval and praise of others, to place the foundation of my identity in everything outside me. *Get their approval and do what makes them happy. Then you'll never be abandoned, unloved, and unworthy.* Yet in my physical pain and depression, it often felt impossible to play the part. Living in a fishbowl is dangerous if you haven't learned how to swim yet.

My confidence began to waver. I began to feel "less than" others in my presence. Sometimes I even stumbled in knowing what was expected and appropriate in formal settings. I didn't know which utensil to pick up first. I didn't know I was supposed to place the napkin on my lap as soon as I sat down. I didn't know my $20 gala dress and fake leather purse were not good enough. I didn't realize that expensive clothes and squeezing myself into the upper-class mold were not things of true value in the first place!

I was so naive and unprepared to live in the public eye, the crap my mind made up was pure insanity. Maybe it was also the local press's critiques. Maybe it was that my entire professional identity was unseen. Maybe it was the fact I just needed genuine authentic connections.

I let my self-conscious mind be infiltrated with messages that I was an "outsider, visitor, undeserving, and unwanted" for years. As a result, it seemed impossible to build true friendships with anyone.

What eventually happened? Alcohol became my best friend and confidant. My father could relate to that. It appeared to easily solve the social anxiety and physical pain. I was ready to face the world or run a marathon with a drink.

Give me the IV, and I'll be, go, do, play any role you need, the disease promised. It was self-will run riot, believing this is how we are supposed to live and deal with physical pain and feelings.

Work it off. Numb it out. Just get it done and move on.

You can handle life this way, rang out in my head regularly.

Soon enough, however, a whole other layer of complications from deep in my psyche added to the fires. I began to have flashbacks from childhood trauma. It was as though the age difference in our marriage abruptly became a problem.

One night is clear to me. I get the chills trying to describe it here. I don't want to. We were being intimate, and suddenly I was scared and in tears. The bald head, his ravenous gazing eyes, the shape of his mouth. Bill's profile and body turned into Dr. K. in a millisecond.

I panicked and screamed at the top of my lungs, "No no no no." I tried to push him off. "Wait, wait," he said, "you're making me feel bad," then got up and left the room. I curled up in a ball in another space and time. I cried myself to sleep, feeling abandoned and alone.

Bill had no clue what had just happened. I truly didn't understand it myself. I wish I had been more aware to explain. I believe he would've cared and listened better.

But "dissociation" and "flashback" were not words I knew or understood then. Sadly, that is exactly what began to happen more and more over time.

A drink will help you get through the night, the disease screamed, and one became two, then two became three. We all know, the disease loves PTSD.

Looking back, it is clear that the concussion, brain bleed, and lack of oxygen from the car accident intensified the flashbacks, the robotic and disconnected state. I think I lost most of my good childhood memories that night I died. You know, the kind that others spew off at any moment with detail and glee. The "once I" or "when I was" ones? The ones filled with the feelings of flying free as a child? Like I said, any I hold inside are stories my brothers and sisters shared. They are not organically mine.

How does it feel? Empty, like a blank canvas, a hollow barrel, a dysfunctional compass with no reference point. I don't know what I can't remember. I don't know what to ask, what story to beg to be told.

It feels like I had no home or hometown. No grounding place of solace I can recall or refer to. And if I ever did, my father symbolized it for me. Like a flag posted on a mountain, he was the front door, base and foundation of a physical home to me. After his death, I was floating, not knowing where that was.

After the accident, I had no map or directions from a past life to get back to. All that was left inside were the ingredients of flashbacks. The room in the doctor's office, where I lay, how it felt, what I saw in his face. The closet in my room, where I sat, how I felt, what was going on outside.

It is not fair I only remember these.

It is not fair I don't get to remember a history of glee.

I know it must've once been there. It must've been.

Dear Son,

You eventually filled up my brain's hole with immense glee.

You gave me memories so joyous, detailed, real, and alive, I want to be there in my head all the time. Our walks, drives, backyard life. The sound of your voice, the feel of your hug. Your mouth on my breast, eyes looking into mine, hands in the dirt, all the trips flying. The way you escaped in time, enthralled with an idea in your mind.

I am so blessed to now have these memories in my head.

It is only through you that my sense of childhood glee returned.

I remember more now . . . it's slowly coming back.

Thank you, dear one, thank you so very much for that.

Love, Mom

***

After Diego entered preschool, we started traveling less.

I started feeling more grounded at home, which reduced

the depression and allowed me to get some help from Kaiser, if even a little. I didn't get close to doing enough, but I started drinking less, and working out more.

Soon enough, a deep, healthy longing for professional work arrived. After doing a little part-time work on large childhood molestation cases, I was beyond blessed to be hired to head up the Alameda County Family Justice Center (ACFJC) by District Attorney Nancy O'Malley, one of my heroes. It truly was life changing and everything started heading in a healthier direction.

At the ACFJC, I finally returned to a sense of working in my element, making the world a better place. I'd work hard in the day, then pick Diego up from school with a sense of having given back to the world. I felt connected to people who genuinely cared and still was able to be an active, present mother. I started to make a few friends outside of work too, like Jackie, Loretta, Lori, and Fariba. Bill and I had mutual work projects we could talk about.

In a healthier, happier state of mind, flashbacks lessened, physical pain reduced, and our marital connection improved.

The ACFJC is a groundbreaking conglomerate of co-located government and non-profit agencies offering coordinated and comprehensive services for victims of interpersonal violence. It is a complete overhaul of victim service delivery and a model throughout the world. As Executive Director, I had the honor of using every God-given skill I had. From bridge building and cross training, to fundraising and grant writing, I thrived in the position and loved it with every ounce of my being.

My office was on the first floor next to the main lobby. I witnessed firsthand the unmatched dedication, hard work, and life-saving skills of front liners. The Oakland Police Department's Special Victims Unit was located on the top floor in the opposite wing of the County's largest victims' rights advocacy center. Collaboration respecting privacy rights enabled decisions regarding whether arrest, emergency relocation, safety planning, a restraining order, or doing nothing was in the victim's best interest at any given time. Angels every day of their lives, the ACFJC team of unsung heroes restored my belief in creating good, warmth, and justice in the world.

I saw them push themselves to save a life without physical or mental breaks for days. They had to look a person straight in the eyes and gently try to encourage them to leave before it was too late, only to find their stabbed corpse a week later. They had to stomach the memories of bloodied scenes when inputting details in a report only to know a life would now be a number. They sat with battered children in special interview rooms with the challenge of helping them feel safe enough to share about abuse without re-traumatization. There was Hillary in Highland Hospital ER conducting forensic exams of intimate injured parts while also gently trying to explain there are people who can help. Anissa, in Victim Witness Protection, ready at any moment to create a safety plan and show the way out. Rodney in the Special Victims Unit, Marsha at Bay Area Women Against Rape, and Nola, who turned her own tragedy into a leading model, helping sexually exploited minors escape and build new lives. The list of heroes is endless.

Over the next year or two, as a result of my increased sense of purpose and social interactions, things improved in and outside our home. There was finally a cherished rhythm to daily life.

Bill and Diego were thriving and happy.

And I was a bit better at living more healthfully.

CHAPTER 10

Dear Son,
you can make it through anything in life,
and are never alone.

Just when it seemed life had fallen into place, bombs came raining down everywhere, in every way, breaking into pieces the cherished peace and happiness present at the time. Within less than a year, three major events happened back-to-back and out of the blue.

Arthur Carmona died.

We lost a child.

And my brother attempted suicide in our home.

***

"Arthur died" is all I heard on the other side of the line. "He was hit by a truck and didn't make it."

No "goodbye," or "see you on the other side" chance given.

Daddy, gone. Priscilla, gone. And now Arthur?

All I remember is the feeling of falling into a black hole and onto the floor. *God, please, no, please. Don't do this again to his mother, and to me. Why him, God, why him? No, no, no, no . . . my God, how can it be?*

As I sat on the floor, my face buried in my hands, Diego kneeled down to me and asked, "Mommy? Mommy?"

I tried to find my voice. It was nowhere to be found. I tried to hide my tears. But I was drowning in them. Then he placed his head next to mine and stayed there, waiting.

I finally mustered up the ability to say, "I helped a little boy. But that little boy is gone now. He went to heaven."

Without hesitation, my dear son said, "Mommy, I'm going to bring that boy back to life for you." The power in his innocent words was unforgettable.

Thank you, dear Son, for being there for me.

But my mind went to work, punching me inside immediately.

If I had not helped to obtain his freedom, he'd at least still be alive in jail.

If I had not initiated the train to get him out, his mother would still have a son. Arthur was hit by a truck just like me. Why did he have to die and I get to live?

How is it that I did something good if it landed someone dead?

How can I live in peace knowing the dirty cops won in the end?

How do I convince others to do what's right when death has the last word?

What can I say to his mourning mother when there is no light left?

A memorial service was held for Arthur. I wanted to truly grieve, but I couldn't connect to anything real. The sudden shock of a dead body in front of me brought me right back to the memory of my father's and Priscilla's deaths. So I went back and forth between numbness and flashbacks inside. I was not present.

The graying of oxygen- and blood-deprived skin. The hardening of hands that once were soft and caring. The stiffened lips on the mouth that once spoke words of hope in the world. A dead body doesn't help you sense the soul it once carried.

I did not know the thing that lay in front of me.

Where was Ronnie Carmona's little boy? Where was the young man who had a hero's journey untold? Where was the courage I saw in his eyes? The calm in his voice, and kindness in his acts? Where was the stature of a man standing tall who meant so much to those who cared for justice?

It seemed the cold, pale, hardened body before me was more of a cruel reminder that there is no ability for real freedom in this life. *There is no way to connect safely. If death is always lurking around the corner and in control, why even try to get close to another soul and know your own?*

When I returned home, I was jaded and in shock.

I felt stuck inside in more ways than one. At some point, chronic pain easily took control again. When disconnected, it is as organic to life as the blood running through my veins. As it intensifies when in this state of mind, I do not recognize the severity until it is too late. Perhaps even worse, my memory and flashbacks began to interfere with life. My sleep was interrupted, so an overload on energy drinks helped me get through the day's acts.

I had to reread things more than once and go back over my notes to remember something I said or an idea I had. Forethought was constant until afterthought took over. There was no living in the present unless I escaped in the presence of Diego or under the guise of a drink.

At the time, I simply wasn't fully aware of the pattern of unhealthy living I was settling into again.

***

My dear brother is my hero.

He is a beyond unique human being and anyone who knows him is blessed to have him in their lives.

After receiving several degrees, it appeared he had a seamless, normal evolution as a single educated man. A great job, friends, and travel. But what is normal? Why was that word ever created? According to society's expectations, he "should've" been happy. Screw that! He was actually struggling in his head.

I don't know when it began.

I don't know if it was always there or came and went.

I don't know where he found his source of strength.

His friend called me out of the blue one day, letting me know that my brother was greatly struggling and needed support.

I called my brother. Thankfully, he called back. We set up a time to meet at a restaurant.

He opened up to me for the first time about his struggles.

It got so bad, he had resigned from work and was finding it more and more difficult to leave his apartment. He could barely sleep, eat, or drink. Courageously, he already had reached out to a doctor for help.

A week later, he called while admitting himself to the emergency room. He couldn't take it anymore. Suicidal ideation was ever present. I went immediately to the hospital. His friend joined me. Thanks to that person, my brother was safe.

He wanted to live and had the guts to get help.

Heroic is an understatement.

His ability to acknowledge the need for help, let alone reach out for help, was incomprehensible to me at the time. How did he do it?

My brother returned to his apartment alone. The option of moving in with us was given, but he desperately wanted to hold on to pieces of his "normal" life. He felt like a failure in society's eyes. *Oh dear Brother, the agony you went through.*

Who was I to force him to move? Or consider inpatient help?

Within days, however, he wasn't answering calls. I went to his apartment and was frightened to death of what I might find. There he was, curled up in a ball, freezing and pale, buried in dirty dishes and laundry. The fear and desperation in his eyes were beyond painful to see.

Worse, he felt ashamed. He was now completely incapacitated by something he had absolutely no control over. I wanted to zap it all away and just hold him close for the rest of eternity.

To see someone you love suffering in this way is beyond heartbreaking. *Why did you have to curse him?* I asked over and over in my head. *He is a good person and has done nothing wrong.*

My sister Marisa thankfully flew up immediately to help. It took us a few hours just to get him out the door, down the stairs, and into the car. We had to stop every few steps because he thought people were laughing at him.

I took him home and set up a room for him downstairs.

One day I was trying to help him feel safe enough to get out of the car. Professionals were waiting to help him inside. Sometimes, his hand would shake and quiver. That day, it was so intense it made it difficult for him to undo his seat belt.

"They are laughing at me," he said. I touched his arm and tried to guide him back to me. "You are here with me. You'll be ok." Slowly, oh so slowly, he returned.

Working full-time and caring for Diego, Bill, and the house, it became more and more difficult for me to ensure my brother's daily medications, meals, cleanliness, and human interactions. I spent hours on hospital admissions, insurance, disability, and social security paperwork. Still, at times I just felt like I wasn't doing enough.

Several visits to the ER, medication concoctions, and in-patient stays later, nothing seemed to help. Every time I had to leave him alone in one of those crappy and cold mental health facilities, it felt more like I was leaving him in a morgue. Beyond dehumanizing, to believe it was "necessary" made no sense at all. A sense that I was failing him was constant.

When the time came for a trip to China for Bill's work, I made arrangements to keep my brother safe with family in Southern California. I flew him down and insisted he stay the full duration, explaining his situation to family.

But they let him fly back early. I was furious, angry, and deeply concerned. Bill and I were oceans away and no one up north knew he would be there alone. I called our neighbor to check on him. But when she did, she said no one was there, at least it appeared so.

We flew back home, and the flight arrived an hour early.

I opened the front door and immediately ran to his room downstairs. There he was, my dear brother, pale, cold, and lifeless.

"No, no, no, no, please God, please, not him too, not him too, please!" I cried. I tried desperately to wake him up, desperately to bring him back to life, but to no avail. I screamed for help then just broke down sobbing on his chest. His smell. His cold hands. His tousled hair lying down. I remember it to a T, vividly.

I looked up in agony and saw a note on his keyboard nearby. A paper with his handwritten words, teardrop stains smearing the blue lines.

> *Nadia, this is not your fault. this is my choice*
> *thank you for everything . . . luv, x*

Paramedics arrived and my brother was taken and put on life support. He struggled to come back. Thankfully, he did.

It took a few weeks for his body to recover. In the following months, a doctor finally found the right medication concoction and connected better with my brother. Without the proper formula prior, he had constantly felt severe sleepiness and mental fog, which added to his depression.

Still, it would take time before I saw that spark in my dear brother's eyes again.

***

Several months passed. Inklings of light and hope returned through Diego, purposeful work, and my brother's recovery. I was deeply grateful that Diego began creating a closer bond with his uncle. As I observed them interacting, the thought of giving Diego a sibling even returned.

When I mentioned it to Bill, he initially flat out said no, without any opportunity for a conversation. No look in the eye, acknowledgment of the longing, processing of the yearning, or mutual understanding. *Ok*, I thought. *Suck it up, grin and bear it.*

He had legitimate reasons to be opposed. But it still would've helped if he offered a shoulder to cry on. By that point, I had stopped asking and cried myself to sleep instead. I think he knew, but never said a thing about it.

Adoption came to mind. We were beyond blessed and able to give a child a good home. I even attended a class and came home with a binder. Bill didn't say anything. At some point, he came home and abruptly announced, "Let's make our own." I stopped taking birth control and within a month, I was pregnant.

At the three-month mark, I told Diego and my office. Bill's staff even sent home a pair of baby shoes as a gesture of congrats. I happily consumed myself with organizing the 2nd Annual ACFJC Gala at the Oakland Rotunda.

When I was five months pregnant, I actually began to let myself feel the joy and embrace the reality that I was having another child. Diego and I started talking about all the things we would do together with his little sibling.

The happiness in my heart was overwhelming.

***

Yet suddenly, out of the blue, my baby girl's heart stopped beating. Just like that. Bam! Your baby's dead.

My heart stopped along with hers.

I might as well have been lying back there in the embankment.

All I remember was seeing a tiny lifeless body on the screen.

I could not move. I could not speak. My head did a number on me. *You stupid fool. Why'd you ever believe? What else did you think? You don't deserve another child. You're not worthy.*

A few days later, I had to stand before hundreds of guests as the Mistress of Ceremonies at the Annual ACFJC Gala. I gave words of hope with a dead fetus in my womb. No one knew but Bill. Many even came up to me and said, "Congratulations on your baby," not knowing we were both dead inside.

Kaiser scheduled a D&C in lieu of induced labor. Bill apparently had to be in Sacramento. I should've told him I needed him to hold my hand and say goodbye together to our baby girl. Instead, I was silent and he was nowhere to be found.

But my dear brother was by my side.

Prior to that, he had very rarely left the house. It seemed his eyes often carried a scared or glazed look for months after the attempt.

That day, however, he came back alive, fully.

They sedated me, but I could feel all the pulls and tugs. I could see her being torn apart through visions in my head. When I woke up alone in the recovery room, tears rolled down my cheek. The kind that just fall without feeling.

Staring at the wall, I thought, *My little girl, where are you? Where do I put this pain? Where will your soul go? Will you visit me later somehow?*

My brother walked in, put his hand on my arm, and did not say a word. His presence alone was immense comfort and enough to break me out of deep sadness. He helped me into a wheelchair and gently pushed me out to the car. Driving home, we remained silent, but he reached out and placed his hand on mine. He walked me with care into the house and tucked me into bed.

When I woke up, I thought only of Diego, longing to hold him. How would I tell him what happened to his little sister? Those same silent tears rolling down my face. The kind that come out when you're so numb with sadness, you don't even recognize you're crying.

Soon enough I heard my brother come up from his room. He walked in slowly, sat down at the foot of the bed, placed his hands on my feet, and asked, "Nadia, are you ok?"

I just looked up at him and into his eyes. My heart was so broken, I could barely breathe. But in that millisecond, I saw my dear brother fully back alive. His eyes showed a presence I hadn't seen in such a long time.

It hit me. Yes, I had lost my child. But I had not lost my brother.

Thank you, Brother, for surviving and being in my life. Your genius and compassionate wisdom today is a blessing to us all.

***

If I attempted to explain the depth of numbing pain I was in at this time in my life, I'd be a fool. Today, I can see how the need to process the loss of loved ones was critical to my mental health. There was just too much of it, back-to-back, and out of the blue.

Instead, only memories of their lifeless bodies flashed through my mind. They darkened and cluttered the path to that home within me where their souls reside.

I didn't know what to do with my pain and broken heart. In my depressed and lonely state, alcohol became my best friend and confidant again.

Buzzed, I felt something at least. I could cry and felt a sense of relief. I could wake up the next morning and repeat the routine all over again. Cook a meal, bring Diego to school, comfort Bill, then with lipstick, makeup, curled hair, heels and a suit, work and lead others in an attempt to save the world. As long as I knew I'd get my relief later that evening, everything went like clockwork, a robot without emotions.

Dear Son,

I know today that death is not something to fear. When we die, we simply fall back to the vast, timeless wholeness of love, light, and warmth. We fall back into our soul selves, untouched by physical life, connected in all ways to every being.

Our true essence is changeless, deathless, everlasting.

Native Americans celebrate death, knowing that it is an end to life on earth, but believing it to be the start of life in the Spirit World. Most tribes also believe that the journey might be long, so afterlife rituals are performed to ensure that the spirits would not continue to roam the earth.

Various tribes honor the dead by giving them food, herbs, and gifts to ensure a safe journey to the afterlife. The Hopi Indians believe that the soul moves along a Sky path westward and that those who have lived a righteous life will travel with ease. To ensure a safe journey, they wash their dead with yucca and dress them in traditional clothes. Prayer feathers are often tied around the forehead of the deceased, and they are buried with favorite possessions and feathered prayer sticks.

The Navajo perceived that living to old age was a sign of a life well lived, thus ensuring that the soul would be born again. Alternatively, they felt that if a tribe member died of sudden illness, suicide, or violence, a Chindi, or destructive ghost, could cause trouble for the family of the deceased. Afterlife rituals could last for several days, with careful thought given to foods and herbs chosen for the celebration, a reflection on how the deceased lived their life.

All these practices embrace physical death, they don't ignore it. They allow the process of mourning, a transition from "goodbye" to "I feel your spirit near."

When death arrives in your lifetime, as your mother, I will do my best to show you that it is not something to fear, nor the pain from it something to shun.

I will hold space for you to embrace vulnerability. To be courageous in the depths of your

tears. *To shout at the top of your lungs, "I am
sad," and wholeheartedly mourn your loss.*

*You'll know love shared in spirit lives on, no
matter what.*

*Our path to that home of love and light
within us can't be marred.*

Love, Mom

***

Months and months passed. News spread that the current
County Supervisor was retiring. She represented the district
we lived in and was a strong advocate for families in crisis.

At some point, I got interested in running, partly based on
a desire to make a bigger positive impact on the lives of those
in need, and partly based on wanting to work away the pain.

The first time I mentioned it to Bill, he was detached and
uninterested. He was silent in fact, and acted nervous and concerned. After all, it would create local political upheaval. An
ex-girlfriend of his, a former State Senator, was already running and would be the obvious front-runner. My brain put
ideas in my head that he must not believe in me or he must be
having an affair.

I went from confident fighter mode, thinking, *I'll just run
anyways,* to the complete opposite lack of belief in myself, *Who
the hell's going to vote for me?* A perfect combo of feelings to
delay making a decision.

I would never have done anything professionally he was
opposed to. Never. Why? He was and still is one of the most
powerful men in the state. I not only needed his support, but
his preferences also always dictated where, when, and how
I'd be. That is partially not his fault, possibly entirely not. The
fault is mine.

Bill ended up making the decision for me. We went to a political event in Sacramento, and he began telling leaders in multiple sectors that I was going to run. I was like, *Oh, I am?* in my head. "Oh, ok," I said.

From there on out, he was entranced. It was as though he was twenty years old again, working on his first political campaign. The machine was off and running in a heartbeat.

Add another layer of public life to our already "under the eye" existence? Add more stress to my mismanaged chronic pain, depression, PTSD, and unprocessed deaths and losses? Seriously, what was I thinking? Obviously, a part of me still found hope through meaningful work and professional challenges. Still, I adored and thrived in my work for the Family Justice Center and fully believe my life's trajectory would have been entirely different had I stayed.

Within a month or so, my face and name covered the entire county. Campaign mailers, yard signs, and newspaper articles were a daily occurrence. I had to be "on" and in "winning" mode at all times. I also still had a full-time job at the ACFJC and as a mother. I couldn't admit, let alone recognize, I needed help for depression, PTSD, and chronic pain.

So there we were, the entire Lockyer family, walking door-to-door evenings and weekends to over 350,000 voters in the district, asking for their vote. It was old-school Lockyer campaigning style. I walked the even side of the street, while Bill walked the odd. Diego rode his bike alongside us, holding the bag of mailers.

Bill showed such an incredible, loving, unwavering commitment to me and the campaign, it energized me to push myself beyond my own expectations. *Thank you, Bill, so much.*

My ground rule to the campaign team was, "Do not make me someone I'm not. Do not market me inauthentically. Do not attempt to win by attacking opponents." Somewhere in me

I hoped people would see my prior public service and dedication, underneath the label "Bill Lockyer's wife."

Thus, the face-to-face interaction helped. It reminded me of my past advocacy work and efforts down south. "My greatest skill is bringing people and resources together," I'd say, true to my heart and record, referring to my collaboration building efforts while on the school board and at the ACFJC, making government services more efficient.

So when the local press colored me as a "Billion Dollar Baby" who intentionally sought out "to use her husband's treasure chest" of political insight, skill, and funds for her own benefit, it cut like a knife. From there on, it seemed as though one local reporter was set on discrediting me, in whatever way possible. It appeared as though I was the first thing interesting to write about in ages.

It felt like he was obsessed with me. It heightened my anxiety to levels highly difficult to manage. He stared at me at public events and it just flat out felt creepy.

But let's face it, my skin was also too thin. It hurt that the press and opponents ignored what I offered in my heart. It hurt that they marred and ignored my record and intelligence. Every day it felt like I was campaigning to prove my worthiness rather than win an election.

Thank you, Bill, for investing in me, whatever the reason was. Thank you, Bill, for believing in me when I didn't have the guts to myself. Thank you, supporters and volunteers, for seeing me beyond the name.

I gave a big sigh of relief after making it through the primary as one of the two candidates to receive the most votes. I still had a full-time job as a mother and leading the ACFJC. I wanted to "reduce stress and drink less," clueless to the severity of my other conditions.

But walking into an AA meeting, introducing myself, and saying, "Hi, my name is Nadia, and I am an alcoholic" was not an option. Anonymity was impossible. What could I have said? "Oh, that lady named Nadia with an identical face on your doorstep asking for your vote is my twin. She's not an alcoholic," and, "Well, me? I just suffer from depression and chronic pain. I'm here to observe." That's not permitted in the rooms.

Worse, it felt like local reporters were on the hunt. They would've brutally shamed me publicly against the sacredness of AA anonymity. That seemed like their sole quest. "Nadia Lockyer is an alcoholic!" would've given them a hard-on. Would they have done the same to a male candidate married to a powerful woman? I doubt it.

So instead, I sought help for all my ailments in the privacy of an outpatient hospital treatment program.

The first day I was there resulted in the worst thing that ever happened in my life. I met a man we'll refer to as "SC." Tall, personable, handsome, and easy to talk to. Over the course of a week, we chatted on breaks, he shared his struggles, and for the first time I actually felt I could share mine. Then he asked me for my number. And that was that.

Soon thereafter, the campaign returned full force. After months of meeting with community leaders, making fundraising calls, walking precincts, joining candidate forums, and giving endorsement interviews and speeches, we won by a landslide.

***

I loved being a County Supervisor. I'm proud of the many things my staff and I accomplished in a short period of time. I truly believe it made a difference in the lives of many and laid the foundation for important projects that continued past my time in office.

As Chair of the Social Security Income Advocacy

Committee, I worked hard to get a third vote of support after many failed attempts by my colleague. It created a fully comprehensive mental health focused program for the overwhelming number of homeless in the County. The third vote was difficult to get because it required a huge County investment. So I asked the CEO to lay it out for me. What was the estimated required investment? What was the realistic one? And most importantly, what would the return on investment be in federal social security funds and when would the County likely see it?

My staff turned the numbers into a visual grid representing the board's choices over a three-year period. Invest this now and we'll see threefold in return within three years? Problem solved. Who could disagree? Assist the homeless with mental health, housing, and more, lower the rate of homelessness, reduce all the other public and human costs such an epidemic imposed, and the return in investment was obvious. This is how I worked, and I loved this type of problem-solving in my core.

I continued to focus on family violence prevention. I invested a ton of time building partnerships between County agencies and local entities focused on juvenile justice and truancy prevention. We even began strategic planning for creation of a youth justice center in the heart of my district.

I also chaired the Public Safety Committee at a time when the legalization of medical marijuana was on the ballot, a touchy subject for those wearing the badge who all too clearly knew how easily everything could take a bad turn. Always looking for a collaborative solution, we ultimately found a way to address safety concerns while enabling legal access to those who medically needed it.

Within a short period of time, I received state and national awards. Stuff like the National Woman's Political Caucus's

Woman of the Year, Alameda County Seer Leadership Award, League of United Latin American Citizens' Hispanic Woman of the Year Award, and others. Positions such as State Senator and higher were mentioned and anticipated.

I was deeply grateful to have such meaningful work, believed I was improving the lives of others, and was beyond thankful for all the honors and blessings.

Still, underneath my suit, heels, and inspirational words in speeches resided a woman who was struggling inside. Just like many other times in my life, I needed help and support but didn't know how to reach out for it. Many walk through life with similar conditions and often alone. Others know when and how to ask for help. I didn't.

It was as though I believed no pain or issue of mine, whether physical or emotional, was worthy of mentioning. I didn't even recognize how bad it had become. My body ached, I had bad dreams at night, and I missed my father and others terribly.

But at that time in my life, I believed I'd merely be a nuisance and lose the love of others, that asking for help would be a sign of weakness, and I was undeserving of having my struggles acknowledged, even for myself. I didn't want to lose my roles and identity that gave me a sense of being loved.

I never thought of sharing my struggles with Bill, or calling a mentor, doctor, friend, or sister. Today I at least know the source of that mode of living and can do something about it daily.

No titles, accolades, ribbons, or lace could cure my struggles inside. A list of physical, mental, and emotional diagnoses were raging behind it all.

Layers of unprocessed pain, loss, and trauma rolled out on teary drives home. Wearing masks for the outside world, my physical body carried the load.

Diego was my one true refuge while Bill seemed off and in his own world.

So on the day that SC contacted me, I was a deer caught in the headlights on the road.

CHAPTER 11

Dear Son,
if anyone hurts you, I got your back.
Our Creator takes care of the rest.

You do not need to invite in an enemy or call on bad luck to have trouble in your life. You are already in trouble when you let your mental intrigues go unchecked.

If your inherent creativity expands that intrigue, your mind will spin it, magnify it, and spread it in every direction. It will weave that intrigue into your words and project those words to every part of your mind. The result is that you lose track of your real self and become shallow, hollow, and full of games. You lose your power of prayer. You lose your innocence.

There is no one who can save you from this
mess other than yourself.
—*Yogi Bhajan*

I'm going to tell you a story. The most difficult one to share.

For many years I couldn't. I didn't know how, to whom, or where. Worse, everyone else made up "a story," but it was far from the truth. Their story was written, published, and read. Many believed it to be true.

Their story nearly killed me. My heart and soul were beaten down. Over and over it was repeated. Every corner I turned, it showed up.

The world was dark and empty. They hung my body in bright light. Buried in public shaming, I lost all hope and faith inside.

The true story isn't a normal story. The kind with a beginning and an end. The type where a girl meets a boy and he breaks her heart again. Those are easy to navigate and even easier to understand.

This is a story, within a story, within another story of fraud.

The beginning was not known until now and the end has not yet arrived. The truth continues to reveal itself the more time passes by.

This is a story of deception used to further deceive. The terror, pain, and darkness are so very deep. There is betrayal beyond betrayal, hidden under layers of lies. There is blackmail, exploitation, assault, and many other crimes. There is injustice and broken systems way beyond belief. There is chaos that's hard to follow, making it hard to breathe.

I don't blame anyone or anything for all that happened next. I created the mess all by myself when I let pain and shame rule like beasts.

We don't need to invite a bad person in for our troubles to

arise. I was already in trouble when the bad guy came to live in an unchecked mind.

Today the wounds are daily reminders to check and clear my head. To stay connected to our Creator, where no fear or judgment exists. To never forget that "It" resides in me and my true self remains the same. That home within is my armor now and the story serves a purpose beyond me.

I hope someday it proves to you that we are never what anyone falsely claims. I pray it helps you realize that your truth and strength always reside within.

***

The real story began with a phone call. "Wow, you're a County Supervisor now," SC said.

"Yes, I am," I responded proudly.

"I'm happy for you," he replied. "Let's have lunch to celebrate."

"Sure," I replied.

The last time I had done something normal and social, like having a meal with a friend, was probably seven years prior. I allowed this to happen in my marriage. It just didn't seem like it was an option to exist outside our home in my own personal identity and friendships. I was thus drawn into having a normal social interaction with someone who was a peer and outside our world.

So I met SC for lunch at a local restaurant. We both loved hiking, nature, and Mumford & Sons and could sing a tune. And like our first conversations had panned out, he told me again how he longed to have his own family and settle down.

He said he struggled with "demons" like depression. I listened. It was a relief to hear someone talk about such real-life things. I thus felt an ease and comfort in opening up that I

hadn't felt in a long time. I told him about the pain in my heart
from past losses and hurt. He encouraged me to let it out, saying, "You're safe to cry with me."

I had never been told that by anyone, let alone a man.

And I naively believed him. I believed everything he said.

I naively trusted him, and who he said he was.

We met again a few weeks later. He was down and told me
his ex-girlfriend was breaking his heart. He showed me pictures of them laughing. He read poems he'd written for her. He
said he missed her hair and feared he'd never love again.

I told him that I didn't really know what true love was,
other than the love I had for my son. That I loved Bill, but didn't
think I was in love. That we seemed so very distant. "Maybe we
can find a way to give love to each other," he replied.

I thought, *Yes that would be nice, but love is just not meant
for me.* I said, "I am married and have a son."

He said, "Friends can love each other too. How about that?"

"Ok," I said, and that was that.

And I believed him.

I believed everything he said and presented as truth.

I trusted him, and who he said he was.

Life went on. I'd work all day, hiding my depression,
loneliness, and physical pain as best I could. When I got
home, I'd escape in Diego and later have a drink. When Bill
came home from a long day's work, he had lots on his mind.
Understandably, he needed to relax, eat, then watch TV. I supported this wholeheartedly. But I also allowed it to create an
impression in my head that I couldn't open up to him, that it
would be met with annoyance or impatience. On reflection, I
regret not giving Bill another chance to be there for me at this
time. My heart breaks and aches just thinking about it.

Fact is, I created a reality inside me completely vacant of
any interpersonal connections and void of a source of spiritual
solace. That is my fault. I created the walls.

I know now that I put myself in positions that mimicked exactly how it felt to hide in my childhood closet or be alone in Dr. K.'s office. Those states of being carved an understanding of the world and of others in my psyche. I did not know any better then. I was completely unaware.

The terrible reality is that SC fit into the mold. He maneuvered right into that space I had made alone. So when he began to text and call me more often, saying things like "just checking in on you," it was like pouring water into a dry well. My brain went, *Wow, he actually cares.* I thus began to naively share details about my struggles, sometimes specifics about my depression, or a nightmare I had. The hole inside me began to feel quenched, less deep. *I finally have a friend and confidant,* I'd think, *and he doesn't care about all the public stuff, just real things.*

I believed he was in every way the person he presented to me. I began to care deeply for him. I began to convince myself I hadn't passed beyond the gate into infidelity. I did not know he was a sociopath planning my destruction.

Then he called one day, out of the blue, in a completely different state. He was anxious, worried, and desperate, like the world was about to end.

"I need you. I'm dying here. Please come now and help!" he begged. I made the grave mistake of going to him, locked up in a hotel room, sobbing.

He said he was "in love" with me and repeatedly apologized. He said he couldn't live without me and was thinking about taking his own life.

He said he wanted to bring me "nothing but happiness" but felt that was denied. He said he wanted to take my pain away and "catch every tear" as it fell. He said I deserved to be happy. He said he had nothing but "goodwill" for us planned.

And I believed him.

I believed everything he said and presented as truth.

I trusted him, and who he said he was.

He poured a glass of wine. We drank and he kissed my face. We cried in each other's arms after I said, "We can never be." He said he had "to use" because he couldn't bear the pain. I didn't understand, but then he pulled out a glass pipe. He held it up in his hand and placed a lighter underneath it. Something bubbled inside. He inhaled and made white clouds.

Just like years before, my diseased body screamed so loud, *Give me the IV line of morphine. Put the button back in my hand.* He could see I was entranced. He grinned and lit it up again. "Why don't you give it a try? It can't hurt you in any way." I had never smoked the demon before. Inhaling it was like a surge of fifty thousand white lines. I will always regret this moment for the rest of my life. He easily could have taken my clothes off as my body dove into a high. The drug I call the devil is very powerful.

At that point, he knew he had control of me with every single touch.

I cannot turn back time, dear Son, I can only give you a living amends. I feel disgusted and enraged with myself with every word I write. I was a naive, desperate, and stupid blind deer and fell into his trap. I immediately fell into a noose of shame, self-hate, and regret. Sometimes I think I deserved his abuse and all its torturing ways. At least, I thought so intensely then, during the agony of trying to escape. Addiction destroys so many lives. It cuts through homes and children's hearts. A physical allergy, mental obsession, and spiritual malady, they say it is. Coupled with a sociopath's acts, it's a miracle I escaped its reign. I am so sorry, dear Son. I am so very sorry. I am

so sorry, Bill. I am so very sorry. I am so sorry,
Daddy, Mommy, and family. I am so very sorry.
I am so sorry, friends and loved ones. I am so
very sorry. I am so sorry, constituents, staff, and
colleagues. I am so very sorry.

***

We began seeing each other every other week or so. Every time we did, he gave me the devil's drug and we got high. My body craved that drug from miles away, and I did not know how to control the urges. He would even tell me he had it ready for me. The following day I'd crash and use energy drinks to get by.

A mental obsession for the drug would rage for days, just thinking about the next high. I know today that SC clearly knew what he was doing with that drug. He had already mastered his MO with many women prior.

A month and a half passed. I clearly remember one morning when I woke up to my values screaming in my head. My soul shouted, *What the hell are you doing? This is not you.*

On top of that, my gut instincts kicked in about who he was saying he was. While he continued to tell me "I love you" and "I am your protector," I began noticing inklings of inauthenticity and instability that he had kept well hidden. He'd call, distraught, and say he was stuck somewhere without gas, money, or food. Five minutes later, he'd text that he was going to a bar alone to have fun because I wasn't there for him. It was juvenile and stressful. He'd say one thing and then another, catching himself in a lie.

So I stopped contacting and responding to him. Entirely. But as soon as I did, his "crazy making" began. I struggled to fulfill my duties as a County Supervisor, mother, and wife throughout the weeks and months of terror that followed.

***

First, he said I was "rejecting" him. I'd try to convince him I truly cared, but had to end it for my child's sake. In response, he'd say, "You made me do this," and send audio recordings and pictures of him having sex with another woman. My heart was stabbed every time. But it wasn't just stupid and basic mocking. It was repetitive and vivid harassment. Worse, he always ended with a voicemail, sobbing. He did this repeatedly. My head twisted such statements into *See, you've never had any worth.* Mental intrigues kept me trapped in trying to prove his love for me.

Then he said I was "abandoning" him. In response, he sent strange texts indicating he was stalking me like, "You took a different route." My head would spin in paranoia and panic every time.

For years thereafter, if someone said something similar to me, it would cause a set of bad memories from this time to return. Somewhere inside, a sickness translated it all into, *He doesn't want you to leave and must really love you.* Mental intrigues kept me trapped in thinking no one else would.

Still, I tried my best to have no contact. I tried my best to not respond. But the more I did that, the more terrifying his texts became. Sickeningly and ironically, I felt I had to respond. That if I did, he would calm down and stop the harassing, painful texts and indications he was stalking me. I knew the panic, anxiety, and mental stress would subside and make it easier to get through the day. It wasn't a conscious choice. I simply ended up trying to manage the chaos this way.

Next, he started to say he was going to kill himself if I didn't respond. The words and photos he texted to me are permanently marked in my brain. He knew I had found my brother after he attempted suicide, so he'd say, "See, this is your fault. Just like it was with him," followed by a picture of a razor blade on his wrist and what appeared to be blood dripping. My heart would sink in guilt and self-blame every single time. My head defined me as selfish, saying, *You selfish woman. You're causing him to suffer.* Mental intrigues kept me trapped in thinking I had a duty to save his life.

When I finally had the guts to block his number and trust my instincts, the evil and sheer terror of his acts rose to a level I never imagined possible in a human being. From a random number, he called and said, "I hacked into your email. Watch me. Now you'll get what you deserve." There is no way to explain the depth of agony and despair on this day. I felt my entire life was being bombed and destroyed, yet I believed I had no source of help to turn to, nor did I understand the internet, online accounts, and my rights enough to do a thing.

But it got worse. When I didn't respond, I received texts saying, "Tic, toc, tic, toc, you're going to go viral," a warning he was on the verge of doing something to harm me. I had chest pain and started fainting in Diego's room. Back then, my head spun, *My God, my God, please dear God, help me! What the hell is happening?* Today I know that on this exact day, intimate photos taken of me without my knowledge were posted without my consent for sale on Craigslist and sent to that same local reporter that had hounded me.

To this day, anything I see on TV, my phone, or the internet that reflects this causes a flashback. Back then, my head spun. *What is happening? My God, my God, what is he doing to me?* Mental intrigues kept me stuck in terror.

All of these things happened multiple times over months.

Do you see the mind games?

Do you see how he caused me to lose my way?

Do you see how it felt impossible to escape?

Does anyone see the torture?

Please, oh please, please tell me you do.

Because back then, no one wanted to know the truth.

***

My Journal Entry

7/22/11

> After I held you in my arms, curled up in a
> ball of despair. Your endless tears, screaming
> to die, to end your own life. You said you were
> tired and sick of "the demons." You sobbed and
> sobbed. Then hit yourself, over and over. Still I
> tried to convince you that you are not all the
> things you say. I held you near and caught all
> your tears. I told you I needed you here. Why,
> oh why, are you hurting me and destroying my
> life like this?

SC Texts

8/27/11

> 8:20 p.m., "I will not take 'no' for an answer . . .
> or else you will see."
>
> 9:11 p.m., "If you're not here by 10 p.m., you are
> making me do something else."
>
> 9:30 p.m., "I hope you're driving."
>
> 10:12 p.m., "You just lost me . . . and now you'll
> lose your mind."

9/11/11

"This is my theme song right now. Dedicated to you Nadia, Eminem's 'Where I'm at,' so many of these lines describe exactly what I am feeling and going through. I'm haunting you bitch, everywhere you turn. I'm following you. 'Cause I loved you with every ounce of me, you know it's true. It's killing you now, yeah. I hope the ho dies slow in you . . . Revenge is mine."

9/14/11

"I love you more than anything, but last night I really came close to letting it happen. I am so scared right now. I am so fucking scared it is going to happen.

I needed you last night to comfort me. And when I called and started apologizing, I NEEDED YOU . . . I'm not going to do anything to jeopardize your life, ok?"

9/29/11

"I FUCKING HATE U!!! Fuck off Nadia. You wanna be cruel? I can too."

10/11/11

"YOU ARE NOW BLOCKED FROM ALL YOUR ACCOUNTS, FB too, I own them now."

10/14/11

> *"If you come here, I will correct it. If you come here, I will stop it. I will erase it all. I will destroy everything. I need to protect you from me."*

SC Voicemail

11/2/11

> *Singing . . . "I don't care if you're dead. I want you dead after all.*
>
> *You're a stupid bitch if you don't do what I said."*

SC Texts

12/21/11

> *"Something happened, and I will never look at you the same again. I'm going to do actions that hurt you."*

12/22/11

> *9:08 a.m., "Since you're not coming or responding, I don't need to tell you who contacted me."*
>
> *9:51 a.m., "This time I will seek revenge on you."*
>
> *11:11 a.m., "It's too late."*

My Journal Entries

11/11/11

*For your cold, cold heart, that couldn't give me
the respect of letting me go, letting me know . . .
about your plans to destroy my life for profit,
the evil and pain you would bring. For your
cold, cold soul, that will sadly end up stabbing
you in the back. I am sorry I didn't save them. I
am sorry I didn't know how. But your heart and
soul were dead long before we met.*

12/6/11

*Oh what a fool I was, what a fool I have been
. . . duped, conned, betrayed to the fullest extent. The core in me is dead now, my spirit lost
in nothingness. I cannot continue being who I
was. Once believing in the goodness of others.
No one could derive such evil intentions. I am
numb, breathless, unable to move. But for my
son, my dear son, I will try again, once more. I
will try to find me again. For my son, my dear
Diego, I am alive with him, with all my heart
and all my mind, a soul alive by his side.*

I surged deeper and deeper into psychological isolation,
desperation, and terror. I tried to protect myself in the only
ways I knew how or was capable of at the time. I could not
shake the mental and emotional anguish caused by what SC
was doing to me online.

I fully believed I could not turn to the authorities because
I was an elected official and the man haunting me was a drug

addict I had personally been involved with. I was further forced to change my cell number multiple times or to turn it off entirely, making it extremely difficult for loved ones who were trying to help to get a hold of me.

My poor staff was at a loss as to what was happening as they observed me losing weight and having difficulty concentrating during important meetings and community gatherings. Every time I had to be at the office or a public appearance, it took an extreme effort physically, mentally, and emotionally to even walk out the door and feel safe.

I finally admitted everything to Bill. I apologized vehemently and begged for help. But every time I brought it up, he would get angry. He eventually became so fed up with my extreme state of anxiety and panic, he began staying in Sacramento, leaving Diego and me all alone in the Bay Area. I don't blame him for anything, and I owe him lifelong amends. Yet back then, it felt like he was all I had to run to for safety. When he left, it was devastating.

My addiction blocked me from seeking help from others, my mind filled with shameful thoughts: *You're a dirty, damaged little girl and deserve everything that's happening.* I never even once thought about turning to the victims' rights and public safety community I knew so well.

How could I explain the mess I had gotten myself into? That I consumed an illegal drug? That I was the one who needed them although I was supposed to be leading?

My mind blinded me to the truth within. Yes, I made a grave mistake. In fact, I made many. But I was still Nadia, the human being, deserving of help and worthy. I just didn't know it then.

By the time Christmas Eve arrived, Bill and I had managed to agree on giving Diego a united front. So we headed south to my family. Prior to leaving, we placed a key underneath the doormat so that our neighbor could get the mail and feed the dogs.

She called later that day and said she could not find it. There is absolutely no way to describe the terror I felt at this time. I immediately surmised that SC was watching us and had taken it. Everything before had been threats on my cell or online. This meant SC might access the house. But when I mentioned it to Bill, he didn't seem to think it was a big deal. I passed the next hours of the holiday in a numb, robotic, completely zoned-out state.

When we returned home, what we found was horror. There sitting in the middle of my bathroom sink was a letter from SC, stating, "You should've never underestimated me." I ran to show it to Bill in the office, and there he was, holding up the key in his hand. "It was on the keyboard and something is really wrong with the computer."

It was a state-owned computer. The program icons were now in varying sizes, the screen was off-center, and nothing opened properly. "Oh God! It was him!" I said. "It's obvious he used the key. Call the police. Please help me, please help us! What more proof do you need? Crimes were committed against us!"

"It's just a stupid virus that got on the computer," he said.

I thought I was going to lose my mind, if I hadn't already. I showed him the letter left in my sink. "What about this?" I asked. "He broke into our home, Bill. We have to call the police, don't you see?"

"No, no, we don't," he said.

"But he tricked me, to hurt us! Don't you see? Remember all his threats?"

"Shut up," he said.

Thereafter, if I expressed any single concern about it to Bill, the whole ambiance in the house shifted. His anger was impenetrable. By the end of January 2012, the home was full of strife, contention, and arguments between the two of us.

I wish I had been able to say, "I am an elected official and married to the State Treasurer and former Attorney General. If I were Maria Shriver or Gavin Newsom's wife, would my husband respond this way?" But instead, I had no words and never dared to open my mouth.

I found out later that SC had attempted to blackmail Bill, putting a slip drive of personal images and what felt like a threatening letter in our mailbox. Bill never went to the authorities. He merely sent SC an email stating, "Consider this your last warning to immediately cease and desist providing or manipulating, in any format whatsoever, any documents and materials of a personal nature."

I wish he had told me then that I had a bit of someone on my side. It may have postponed the point when I started losing my mind. Looking back on my condition at the time, I clearly see and admit how very selfish, and self-centered, I'd become with Bill in the midst of SC's terror.

There wasn't a quiet millisecond. SC had complete control of my every breath and thought. My brain kept trying to connect the dots. Every time it tried, it didn't know where to start. What came first? What happened last? I walked like a zombie doing my best to care for Diego, Bill, my brother, the entire district, the dogs, and the house. I couldn't eat or sleep and when I did, nightmares haunted me—pictures of threats in texts, his slit wrists, the words "tic toc," and more. I didn't sleep a full night for weeks at a time, regularly waking up startled from a nightmare.

I just need a drink, to be able to think.
I just need a drink, to get through the day.
I just need a drink, to be calm at home.
I just need a drink, and I'll make it through.

The disease, oh how it loved what that man was doing to me!

***

On February 3, Bill called while I was driving home from picking up Diego at school. "Have you been trying to get into our B of A account online?" he asked angrily.

"No! No, Bill, why?" I asked.

"Someone has been and I was notified. I'm on my way home," he said.

"You know who it is, Bill!" I said.

"Why? How would you know? Have you been in contact with him? Why don't you just go ahead and commit suicide!" he shouted then hung up.

Left with nothing and no one, I was already dead inside. I couldn't go home because Bill would be there. I didn't want to argue and have something bad happen. So I booked a room at an Extended Stay in Newark and drove to Target to buy what Diego and I would need for a few days. Food, cooking supplies, shampoo, and a few toys for Diego. I found comfort in knowing that the room was a place we could stay for a while. No one would know and I told myself I'd finally figure out what to do. The front door was in a separate and secure hallway. The room was equipped with a family room, fireplace, couch, little kitchen, and separate bedroom. I turned off my phone and cooked dinner while Diego played with his new toys. We ate, snuggled, then watched a movie on the couch's pull-out bed. *This is all I ever wanted,* I thought. *Can we stay like this forever?*

Eventually, we fell asleep together side by side, warm, safe and sound.

When I woke up hours later, I changed into my sleepwear, brushed my teeth, turned on my cell phone and set the alarm. Someone had called from an unrecognizable number ten separate times between 4:19 p.m. and 11:54 p.m. Then the phone went crazy in a slew of incoming prior texts.

It was obvious the calls and texts were from SC. His words went from apologetic to accusatory, from endearing to hostile, from threats to harm me to threats to harm himself. Toward the end of the list was "I know what you're afraid of. I can stop them. I can help you stop them from destroying your life." *Whoa! Them?!* I thought. *Who? What? How?*

In my confusion and fear, his manipulation sent questions raging through my mind. *Oh my God, is it someone else who has been threatening me and Bill with blackmail? Exploiting me online? His friends, his roommates? Has it been someone else all along? Is he all I have who can help me? Is he all I have who can put an end to it all?*

I needed safety. I needed answers. I believed the only way to them was through him. *If I do what he wants, maybe he'll stop.*

So, in a heartbeat of desperation, I responded, forgetting every strange, concerning, stalking-like word in his prior texts. And sure enough, it was SC. "Oh thank God, it may be too late. Hurry up, Nadia, let me in. We're running out of time. I'm outside and will keep you safe and fix it."

And I believed him. I believed everything he represented as truth. To my grave dismay and heartache today, deceived, manipulated, and duped, I still trusted him, a sociopath in disguise. I still believed he cared and would protect me, despite the magnitude of his fraud. *My God, to be held and feel everything will be ok,* I thought. *I have nobody else to turn to, no one else who understands.*

When I let SC in, Diego asleep on the pull-out bed in the front room, he quickly gazed around then rushed to the back room, closed the doors, and did not look me in the eyes.

He threw a backpack down and started searching inside.

"What are you doing?" I asked. "You said you would help."

"Wait a sec," he said, frantic and disheveled.

Something was off. Nervous, I walked to an open area in the same room to get distance. "Please just tell me what's going on. Please help me," I said, facing out.

"Let me show you," he said, pulling out a laptop.

"Show me what?" I asked, then immediately saw a glimpse of truth in his eyes. It was a smirk, a "tricked ya!" look.

"What did you do?" I asked in a desperate cry.

And he switched immediately.

"How could you think that of me?" he asked angrily and charged my way. The only place for me to go was backwards, into the toilet and shower area.

Nothing but rage, nothing but rage, he was under a spell and grabbed my neck with his hand. As I struggled against the wall and his grasp, his eyes, his eyes, I'll never forget his eyes. He dug his thumb into my flesh. It's stamped in my memory, and haunts me to this day. *I cannot get it out and escape. Can someone please cut it out of my mind? I want to be free of it.* I pulled and tugged at his shirt, I tried to fight. But then in a millisecond, he straightened his arm, grabbed more flesh, tightened his grasp. *I'm going to die.* I collapsed on the floor and blacked out. I do not know how long I lay there before I awoke, coughing and barely conscious. I will never forget that moment. SC was kneeling beside me, and he immediately grabbed my head, then began bashing it against the floor. Everything went black again. When I eventually came to, I just remember feeling like a dead fish. I could not move. I could not speak. All the while, I wanted to fight back in complete and utter fear for more life. Yet there he still was, now sitting back on his feet. "No, no, no, no, no," he kept saying, over and over, shaking his head in his hands, then looking at them, as if in disbelief of what he had just done.

Soon thereafter I heard Diego shout, "Mommy?" and a tiger-mama fire fueled me. Still lying immobile on the ground, I mustered a scratchy, barely there, "Get out!" to SC, now standing above me nearby, frazzled, confused, and delaying.

"Mommy?" Diego went again. I stumbled, dizzy and dazed, yet managed to pull myself up to sit on the bathroom floor.

With the aid of the toilet to hold on to, I pushed myself to standing. Wobbling like a dead man walking, with a surge of mama will. "Get out!" I said as loud as I could and yanked him by his shirt toward the exit. SC ran out and the door slammed shut. I made my way to the front room and collapsed next to Diego. In complete shock, my mind went blank as my neck swelled, head throbbed, and body shook. I just lay there, having no idea the magnitude of what had just happened.

A knock was heard within minutes. I could not move. I was terrified. "Police!" The people next door had heard the attack and called 911. *Please help me, please help me, please help us, please help us,* is all I thought. I struggled to find my sight, my feet, and then my balance and remember stumbling to open the door.

And there they were, like saviors entering my dark and frightening world. The ones I wish I'd had the guts to reach out to before.

The Newark Police Department came in like a SWAT team and surrounded us with care. I see now how they were the only human beings that ever believed me, that protected us in any way for a long time thereafter.

I remember an officer looking at me, his eyes on my neck, and within a split second I collapsed into his arms. Next thing I remember is being rolled out on a gurney, repeating, "Diego, Diego, Diego," over and over and over again.

In a half-conscious state, the pain in my heart was so very deep. I can still feel it today as I write and cry, the desperation for him and his comfort in that moment was all I could think of. "Oh God, Diego," I sobbed.

All I remember about that night is crying alone in the emergency room. They examined my neck and head. I'd suffered multiple head and neck injuries, including a concussion and intense swelling and bruising that made it difficult to breathe. Aching, bruised, swelling up, and shattered, bewildered, and beaten inside, I felt more paralyzed there than I had when I first woke up from the coma after the car accident. At least then I'd had an inkling to attempt to move. There in the ER, I had no idea where or what to move to. *My future? My present? My past? No, thank you.*

Sometime during the night, I recognized that a flicker of human warmth was there. A frontline angel, Officer Horst from the Newark Police Department, sat outside my curtain the entire time, keeping guard. A complete stranger, he knew more about my life in those hours than anyone else. He was the first and only person to truly protect me in this situation during that time. Without a word, he communicated through his eyes: "I know what happened to you. And I believe you." I didn't realize then how much this saved my life. *Thank you, Officer Horst, for being the first person to validate the harm caused by SC.*

In the morning, a nurse and doctor entered the room to examine me. They had a long conversation outside without saying a word to me. The doctor reentered and gently asked, "You probably want to go home now, right?" I nodded and did not speak. By that point, the swelling and bruising were throbbing and excruciating, but I was also desperate to hold Diego close. The nurse standing by his side, the doctor stated he understood but reiterated the gravity of injuries sustained and the need for rest.

Hours later, Officer Horst walked me gently to his patrol vehicle and drove me home. I was numb and tears rolled down my face. He walked me to the door and knocked. Bill opened the door and was a bit in shock when he first saw me. I walked quickly past to see if Diego was there, then lay down on the bed.

He and the officer chatted before he came back and said, "You are lucky you're alive. He said you could've easily been killed."

After a few hours of rest, I got up to use the bathroom. Suddenly at the doorway, I could not enter. This is a memory I will never forget. The sight of a bathroom, toilet ahead, a tiny space within four walls where I had almost been killed. Bill tells me I just stood there, stuck in time with SC's raging eyes and hand around my neck. Frozen, I couldn't be brought back to the present. Bill spoke several times to me yet states I didn't respond until he placed his hand on my arm.

"Nadia?" he asked, as a surge of breath quickly exited me. When I saw the unique blue tiled walls that set apart our home restroom from any other, I was finally mentally able to return to the present.

Before entering, however, Bill cautioned me. "You might not want to look in the mirror." But of course, that was the first thing I did. Blue, purple, and red markings colored my neck and head. Thumb bruises and fingernail marks were chiseled into my flesh. I covered my head, ran to the hallway, sat on the floor, and cried. An avalanche of that dreaded memory came crashing down again. For years thereafter, and sometimes still today, I could be back there in an instant. It is not fair to have to live with this in my head.

Later that day, Bill took photos of the assault injuries I had sustained. They spread the gamut of inches over my entire neck, from the left ear down to my mid-chest plate. The right side of my forehead had a three-inch-long bruise. These photos were eventually printed in the press and I still have some of them somewhere today.

Newark Police Department, specifically Officer Horst, immediately received an Emergency Protective Order (EPO). A few days later, Officer Horst called and asked me to come to the police department to answer some questions. I went in as best I could and asked if SC had been arrested, expressing my fears for my safety. He said no but that SC had promised to come in several times and not shown up. Then he handed me a "Victims' Rights" brochure and said, "Thank you, get help, hang in there." In the meantime, I heard that SC was bragging online about hiding and evading the police.

The reality is my life would've turned out very differently had Officer Horst been able to find and serve SC the EPO. Any and all contact made thereafter would've been grounds for arrest and probable prosecution. Someone with a phone number based in South County was repeatedly sending me texts, sometimes more than sixty a minute, and appeared to be tracking my phone. In fact, we later discovered through Verizon cell phone records that SC was tracking my exact location hours prior to and days following the assault.

***

As days passed resting at home, it was clear I needed serious help and support. But I was deeply torn as a mother. Get help and have to leave my child? Stay with my child while in need of help?

No mother should have to choose between getting help for mental health, trauma, and addiction and being with their very child! It angers me that this choice is imposed on families today. Why on earth do you think so many never get the help they need? There should be places for parents of young children to go where everyone can get help and support. Why is the family forced to separate; why is generational trauma acceptable? After Bill convinced me Diego would be ok, I ended up going. But the marking of separation, confusion, and shock in Diego's head is not something to just quickly gloss over. Hands down, as a society we must increase trauma and addiction treatment options that support parent-child relationships.

A couple key supportive women from the local victims' rights community came to my home with information about a local Bay Area center. My time with Diego would be limited, but I'd still get to see him. I was desperate, so I said yes, sobbing.

Upon arrival, I was immensely weak, sleep-deprived, distressed, and distraught.

After going through the motions of the intake process and medical screening, I was given a room to myself and collapsed on the bed. I didn't unpack my suitcase for days. I did not get out of bed or dare look out a window for fear of what I might find. The outside world was frightening, and I just wanted to stay there in that room and leave it all behind.

My body ached from the assault, while my brain was in shambles. I didn't sleep well for a week, the memories just wouldn't let up. The nightmares and flashbacks were too overwhelming. A snapshot of a threatening text, a photo of the blade at his wrist, the look in his eyes, the feel of his hand on my neck. I could go on and on. It was endless. I could not escape my head.

The first time I tried to get food in the eating hall with other patients, I panicked and ran back to my room. The sounds of utensils, voices chatting, a look, an arm move—it all scared me to death.

I was scheduled for a therapeutic massage and was asked to lie down on my back. The therapist began leaning toward me with her hand wide open. Covering my eyes with my hands, I screamed, "No, no, no, no, no." I stood up and ran out, half-dressed and bewildered.

After a few weeks, they eventually diagnosed me with severe PTSD and dissociative disorder. I began working with a therapist. She said I suffered from the effects of an "abusive dyadic relationship," insisted I stay for months of intensive trauma treatment, and wrote the following in a letter I still have:

> *Often dominant partners seek to continuously*
> *undermine the other person's ability to think*

for themselves. Attempts to degrade and ma-
nipulate the weaker party can be achieved by
introducing drugs and sex into the relation-
ship, rendering the weaker person even more
dependent on the other person's effort to main-
tain and experience pleasure and stability in
their daily lives.

Even more frightening, individuals who
seek to acquire the "upper hand" in a relation-
ship typically empty harmful and degrading
assaults on the partner's ego through any and
all means. As one partner begins to depend
more and more upon the other, the dominant
partner seizes the advantage and takes steps
to acquire complete control over the person's
physical environment, social relations, and/or
cognitive processes of reality-checking.

In real time, it was completely overwhelming to carry such
a weight and was utterly impossible to understand the magnitude of SC's abuse. The findings and facts didn't begin to crys-
tallize in my mind until months after the assault.

To this day, as far as I know, SC has never been arrested or
prosecuted for anything.

Instead, the press had a heyday and created a scandal with
my pain.

Public shaming nearly killed me. I fell into suicidal ideation more than once as a result.

The rest is the truth played out behind the scenes of "a
story" they made up.

***

The most severe pain of my life evolved from how I believe

the press empowered SC. When all of us treatment center patients had to write our life story, we were given access to computers and the internet. When opening a search engine, I immediately saw an onslaught of articles about me from local media—they were filled with SC's quotes claiming we had a longtime consensual affair and completely disregarding the assault, stalking, and exploitation committed against me. SC bragged in blogs online about how he was "hiding in his man cave" from police with the press in his back pocket. Comments online branded me a "slut," "addict," "infidel." It was implied I deserved it all, and psychologically it tore me to pieces. The visual memories of what I saw in the press and blogs online added layers of trauma that unfortunately last to this day. At the time, with the press having empowered SC even more, I became gravely suicidal. My life was never, ever, ever the same.

Dear local reporter,

> *You gave SC power to exploit and impose a thousand acts of mental terror. He threatened to talk to you when I tried to leave or did not respond. He claimed he would stop you if I went to or responded to him.*
>
> *When you published his words, you marred the facts and influenced public perception during the investigation. When you published images of me, you violated my privacy, dignity, and body just like he did. You exploited and commodified me just like he did.*
>
> *I am not a body. I am a human being with a soul.*
>
> *Do you acknowledge that? Do you see me at all?*
>
> *Nadia*

While I was still in treatment, the District Attorney issued a warrant for SC's arrest. Tragically, any chances for justice and safety came crashing down when the press claimed DA O'Malley had a conflict of interest because I had worked for her, helping victims, and because Bill was a political donor. A harsh truth to accept. But yes, that is what was said. The case was taken from her and sent to the State Attorney General's Office. Yes, it's beyond belief.

The Attorney General's office began a new investigation. Everything was delayed and eventually, I believe, heavily influenced by the press and SC's scamming. Weeks passed and the public began questioning, "If a crime was committed, why hasn't he been arrested? Why the delay? She must've made it up."

From his man cave, SC orchestrated a scam of a defense. From Sacramento, investigators watched the press clobber my reputation and credibility. While printing SC's words and intimate photos without my consent, they never asked me for the truth or my side.

The list is endless.

"It was a long-lasting consensual love affair," he said, void of the truth of his threats whenever I attempted to end it.

"She went to meet him at the hotel," in reference to the night I was assaulted, void of the truth that he actually tracked my location and scammed his way in.

"She was a jealous, angry woman and the one who stalked and harassed him," void of the truth of his documented threats to harm me if I did not respond and of the heart-wrenching slew of his endless messages.

"She consented to the sex tapes and photos taken," void of the truth that I was either completely unaware or under the influence.

"The district attorney's office found no evidence of stalking," void of the truth of his physical and online stalking.

While in treatment, I called my campaign manager and asked her to release a statement admitting my addiction and need for treatment, as well as the trauma. Still, I felt I had no ability to defend or speak for myself. No one took the initiative to do so for me. We had the funds to hire a lawyer or spokesperson. Bill would've done that for himself. But he didn't for me. My fears started to grow into resentment.

I began making references to suicide in group during treatment and was privately asked by the staff to stop. They said that I would be discharged if it continued. Back then, it didn't occur to me how unprofessional and unethical that was.

Today I wish I had said, "Well, I'm sorry if I offended you. But the man that almost killed me is telling the public lies and now they believe I deserved it. If you knew what I went through, you'd want to kill yourself too. Instead of banishing me from the very help I need, why don't you tell me I deserve to be protected, that I deserve to live? Because right now public shaming, nightmares, and flashbacks are killing me and I see no way out."

My Journal Entry

Bayside Marin, February 25, 2012 (three weeks after the assault).

I am haunted by the lack of answers and unfilled blanks on the pages of my life when SC was in it. I see his hand on my neck, his other on my head, and I am begging for answers—it is a nightmare that repeats over and over until I pass out.

As a child, I was curious, enjoyed diving into encyclopedias and newspaper clippings, finding solutions to quandaries that baffled others. That skill was further trained in law

school and is marveled by the legal world. I
inherited this trait from my father. But now I
often pray that it would go away.

My mind won't stop. My brain gets tangled
in deciphering what is truth versus fabrications
in the piles of SC's cons and scams. I need my
head to leave me be. How desperately I wish it
would. I can't stand this torture any longer.

The only thing that brings me a sense of
relief is this: every day I visualize an old rect-
angular tape recorder—I push rewind, listen to
the dark brown tape roll back with every turn.
My body jolts a tad at its sudden stop. I press
record, and just sit there watching the wheels
turn, round and round, slowly attempting to
erase every moment of the past year of my per-
sonal life, all that was born from his lies, scams,
and fabrications, all that never existed in the
first place. Slowly, slowly, it is all erased away
until I am ok with having absolutely nothing
but the sound of air floating in my head.

I begged Bill for help, any help. Can you please speak for
me? He flat out said, "You narcissistic bitch," and hung up on
me. My choice was clear. I began tearing a sheet into pieces and
tying it together with the intention of hanging myself from the
balcony. I even imagined them finding my body hanging there.
Just like I was hung out naked in the local reporter's article,
they'd find my corpse hanging out in bright light like the com-
modity they'd made it.

It'd shout to them, *See, this is what you did!*

Sobbing made it hard to write the letter. Diego filled my
mind.

I thought he deserved a mother who believed she deserved
to live. Everything outside me was dictating that I didn't.
Everything inside me didn't match the dark and evil in the
world around me.

But I could not find the words to justify what I was about
to do to him.

My handwritten letter (I still have it):

*In these depths of pain and hopelessness, I find
my healthy, sober self crying for comfort, calm
and safety—serenity, warmth, light and love. I
can't find it here with his violence and fraud
unpunished, his deceit and selfish purpose running free while I lie here imprisoned . . . and my
dear son, my dear son, oh what has he done to
my son's future?*

*The tears feel like blood dripping from my
eyes—did I survive, really survive the car accident? Or was it a lie too? Did Daddy really die?
Or was that a lie too? Did Priscilla, Arthur,
and my baby really die?*

*I know what is true and what is not—to
ask me to accept [that] an attempt to kill me
[will] go unacknowledged by the world and be
called "nothing" by my husband is to ask me to
change my entire understanding of what is real
and true.*

*An injustice is an injustice, and his crimes
continue every day. His plot to destroy my life
and profit runs free and I suffer here without
my son. I can't do this life anymore this way.*

Diego, Mommy is with you in your heart

forever, an angel by your side. Anja—please fight for his custody and raise him as your own. Don't tell him what happened until he is much older. Tell him every day how much you and the family love him, how much I would've showed him.

Mom—I am so sorry.
This world is too painful.
I don't know how to live in it and be ok.
I am defeated by their injustice and cruelty.
Diego deserves a happy parent.
Please bring him happiness forever, please . . .
Nadia

I don't know if it was God, Daddy, an angel or all of the above, but suddenly my therapist came walking in as I completed tying the noose. The balcony was a few feet away. It could have happened minutes earlier, but the thought of Diego had delayed me.

My thoughts whirled: *He needs to know who his real mom is. I am not what they have said. Do you remember me, dear Son? Do you at least remember who I really am? I am a good person, a good mom, a caring and kind human being. I cannot let SC beat my son down too. Don't do it for him . . . don't let SC win.* The therapist ran to me, pulled me in, and held me close. I just sat there in his arms, sobbing.

***

I own my bad choices. I know it was wrong to get involved with SC and use drugs. But does that mean I deserved to be abused, exploited, blackmailed, and assaulted? No. Because it seems the press and authorities did not care that a criminal was and likely is still free. It seems there is no public information, legislative, and criminal justice accountability.

Without public accountability, the survivor's autonomy over their life is often stolen. Why not pass legislation, strengthen and enforce laws that better protect individuals' privacy and identity online? That automatically require websites to conduct slander, fraud, and exploitation prevention tactics before posts are permitted? In my case, what remained online and unprosecuted crimes left me unable to fully heal, recreate my life, and leave the past behind. I no longer had the privilege of beginning a partnership, friendship, or professional opportunity with an empty slate. Once people googled my name, which everyone seems to do these days, they not only read the lies and scandal, they more often than not believed them. As a result, they treated and looked at me differently. Shame was shot my way. It took years of work to dig my way out of it.

Without public accountability, the wounds and needed healing journeys of survivors get forgotten. Why not cover those stories in the press more often so as to educate the public regarding signs of abuse? Why not give the facts and rates of interpersonal violence as well as ways to help others suffering in it? Personally, I felt as though I would never truly live free of anxiety, fear, and nightmares again. Anything could trigger a memory of the horrors of SC. That common hand-on-neck attack in movie scenes. A screenshot, the sound of a cell phone text. The lyrics of a song, the look of a certain car. Someone's words and tone, computer pop-ups warning of a virus. Internet connection delays and certain online ads. I longed for the day when I could go about my life unaffected by such things.

My mind checked out; it went somewhere I didn't want to be. My body was here, but I wasn't, as though real time no longer existed. Even today, people say they can see it in my eyes when it happens. If I am lucky, they ask, "Nadia, are you ok?" or "What's going on?" I try to explain what was triggered inside. In the past, it just sent people away, I felt abandoned and alone. Today the people in my life are far more supportive than that and I am never alone when connected to a home within me.

Dear Son,

> *You probably wondered sometimes what was going on inside my mind. I did my best to move on in life. But it took a long time to lift the layers and build up my armor inside. I did my best to be fully present for you while reminding myself of the truth. Today I'm better able to walk away from anyone who judges. Today I'm better able to find a safe place when a memory is nudging. Please know that your mother is stronger now. I know now what real life is. I found my home within again and together there we will remain.*
> *Love, Mommy*

***

Sadly, even after admitting my bad choices, a near suicide attempt, and while getting the help I needed, the press printed a photo of my empty seat at the Board of Supervisors' meeting and regurgitated SC's lies about the relationship. In response, to my grave dismay today and against the heated advice of my therapist, I discharged from treatment after merely thirty days in an aimless effort to redeem myself, speak my truth, and fulfill my elected responsibilities.

Little Nadia was alive and kicking. *I'll prove them all wrong. They'll see. I'm a good person inside and worthy of love.*

I'll continue fighting for my district and do what I was elected to do.

I was gravely ill-equipped to handle the press invasion of everything in my life immediately thereafter. They followed me, even parking outside our home and randomly knocking on our door. In response, I issued another public statement owning all my actions and calling upon the County to address the epidemics of addiction and exploitation of women. Then I focused immediately on the most important matters at hand, including working to stop a hospital's closure and a freeway being constructed in the middle of my district and attempting to save the homeless and troubled youth through targeted efforts.

I went to the next board meeting and stood tall before the public, knowing my truth and believing the justice system would find and fight for it. While cameras all around pointed at me, the truth was my rock, and my rock was the truth.

Put on a poker face, Nadia, I told myself. *Shut down all emotion and signs of weakness. Shut 'em down. Just shut it all off.* All the while, my psyche was saying, *Run and hide away for your safety! That man is out there and preparing his next move.*

To my utter dismay, the press never let up. They jumped on a wild ride, creating a long, drawn-out "drug and sex scandal." I watched in horror as the local reporter continued to focus solely on the photo of my breasts (which he never should have had in the first place) while setting aside those of my strangled neck and bashed head. The stabs and stabs just kept coming, day after day, week after week. My already damaged heart and psyche were buried deeper and deeper under more and more pain and shame. My thoughts scattered.

Don't they know they're slowly killing me? Don't they know he almost did?

Where are you, Dana Parsons? Where is the truth seeker in the press? Where is the justice seeker? Where is justice at all? I fought for another's justice and the truth. I convinced others to believe in our judicial system. I even convinced them to believe in the press. Why is justice betraying me, the press persecuting me? Why do they criminalize women and let the bad guys go free?

Dear Son,

When we are young, our elders advise and direct us to tell the "truth." What does that mean to you? Is the truth a thing? Something that cannot be changed? Something that we commit to?

As a young girl, I thought the truth was a moral thing. Like a commitment to be honest and good, even when we make a mistake. Later in life, the facts became the truth, the goal, the common standard. They are what they are and cannot be changed.

But today, the truth is a matter of life or death for me. The truth is the source of all power and existence. Someone can lose their freedom if all the facts are not presented in court, or if they are ignored by a court for that matter. Someone can be shot to death on the streets by the police because an assumption erased what was actually happening. Someone's entire life's purpose and reason to live can be stolen when a lie is printed, read, and believed as the truth.

But please don't give up on it, ever, dear one. It is with truth that we rise up and bring evil down. It is in truth that we find strength and grace to never give up. That begins by connecting to our own within us.

Love, Mom

*****

Meanwhile, inside our four walls of home, Diego needed privacy, extra love and care, and soon professional help. Whenever I walked into a room other than the one he was in, seconds later he'd shout out, "Mommy?!"

"Yes, dear," I'd reply.

"Just checking on you," he'd say, with the anxiety of knowing a press van was outside, careless of what they were doing to such a little guy. This happened every day for several months.

Bill understandably wanted us to "move on" and leave the past behind. But when the past is being shoved down your throat on a daily basis by the public outside, it is impossible.

Sadly, soon my colleagues on the Board of Supervisors began believing the press. Nate Miley, president of the Board at the time, walked into my office one day, sat down, and said, "We need to talk," nervously shaking his leg and talking fast.

"I am asking you to resign. This is all too much. If you don't, I will move for your removal. It's your choice," he said. Here was a man sitting before me who had had a public scandal himself.

In his case, the press and everyone else soon let it go and moved on. Like with Clinton, Trump, Newsom, and all the other male elected officials I could name here. But me? I was "female, young, beautiful, a rising star," and they never stopped.

I hastily explained to Nate that the truth was going to come out. That what was being said included mostly lies. That multiple crimes had been committed against me and I'd tried to get out. My words went nowhere. "The choice is yours," he repeated, and left. When I got home that night, I called and informed Bill of the conversation, asking for his advice. "You should resign," he said.

There I was, a grown woman who once was a little girl who

only wanted to help others and save the world. Who once had dreams and then made them real. Who worked so very hard to get to where she was. All of it destroyed due to a single inhale.

On the day before my 41st birthday, I submitted my resignation and have never returned to public office or a full-time professional position since.

This was the statement issued: *"For my child, and in the spirit of Mother's Day and National Victims' Rights Week, I hereby announce my resignation from the Alameda County Board of Supervisors in order that I may focus on the well-being of my child, recovery from chemical dependency and interpersonal violence, and transitioning to work in the private sector. It has truly been an honor serving as supervisor for the constituents of District 2 and for this, I am eternally grateful."*

In response, a blog post stated, "Drug Addict Democrat Slut Nadia Lockyer Resigns as Alameda County Supervisor." No matter what I did, I couldn't escape, and nothing was ever enough for them to stop and let me and my child recover in privacy without the public shaming.

Bill decided to stay in Sacramento again, leaving me alone to care for Diego in the middle of what felt like a war outside. The pain was so intense, I could not eat or sleep. I cried all day and night until I could not cry anymore. I did not leave the house except to take Diego to and pick him up from school. I couldn't bear to face the cameras and the world. I used what we had in the pantry and freezer until we had no more food, then asked my brother to get groceries for us when needed.

The psychological layers began to drown me. Nightmares and flashbacks flooded in. I wanted to turn to Bill for support and for advice, but my guilt for the pain I'd caused him was overwhelming, so I didn't dare try. A double whammy of disconnect and disassociation. I was in a hell I had no inkling how to get out of. I was nowhere to be found, but in everyone's face, I was naked in print.

Investigators from the Attorney General's office eventually interviewed me. I was terrified and asked my therapist to be there. I did not know if I could do it—explain what happened, put it all into words, remember every detail.

Initially, the questions were basic. I went through a timeline as best I could of that night. Describing the assault was the most difficult of all.

But then they asked me, "What were you wearing?" I was confused about why they were asking me this, but answered the question anyways. Today, I think, *How was this relevant? If a woman is wearing clothes you approve of, is she more credible? If she isn't, is she less? Did they ask SC the same question? I doubt it.*

An investigator in the AG's office also asked, "Have you had sex with anyone since the alleged assault?"

The shock of his question was horrifying. Today, I think, *How was this relevant? If a woman does not have sex after an assault, is she more credible? If she does, is she less? Did they ask SC the same question? I doubt it.*

My mind was spinning by the time the interview was over. Their questions made no sense to me. I felt cross-examined as though I was the suspect.

A few weeks later the Attorney General's investigators came to the house. They looked in my eyes and said, "There will be no prosecution."

I wailed, ran to Diego's room, and fell to the floor in a fetal position, sobbing. One of the deputies peeked in and began to speak nonsense, attempting to justify the decision.

"How do you expect me to live? How do you expect me to breathe with the memory of his hand on my neck?! How?! How?!"

Three reasons were publicly given for not prosecuting SC: "She let him in, is unstable, and is an addict." To my knowledge,

SC was never arrested or prosecuted, and continued to exploit me online, as well as other women, using the exact same MO he had used before he met me.

> *Dear Son,*
>
> *What is the meaning of the scales of justice?*
> *They say that since the first modern-day legal system began in Rome, the scales of justice have been used to symbolize the balance between the truth and fairness sought in the justice system. It also represents the balance between the support and opposition a case has, with the scale responsible for weighing the two and reaching a fair and just verdict. The scales are held by Lady Justice, or Justicia, the Roman Goddess of Justice.*
> *But here, the Attorney General's office cut off Lady Justice's arms. They denied her power and disrespected her role. Without any effort to seek the truth behind it all or gather documentation from me, they blindfolded and silenced her, then locked her up far away. I can still hear her screaming, "Enough is enough! Send him to prison!"*
> *Love, Mom*

I felt as though any and all hope for truth, justice, and safety was obliterated. Evil and darkness had won. I immediately thought of suicide again and took measures to begin the process.

A knock was soon heard on the front door. When I opened

it, Officer Horst from the Newark Police Department, the one who stayed by my side all night in the emergency room after the assault, was standing there alongside several others.

He sat me down. I just cried and cried. "Why? Why? Please tell me why? He hurt me, he tricked me, he violated my entire life, I almost died . . . ," I muttered, over and over.

He interrupted, "I know, Nadia. I know what he did to you. And I am so sorry. You need help. Your son needs you." He got my attention and offered to take me to Kaiser Mental Health Center.

I went into the safety of Kaiser for forty-eight hours, searching with all my might for an ounce of strength to continue my life for the sake of motherhood while the man that almost killed me was free to continue living just as he was.

Upon discharge, the case manager handed me back my cell phone. But the moment I turned it back on, an inundation of texts and calls from a South Bay number came in. I drowned in fear. I didn't want to leave the facility. It was the safest place to be, away from the press's crucifixion and SC's continued stalking. Desperate to be with and care for Diego, I forced myself to leave. As soon as I got in the car, I told Bill about the texts and showed him the phone. He just told me to be quiet and "move on." Minutes after we arrived home, another call came in. I answered. "I'm so sorry. I'm so sorry, Nadia," he said—it was him, SC.

How did he contact me? Am I losing my mind? I thought. I curled into a ball and sat on the floor, and very clearly stated with fervor, "You destroyed my life. I will never let you hurt me again!" then hung up. Minutes thereafter, SC made the mistake of calling our home number and Bill answered.

Thankfully, that convinced Bill to support me in getting a temporary civil restraining order. But it had to be handed to the person being restrained in order to be enforceable. SC could not be found. In the meantime, he mocked these attempts by bragging online about how he was avoiding being served.

SC post on Facebook, 5/31/12:

Time to go back into hiding.
I hope nobody finds me in my man cave.
There's investigators out there looking
for me—
oh no, I hope they're not the Matrix agents.

Bill escaped again to Sacramento, living there with a friend. So Diego and I spent his 9th birthday together with his friends. I tried my best to make things appear normal for him. For brief moments, I could even imagine everything was ok. But I was never able to sustain it for long. There was always a lurking fear knowing that SC was out there and online. My nightmares and flashbacks intensified, and I simply had no idea how to manage daily life. Every night after I put Diego to bed, I drank my pain, fears, and shame away. I just didn't know any other way to escape.

Soon enough, I packed everything and drove Diego and myself to Southern California, closer to family. Tragically, prior to leaving, I found an old bag of the devil's drug hidden in the garage. I kept it with me like a safety blanket, thinking to myself, *Don't use it now. Just make it to Southern California and you will be ok.* It felt like the friend I had been desperately longing for was in my bag.

I was going to build a new life for us with the support of my family. I needed to return to my roots. I planned that Diego and I would live with my sister until I figured out how to support our lives as a single mother without Bill's help. I would find work somehow. Maybe I would even change my name.

I was willing to do anything to just get away from it all and build a safe, healthy, peaceful new life.

I set up our room, making it cozy and quaint. I enrolled Diego in homeschooling and made a desk area for him. We got through his daily homeschooling assignments then played outside. We ate dinner with my family and tried to return to a normal life.

But shame had me running to stand still. I could not shake my obsession with justice, redemption, and the truth being known. My mind told me that the labels "addict and slut" defined my worth. Little Nadia was screaming, *But I am a good girl inside! He hurt me, he haunted me, and I did my best to get out. See me, hear me, please don't let my truth be denied.*

I began gathering evidence and putting it in a binder. I spent long days working to print out proof of SC's online stalking, exploitation, threatening texts, and more.

Also, the Verizon Fraud Unit advised I provide the local police department with a copy of the temporary civil restraining order, even though SC hadn't been found. So there I went to the Orange Police Department as an empowered single mother creating a new life with my temporary civil restraining order in hand. A kind officer sat me down and spent a good hour going through my binder.

I clearly remember him saying, "Wow, this is a whole lot you've dealt with. We can help." He had sincerely listened, read the documents, and completed a report. I finally felt a sense of hope for a new life in Southern California. I finally felt I had the help of law enforcement again.

But when I stood up to go back home to Diego, another officer walked up and told me to sit down. I smiled, thinking, *Wow, they're taking this seriously finally.*

"You're not going anywhere," he said with almost a sad look on his face. "You're under arrest for possession of an illegal substance." I had hidden it in a boot in a shoebox high up in the closet.

I literally fell into a black hole within myself and fainted. I woke up a few minutes later in a holding cell, completely and utterly defeated. Later I learned that my sister had called the police while I was at the department attempting to enforce the temporary civil restraining order.

That was August 28, 2012. I am now over ten years sober from the devil's drug.

I own each and every part I played in sealing the deal of SC's destruction of my life. It hurts even more knowing that my untreated trauma and disease caused me to become the non-credible, unstable, fragile addict everyone said I was. This is what a survivor does when her truth is denied and she is brutally shamed. This is what happens when we can't find our true worth underneath all the pain.

***

I say loud and clear, no matter who you are, where you come from, what gender, race, sexual orientation, creed, or religion you identify with, if you have struggled with surviving inter-personal violence and related addiction and are calling out for help, please know I hear you, I see you, I believe you, and I know you are so much more than what anyone says or does.

There is a home within you that holds the truth of what you are—an infinite being of love, light, and warmth that nothing can change or hide. It is here where you'll find freedom from the dark and begin to feel alive.

CHAPTER 12

Dear Son,

guilt is ok.

Shame never is.

They say every seven years we experience a new cycle in our state of consciousness, that the key is opening up our inner connection to something beyond us that places spiritual directives along the way.

I believe that something, or "It," is beyond, around, and within us. "It" made us and is us. "It" feels like a home within me. When I died in the car accident, I was thrown into "It." I know "It" to exist with my whole heart.

It is the home I've always desired to give my sons in both the physical and non-physical forms. Yes, the quaint abode with a garden and playground. Yet that is impermanent. More importantly, an understanding and relationship with a grounding, intuitive, and illuminating higher power. A place of truth inside them they can connect to anywhere, anytime, that flat out shuts their minds up when thoughts begin to harm them.

When connected to "It," my fear- and shame-based thoughts are noticed and banned more easily. When disconnected, on the other hand, I live in a body-focused reptilian brain. The sole focus is survival in states of flight, fight, freeze, or fawn modes, depending on the situation. When living this way, I can become highly vulnerable to any one of my diseases.

When life hit me hard with heartache, back-to-back and out of the blue, I ran to stand still. I'd sometimes reach stillness, but then something would knock me off my feet again because I had no home base within. Even when I heard my father's spirit calling, I did not know how to stay connected to the truth within.

It took the next seven years to find and fully return to that home within me. It was filled with layer upon layer of challenges and complications. And even more, my true self and ability to open up were buried deep down in fears, shame, and pain.

***

I was sent to Santa Ana jail and, due to the press coverage of the arrest, placed in protective custody. Frankly, I see now how a single article was far more of a sentence than anything I was facing in court.

I remember overhearing the girls in another holding cell within view asking, "Who is she?" and wondering why I was placed alone. I thought, *I am no different than you. We are all just trying to do our best in life, right?* All I wanted to say was, *I am just a normal person, so why can't the press just leave me alone? Why can't I walk through healing in privacy, without the public shaming?* Every woman appeared desperate for love in all the wrong ways, and those ways had gotten all of us behind bars.

I was medicated and slept for I don't know how long. I woke up to tears, my body shaking in the cold, bones aching on the metal bed. The sound of keys clanking and voices echoing brought me to dark places imprinted in my head. The bathroom, his hand, the razor blade at his wrist. I couldn't escape the terror. My mind was more imprisoning than the six-by-eight cell I was in.

When I was able to quiet it at all, Diego was all I thought about. The pain, guilt, and remorse were overwhelming. My mind, in control, upped the ante. *You deserved to be victimized and all that man's abuse. You are a bad mom, a sinner, and should go to hell.*

Unbeknownst to me, my sister Sabrina called the jail and begged for me to be placed on suicide watch. Eventually, I was taken out of my cell and brought to a bench in a nearby hallway. A woman walked up and sat down almost immediately.

She was kind, gentle, and looked me in the eyes. "How are you doing, Nadia?" A bit shocked she actually knew and said my name, I initially just sat there, confused, and in pure shame. She said, "It's ok."

Finally I stuttered out, "I was on the other side of the glass in a suit the last time I was here. I'm so ashamed. I'm not a bad person like they say."

After a couple seconds of silence, she said, "I know who you are. I know what you did for Arthur Carmona. When he was imprisoned, I worked here. You, Nadia, you were his hero."

I broke down and sobbed my heart out. Someone saw the real person within me. In the darkest of places, someone somehow knew the real me. I'll never forget it.

Flashes of the past two decades raced through my head. My father's barrio, local activism, Santa Ana schools, campaigning door-to-door, voting rights protests, Arthur Carmona fundraisers, and workshops for youth . . . all of it literally happened just outside the jail's four walls.

She just sat there as I cried. She held a space called truth. She saw through the outside labels into my soul. Her eyes were like lighthouses in the endless storm.

"Do you want to take your life?" she asked.

I nodded my head. "But I can't. Diego, my dear son, Diego, for him I have to fight again."

I was immediately placed on suicide watch and remained there a few days. I tried to sleep, curling into a ball and crying most of the time instead. A woman's repetitive screaming, "Donna, Donna, Donna," for hours filled my cell with anxiety and panic. I tightened the grasp around my legs, covered my head, and clenched my teeth.

At some point, keys clattered as a guard shouted, "Lockyer!" I tried to compose myself and stood up while he unlocked the thick steel door. "Hands behind your back," he said, motioning for me to exit the cell.

Step by step, he told me which direction to walk until the only way forward was down a long central cement hallway.

Arthur Carmona walked down the same corridor fourteen years prior. His footsteps, breath, and thoughts had marked the same path.

Back then, he was the one behind bars in orange garments.

That day, it was me.

Back then, his truth was unknown.

That day, it was mine.

Back then, he needed me to fight for his freedom.

That day, only I could save myself.

He never deserved to be there. But I did.

He never gave up hope. But I had.

I was escorted to the same visiting cells where I had visited him in the prime of my life. There, sitting on the other side of the glass, was the closest person to actually being my father, Al Stokke. The same man who'd encouraged me to fight for Arthur. The same man who was my father's confidant and friend. The pity, disappointment, and sadness in his eyes were unbearable. My head fell into my folded arms on the table, hiding. I sobbed, unable to look him in the eyes.

All I could think of was my father. The symbolism of the moment consumed me.

All the feelings of loss returned in an instant and then were blanketed in shame.

My mind filled with unspoken words: *Where were you, Daddy? I needed you. Why did you leave me? I've felt so all alone, without a home, for so long. Please come back, Daddy. Please. What have I done to your legacy? Your little girl with dreams?*

"Nadia," Al said. "You have a long journey ahead . . . but you'll get through this. You will make it through. You have to. Remember what your father said, 'This too shall pass.'"

***

If Al Stokke had said to me that the next several years would require multiple admissions to treatment, a few arrests, a conviction, a couple of hospitalizations, forced separation from my child, and another attempted suicide, I would've told him, "Screw you. I'll stay here imprisoned." But I was completely incapable of realizing the magnitude of the challenges I faced.

What could I possibly say to my child? "I'm screwed up, people fucked me up, and I'm sorry I failed handling it over and over again"?

Apologizing to Diego wasn't an option. To him, it probably felt more like a curse. Maybe I should've said, "I will do my best to give a living amends for the rest of my life." But I'm sure he wouldn't have held his breath, as well he shouldn't have then.

And words to reassure him? What could be said? "Don't worry, dear Son, all that Mommy has to do is cure chemical dependency, PTSD, depression, chronic pain, an unhealthy marriage, legal problems, and an obliterated professional life." It would've been frightening for anyone to hear, let alone understand.

And how on earth could there have been a road map or orderly "to-do list" for the job ahead of me? Still, I tried. Indeed, I earnestly tried to make one.

Ok, Nadia, first get sober, get your public reputation back, justice will result, and then everything will be ok. Where was the part about healing my mind, body, and soul so I could be a healthy, stable, and happy human being for those I loved?

Shame controlled my entire life for years. I believed I was merely what they said I was. My soul couldn't cut through to me.

***

By far the deepest pain I have ever felt as a human being is as a mother when separated from my children. Every time I voluntarily sought help or was forced into getting it, the system imposed abandonment on my children.

I am utterly incapable of accepting, handling, digesting, let alone understanding it as a mother. It makes no sense to every inch of my being. There was absolutely no rational purpose behind it. Why on earth would anyone think this makes sense, let alone when sober?

Motherhood should be overflowing with the world's support. It should be heralded as the most special role, all efforts and resources invested in its preservation. When a mother needs help, her children need help alongside her, not to be ripped away. When a mother makes unhealthy choices, her children need to learn better ones with her, not to be separated as though they are the ones deserving of the punishment.

Who the heck ever thought forced separation should come first?

Worse, when she voluntarily seeks help and accountability, why is she so often forced to choose between being with her children and receiving those? This inherently feeds the disease. It empowers shame. It fuels depression.

Providing mothers with a safe place to get help with their children should come first. Why the lack of addiction and treatment centers with on-site childcare and schooling? Think of all the children who wouldn't suffer from the trauma of abandonment. Think of all the mothers who wouldn't wallow brokenhearted and distracted in recovery.

Generational trauma can be quelled, but it won't happen until we put mothers first.

And why is vulnerability punished? Why can't we dive into our wounds and walk through hard truths without fear of being judged? Why can't we reckon with stories written in our heads without the threat of a system judging and shaming us? If we cry, why do they say, "See? I told you so. She's unstable and in relapse. Call 911. Have her locked up. Her children need that."

Why don't they instead say, "Wow, what amazing courage she has. Let's hug and hold the family together. Let's show the children it's safe to ask for help. Let's teach them they can show their pain without fear of being abandoned, punished, and shamed."

Am I angry at the system? Of course I am. Mothers and children deserve so much better. Do I think separation is needed in many situations? Yes. But that doesn't mean all situations require total separation.

***

I was taken straight from custody to residential treatment where I spent an entire year by mandate of the court. Charges for possession and endangerment hung over my head. Without a doubt, I needed to be held accountable for bad choices made. I also desperately needed trauma therapy and mental health help.

I arrived shoeless, without any belongings, and was placed alone in a room in a medical building strictly dedicated to detox and those with chronic medical conditions. The need for physical detox was minimal by that point, but my psyche was severely damaged.

I didn't exit my room for weeks unless I had to. I tried to sleep, but more often stayed curled up in bed. I feared everything and anyone. The daylight was frightening because I feared what was in the news. The sounds of "normal life" scared me even more. They would trigger flashbacks and remind me I was stuck in a time and space I had no idea how to escape.

Nights were worse. Nightmares with a repeated theme played over and over again. My mind beat me to a pulp, trying to connect the dots. Every detailed memory and flashback of SC's actions only reminded me he was still walking free, unprosecuted and likely abusing others. Like a lashing on my heart, every waking and sleeping hour I was afraid.

At some point, I was given a strong dose of psych and sleeping meds. But my body responded with full-body muscle spasms that mimicked seizures. It would start with a warm feeling on the left side of face, then my left arm would feel slightly paralyzed, my hand would curl up, and I'd often faint or nearly lose consciousness. Sometimes, the left side of my face collapsed entirely and would not move. This happened off and on throughout my stay, even after I stopped the psych meds. As a result, I spent a lot of time in the medical building.

A young woman named Kiana, a genius of an artist and singer who suffers from a condition called Ehlers-Danlos syndrome, somehow reached me within. She is the one who finally got me talking and sharing.

We commiserated over cigarettes, puzzles, and painting. Silence was perfectly fine when we both needed it. She patiently heard me tell story after story about Diego, how he built territories, our daily adventures, our frequent "missions," how the pain was so deep in my heart.

I wanted to just run out the doors against the rules and go find him. She would talk me out of it and ask me to watch her paint something for him. One of those paintings was of a howling wolf in rainbow colors that hangs above Diego's desk to this day.

I was moved to one of many homes run by the treatment center, placed in a room with two others, and given a required group meeting schedule and a binder of assignments. We were not allowed off the premises and were taken to group meetings and the grocery store together in a van.

As the number of people and sounds around me increased, so did the intensity of my flashbacks, nightmares, and chronic pain. Triggers came left and right.

The "bing" of a cell phone text, and "Tic toc, tic toc, you're going to go viral" returned. A glimpse at a computer screen, and images of my naked body being hung out and sold glared. In panic, I'd run and hide in my own space somewhere.

Worse, my room was right beside the TV room. A scream from a scene, a man's threatening voice, the sound of a crash, and more would send me running out of my room and pacing the hallways, frantic to get out.

Once, I yelled at the top of my lungs, "Stop!" Another time, I ran out the front door, breaking the rules, and paced back and forth on the driveway, not knowing what to do or where to go.

"Nadia's freaking out again," the girls would say. I'd just stay wherever I was, feeling alone and abandoned, until staff finally came and slowly brought me out of wherever I was in my head.

If I missed group, they all knew what was going on. I was either stuck in another place and time in my head or I'd fainted in a physical flare-up.

Chronic pain is no friend to psychological warfare. An ache in the left shoulder and neck meant a triggered memory of his evil eyes and hand around my throat. It was as though I could never get a break.

You can't get much out of treatment when in this state. And it lasted for years.

I was assigned to a specialized trauma treatment group. I went through the motions as best I could but was never able to benefit. I didn't know where to start. I didn't know what "scene" to process. I had barely begun to feel alive again and wasn't ready to go back there.

Once a week, we'd be taken to a different facility for the whole day. We were taught basic grounding skills such as deep breathing, placing your feet firmly on the ground, or pinching your skin as a way to return to the here and now.

A single client would be placed in the middle of our circle and prompted with questions, sometimes enabling them to connect to a traumatic memory. The hope would be to "rewrite" the ending to the memory so one "escapes" or so there is closure.

One time a young man in his early twenties asked me to play the role of his mother. He was also molested as a child by a professional. He, on the other hand, had told his mom, but she did not believe him. He'd spent the majority of his young life addicted to heroin, full of shame and resentment.

He sat before me as a little boy, crying, asking his mother to acknowledge his truth. *And oh, dear Son, dear Son of mine. It cut me like a knife to feel his pain inside, a pain I could relate with too well.*

I cried and said, "I'm so sorry, dear Son. I'm so sorry. I

believe you. I do now. I do, and I will protect you from here on out." He fell into my arms and sobbed.

Imagine, three little spoken words, "I believe you," could have changed the entire trajectory of this young man's life. Instead, heroin nearly killed him.

*＊＊

Diego was the only thing that gave me hope and brought me back to the present. For the first several weeks, I was unable to have any contact with him, and it was tough. When the treatment center allowed it, I was at Bill's mercy as to whether or not I'd get to see my child. A feeling of powerlessness as a mother and a wife began to evolve and would be ever present for years to come.

What is Diego thinking, worrying about, going through right now? I'm losing our bond, I'm losing him, my mind would say in a pool of shame, remorse, and guilt. Then it'd be, *Has anyone helped him process the sounds of his mother nearly being killed? Does anyone even care about that crime that SC committed against Diego?*

When allowed to call him, I had no idea what to say, how to comfort him, let him know or, better, believe everything would be all right. So I just made small talk in the few minutes we had and gave loads of "I miss you" and "I love you" before our call ended.

The reality was, for an entire year, I fell asleep crying, yearning so deeply in my heart to cuddle with Diego every night and say, "Everything will be ok," and "Mommy loves you more than all the stars and planets in the whole universe."

Bill eventually started flying Diego down on weekends for a few months so we could spend quality time together. I have deep gratitude for him for doing this and thank him whole-heartedly. Eventually I was granted weekend overnights and it was the highlight of my week. I'd plan out fun activities for Diego in an attempt to make it as "normal" as possible.

I had to keep myself busy doing something, anything, with my hands and head for Diego in an attempt to handle the pain of separation. Like a mama bird in constant motion making a nest, or a sea turtle digging a massive hole for its eggs, all intentions and energy as a mother had to go somewhere. So I cut out pictures from magazines that reminded me of him. Trains, dogs, sea urchins, sailboats, lighthouses, all the things he liked. I pasted them into collages and mailed them to him. In December, I made a collage for every day of Christmas with a "Mad Libs" line of questions leading him eventually to where his present from Mommy would be found. Those pages are in safekeeping.

At some point, the advocate and "doer" in me came back alive and kicked into full-fledged "fight" mode just like it had as a little girl. Every morning, I'd rise before all the others, do floor exercises, make coffee, then read lessons. I made my to-do lists, completed an entire binder of focused writing assignments, and even enrolled to get certified as a California Drug & Alcohol Addiction Counselor, eventually finishing all the classes.

With a pat on my back, I'd say to myself, *See, I can conquer this disease all on my own and even teach others how to do it!* I was a perfect student on paper with a false sense of accomplishment in "recovery."

Today it is painful to look back on how hard I tried in all the wrong ways to get better. I was so naive to the many layers of deep, tough internal work needed before any hope of mental health, sobriety, chronic pain management, and clearing away of practical wreckage was possible.

In weekly therapy, I monopolized the time with shame-filled rants. My therapist said, "Nadia, you're not a bad person." I didn't believe it.

On the inside, I was ashamed of my entire life: my bad choices; what I had put Diego and Bill through; and disappointing my father, mother, brothers, sisters, friends, staff, community, constituents, colleagues, youth, strangers, the entire world. On the outside, everything confirmed it—"addict, slut, infidel, loser, failure"—making the internal struggle that much more insurmountable.

Everywhere I breathed, looked, and listened, shame was there. *You crazy, little, dirty, bad, unworthy girl, woman, wife, mother, lawyer. Go wash your face—heck, wash your whole body. You are crippled and will never walk free again,* repeated over and over again in rhymes.

Thankfully, after several months I was able to transfer to a different female-focused program where Diego could miraculously stay with me on weekends. The longer time periods allowed us to cuddle and engage in small talk about his life and why I couldn't be home with him. Guaranteed, every hour together with Diego added up to a day of improved focus on recovery.

I'll never forget when we played bingo with the rest of the moms one evening and he won. Everyone clapped as he proudly walked up to a box full of prizes with a huge smile on his face. He quickly saw what he wanted, picked it up, walked straight back, and set it in front of me. It was a beautiful little snow globe with a small butterfly inside.

"Here you go, Mommy. This is for you," he said and smiled.

Little did he know the symbolism it held of one life ended, another life begun. To this day, that same snow globe sits perched on a shelf of special things.

My Journal Entry

Every night I pray alone to my Creator, with the utmost shame and humility, for repeated

*forgiveness, strength, and redemption. When
I do so, I can't help but envision a scripture
etched in my head as a child, where a woman
praying for forgiveness and the healing of her
daughter tells Jesus that "even the dogs under
the table eat the children's crumbs," and in response to her humility he answers her prayers.*

After a year, the judge finally allowed me to return home.

My initial understanding with Bill was that Diego and I
would live in the Long Beach condo full-time and he would
only come to stay on the weekends. We were to remain physically separated and take things slowly, doing our best to keep
things healthy for Diego's sake.

But it was clear from the moment I walked in the door that
Bill had every intention of staying full-time. It didn't take long
for our marriage to devolve straight back into the same unhealthy patterns we were in before. Same people, same relationship, just a different location.

Still, I decided to stay in the marriage and dedicated my
heart to making it work, despite the underlying unaddressed
issues. I escaped into the happiness of motherhood with all my
heart and soul, earnestly trying to ease Diego's adjustment to a
new home, community, school, and life in Southern California.

I focused on being the best mother I could be. I walked him
to and from school every day, treasuring our little chats along
the way and our regular stops at the neighborhood bakery.

When he was in school, I attended an outpatient treatment
program, a chronic pain management class, and AA, always
ending up standing in the same spot at the school every day
when the release bell rang.

Diego had a hard time making friends at first. He was in
fifth grade at the time. I would spy on him from afar to see what
it was like for him during recess and lunch. One particular kid

was mean, but Diego would still hang around him. When I asked him about it, he said he had no choice. It broke my heart.

So I volunteered as a parent to help on a field trip to a local beach. Diego had been meticulously working on one of his epic sandcastles for a long time. The same mean kid purposely began barging through the masterpiece and went back and forth dragging his feet through the sand. Some others were watching and just sat aghast.

I walked straight up to the kid and said, "Don't you ever f**k with my son again." Rumor had it, "Diego's mom used a bad word."

Afterwards, he seemed shocked anyone had said anything to him at all. Good or bad. His emotions came up like a clogged broken hydrant. He sat down alone, just staring at the sand.

I went and sat next to him. "What's really going on?" I knew something deeper was stirring. "Are you ok at home?" A little nod in return. "Why do you feel a need to do mean things to others?"

A shrug of his shoulders. He said, "I don't know."

"It's ok, and whatever you're going through, it's making you mad. Is that it?"

He nodded, wiping away tears and gathering his composure.

"I get it. I get it. I'm Diego's mom, can you at least tell Diego you're sorry? And if you ever need to talk, I'm here if you need me." He actually smiled. He was accepted as he was and never bothered Diego again.

Dear Son,

Remember to "flip it." Flip the focus back to them. Whatever anyone says has nothing to do with you. They are hurting inside or something else is going on. So say in response, "I am

*sorry you are having a bad day," then smile and
walk away. Try not to brand them a "bully" or a
"jerk." That doesn't help a thing.*
       Love, Mommy

***

Despite my fears of the recent past being discovered in
public records or online, I filled out papers to volunteer at
the school itself. They asked if I had "ever been arrested or
convicted." I had to put the truth. So when I went to the
office to turn them in, my mind went straight into shame
mode.

*They'll recognize your name, google it, see the lies, and be-
lieve all of it. Your entire identity is gone. Your good heart will
never be seen again. You have no freedom from the past. Get
used to it.* So I said, "Never mind," turned around, and walked
out the door, relinquishing the hope. I let shame win.

Thankfully, our Long Beach condo became the base of
the boys' gatherings. Diego found lifetime friends there. Every
morning a few of them came over for breakfast. They'd all
take off together from there. I'd watch them from the balcony. Weeks off from school ended up in two- or three-day
sleepovers. Diego appeared fully adjusted, happy, and thriving,
both in school and with friendships.

Soon enough, over two and a half years had passed since
the day of the arrest. Finally, I felt grounded and worthy as
a mother, while practical wreckage had cleared away. On the
outside, things appeared "fixed" and I appeared "cured."

The press even wrote a couple of beautiful recovery stories.
While the words "sex and drug scandal" never let up, head-
lines like "Nadia Maria . . . Full of Grace" and "Nadia Maria
Davis Lockyer's Comeback" arrived. For the first time, some

of the truth began to come out and I had a sense everything would come full circle at the right time.

When Diego entered sixth grade, walking him to school was no longer an option. He was growing up and beginning to feel uncomfortable with "Mommy" holding his hand.

His sweet youthful confidence was blossoming. I'll never forget the day I tickled him and saw a single long strand of hair growing under his armpit. I thought, *Seriously? Come on, let the kid be a kid a little longer.* But I couldn't stop time. And our dear son Diego was really growing up.

It was time for me to recreate my professional life.

No one can say I didn't try my best. I submitted my résumé and biography to multiple places. I made a couple short lists, was called and questioned. But when asked about the gaps between the years I'd worked, I was honest. "I needed help. I'm recovered and ok now."

"Ohhhhh, Lockyer, right. I remember," they'd say, or something similar. The energy coming from the other side of the line would shift instantaneously. The friendly questions, talk, and conversation ended. I'd never hear back, even though I was fairly confident I was one of the best on their table. It was a cold reminder that what was said about me in the press overpowered all I had accomplished prior.

What began to evolve inside? Shame, fear, and resentment.

Doing legal work with my name on it or walking into a courtroom to speak on the record was out of the question. Plus, how could I walk with dignity into an Orange County courthouse now? My booking photo had been all over the news. Every article from the past, swimming out there online. Who would believe or hire me now?

I tried every other avenue. I enrolled in a course, completed it, and became a Certified Domestic Violence Advocate. *If I can't run the place,* I thought, *I can at least help victims individually.* I offered my services at multiple locations. No one responded. My head told me it was for the same reasons but that may have been an illusion. *I'll never escape what was said. No one wants a labeled slut and addict.*

I volunteered at the Public Law Center and represented an abused, abandoned, and neglected undocumented immigrant child. I successfully obtained guardianship on behalf of his grandmother and grandfather.

I felt alive again during those couple of months, like I had skirted by the sidelines in the privacy of a home computer. While it was a start in the right direction, it wasn't an income source nor a way to establish myself again professionally. If I sought employment there, it was inevitable my past press would crush any chance of being hired, I thought. Shame stopped me from even trying.

The possibility of recreating my professional life seemed doomed.

My Journal Entry

A false personification made by a liar hurts me every day. The real me is ignored by others' pre-conceived judgments. I am forced to crawl myself out of labels every first interaction. Does anyone realize how painful this is? I am still that little girl who just wants to help people. I am still that little girl who was hurt, scared, and abandoned. I am still that little girl who has endless hope in her heart. Why don't they see the real person I am? Please, Creator, please take this away. I want to give light to the world today.

✢✢✢

All Bill ever wanted for me was to be happy. He knew I felt a hole in my heart after running into difficulty finding work. He also knew I received so much joy from being Diego's mother. He always told me I was a wonderful mother to our son, and I'll love him to the end of time for that.

There had been progress, indeed, on so many fronts.

I felt a calling to something I could not pinpoint.

The loads of gratitude, love, and energy inside waited for an answer to come. And so, very gently and gracefully, an inkling to give Diego a sibling returned.

It arrived through a dream. I was with my father's spirit and powerful balls of light encircled us. It was not my first dream of this kind. Sometimes I even have visions while awake at indiscriminate times of meditation. I undoubtedly believe the phenomena is born from where I went when I died.

But they only happen when I'm in a state of internal peace and calm. So they understandably were absent for a very long period of time. Upon return, the dream was unexpected.

Yet it made complete and perfect sense.

Two infinite angels of light were calling and were ready to enter this world.

CHAPTER 13

Dear Son,
you are not mere DNA.

Science is beyond fascinating and inspiring, yet can appear calculated and confined. Curiosity is fed by and answers are found in countless discoveries and explorations. But many place science on the opposing end of spirituality.

I just see spirituality, science, and physics as best friends.

I think of science as the study, exploration, and discovery of the things "It" made and more. I think of physics as the beautiful use of formulas, methods, and principles to understand, explain, and predict the things "It" made and when. Spirituality is just acknowledging and connecting to "It," the infinite source behind it all that science and physics can't explain.

Today, one of my absolute favorite things is listening to Diego talk about anything astrophysics and science related. I stand in awe of his curiosity, questions, and knowledge about physical matter, how and why certain life is supported and where.

While we worked on his college applications together, he said, "Mom, maybe there is another blueprint for 'life' existing in our galaxy. Maybe we are limiting ourselves with a silly, narrow formula for what is itself 'life,' maybe we're looking in erroneous ways, with the wrong tools and incorrect goals in mind."

Maybe, indeed, dear Son. I don't know. But you'll be leading the way in those endeavors soon.

And I do know the answers are not found in mere DNA.

Dear Son,

Oh how I prayed for the days your soul came calling. How I longed for your glorious beauty to shine light all around us. And so, with two different parts mixed together, we made "you" with the help of others.

But think about it, did we? Did they?

What caused the egg and sperm to join together?

What caused your heart to beat? What is behind the biological answer?

If the heartbeat is triggered by electrical impulses that travel down a special pathway we've named the "sinoatrial node," a small bundle of cells located in the right atrium, what triggered the electrical impulse? The energy? Where does that come from?

You can refer to any biological, scientific, or physics data we have, but the answer still remains, what is that source of energy?

With every form of life, what dictated the essential "goldilocks state"?

It most certainly wasn't me, nor the doctor, nor IVF.

You were not merely DNA in a healthy A+ rated zygote.

The "you" I know is so much more, your "Sat Nam," your true self.

You are the infinite being I saw when I died and visited the angels.

Love, Mommy

The practical side of the IVF process is cumbersome and calculated. Giving yourself injections every day to then have your hormones evaluated is no party. But in comparison to all the past medical crises and experiences, it was a walk in the park.

I did not tell Diego, or my friends and family.

Only Bill knew. And to him I'm indebted.

On the day before my 44th birthday, I was lying on the exam table in the medical room with my legs open. The doctor walked in and said, "I'm going to transfer five. We have a couple A pluses and a few As." What does that mean anyway?

I shouted, "No, no, no . . . I cannot have quintuplets!"

"Let me tell you like it is, young lady," he said jokingly. "At your age, there is a 6 percent chance you'll have one, 3 percent two, and 1 1/2 percent three. Plus, whether or not the cells continue to divide? Well, only God knows that. There's only so much I can do."

"Go for it," I said, with all the conviction in my heart, knowing in my gut that whatever happened was meant to be. I was never going to repeat the process again.

After the transfer, I ate a ton of pineapple and stayed on my back, telling Diego something else required it. Blastocysts normally hatch out of their shell and begin implanting about seven or eight days after fertilization. At some point, an embryo had to miraculously "decide" to attach itself to my womb.

Days passed before I went back into the doctor's office. Finally, it was the big day. The nurse was quiet and began the ultrasound with my sister by my side. Gazing closer. at the screen, she suddenly smiled.

Pointing with her finger, not saying a word at first. "What?" I asked nervously. A few seconds passed, then she suddenly said it, "Two, there are two growing in you."

I burst out in joy, knowing it was always meant to be, for I had met these souls before and knew they were calling me.

Weeks passed and turned into months. I started showing in my belly much earlier than I had with Diego.

He always laughed when I purposefully protruded my belly. "Fat," he'd say jokingly and smile as I cuddled him closely. I'd always wonder what he was thinking with a brother or sister in the making.

When I found out I was having boys, I was so thrilled and so excited to tell Diego, that I drove to his friend's house where he was hanging out, placed two pairs of blue baby shoes on the hood of my car, then went up to the house to call him out and surprise him. As he walked out, I just said "hi" and no other word.

When he saw the shoes, he knew he was going to have two little brothers. Imagine if I had to tell him he was going to have two baby sisters! He had been the only child for so long and his life was about to drastically change. Adding more boys to the house made it a little less dramatic. I mean, our dogs and fish were boys too.

Dear Son,

I finished writing this chapter the morning of New Year's Eve. After closing the computer, I picked you up from Daddy's and we went to play at one of our favorite parks. It was a clear blue sky, chill winter air kind of day.

After the swings, hide-and-seek, and some Pokémon play, we sat down and broke out snacks and a "Dino Bone Discovery" chunk of cement. You loved the little hammer and chisel and went right to it.

At some point I asked you, "So, how was the movie Soul?" knowing you had recently watched it with Daddy.

You jumped in with your excited big breath between every sentence mode. "Well, there's this man and he dies and he's deciding what to do and then he meets these littler souls and they have a conversation."

I got chills, then replied, "Well, remember when Mommy visited the angels? You were there too, before your actual body happened. That's where we first met."

"Oh, ok," you replied, and ran off to play. Oh how I love you so!

Love, Mommy

From five months on, the pregnancy was monitored weekly. They would attach nodes to hear the heartbeats and monitor the babies' growth and my Braxton-Hicks.

The doctor always said, "Just make it until December and get them to five pounds each."

By the time my belly wouldn't fit in a full meal, I ate lots of eggs and drank protein veggie smoothies, took a ton of vitamins and brain-feeding oils, walked a lot, and napped even more.

Bill, Diego, and I regularly went to the movies in one of those theaters with large recliner seats. I joked with Diego and put my seat far back, and with my hand rubbing my very visible belly, I'd loudly say, "Oh darn, I ate too much."

"Mom," he'd say loudly, chuckling in that high- and low-pitch kind of way.

We often were unable to control our laughter. Patrons nearby would turn around and "shhhh" us, but as soon as they saw my belly, the look on their faces was priceless. It just made us laugh even harder. One time we had to walk out because we couldn't stop.

At thirty-two weeks, we had a little scare. The Braxton-Hicks were so intense, the doctor decided to keep me overnight. The babies' heart rates were monitored, and my blood pressure observed. I never dilated, but my iron levels were quickly declining.

In the morning, they gave me iron injections but decided not to give me the steroid treatment to accelerate lung maturation. I went home and took it easy, but I was often very tired.

Thankfully, I was able to carry our baby boys up to a day shy of thirty-six weeks. At some point while we were at a movie theater, the Braxton-Hicks returned so intensely and frequently, it was clear I had to go to the hospital.

I was monitored for a bit and we got the news. "They have to come out now." I had sudden severe pre-eclampsia. Kaiser called several doctors, and they rapidly prepped the delivery room for a C-section.

Bill came quickly and was by my side, holding my hand.

His eyes filled with joy as he said, "Everything will be ok."

As they rolled me out, they stopped a moment so I could look to my left. There was Diego, my mother, and three sisters, along with their husbands, all blowing me and the little ones inside my belly kisses.

I immediately called for Diego and he came to my side.

"Dear Son, I'd like you to name your little brothers. Remember the ones we talked about? Pick two on the list, ok?"

"Ok, Mom," he said. "I'd love to."

And sure enough, he did.

I was infused with magnesium, an epidural was placed in my spine, and the doctor immediately said, "Here we go!" It seemed there were twenty nurses and doctors in the room.

Bill sat beside me. But he said he could see everything, and it was a miracle. The tugs and pulls are a strange sensation. We had experienced it with Diego before. This time, it was a bit more complicated and my heart was pounding. I took several deep breaths and closed my eyes.

There he was, with an audible loud cry, 5.8 lbs.

Then one minute later "boy #2," with a soft whimper, 5.4 lbs.

Our beautiful sons, Harrison and Elijah, Diego's chosen names.

Dear Son,

From the moment your soul entered a physical body, something beyond us your heart to beat. "It" creates a life-force energy in you to love, play, give, and receive.

"It" is in everything.

"It" is itself the water, earth, air, and fire.

"It" is the sand kernel, butterfly, volcanic rock, and stars.

"It" is "you" and "you" are "It."

"You" are a microcosmic fractal of a macrocosmic oneness.

Your true self is a beautiful, unique, individual mandala.

Fly free, dear Son, in your one true self,

which always remains the same regardless of
anything that might happen in this finite world
or what anyone says or does. The colors and
hues of your tapestry are glowing. And oh what
a joy it is to see it all flowing.
   Love, Mommy

Harrison stayed overnight in the neonatal intensive care unit and was brought to my hospital room the next morning. Elijah remained in the ICU for several days. Because of weight loss after birth, he required body temperature regulation and tube feeding.

Physically, mentally, and emotionally, the separation was intolerable, and despite the fact he was across the hallway, I rejected it in every way. I had to be "connected" to both my baby boys in some way, every moment of the day. The bond I felt with them was intense and automatic. I insisted and, soon enough, the nurses let me sleep on a chair holding Harrison on my chest as I gazed at and sang to Elijah while he grasped my finger through the hole in his incubator.

When I first saw him in the incubator, I wanted to rip him out. With my breasts calling to do the feeding job for him and my hormones out of whack, I was emotional and deeply upset I couldn't yet hold and comfort him in my arms.

Worse, when Harrison and I were discharged, they said Elijah had to stay. While I understood why, I couldn't take it as we drove away. I'll never forget how much I sobbed. It felt like my heart was being cut out. Like someone was sucking out the life energy behind its pulse. It was difficult to breathe, as though he was me and I was him.

A few hours after we returned home, I drove back to the hospital with Harrison, although it was forbidden after the

C-section. Then I convinced the nurses to let me in the ICU. I sang and talked to both of them, with Harrison in my arms and Elijah holding my hand.

As I breastfed Harrison, I used a syringe to gather drops of my milk for Elijah. Soon thereafter, they let me directly breast-feed him, although they had their doubts it would work. Sure enough, it did.

The day the twins first connected with each other out-side of my womb will forever be treasured and is captured in photos. I placed a pillow on my lap, then Harrison on my left, Elijah on the right, just as they were in my belly. They in-stinctively nuzzled their heads and limbs together as if to say, "There you are, dear Brother." With my bare breasts between them, we were all three physically connected again in our own haven.

Some of the most precious, most beautiful moments ever are in this space. Observing your child move and connect to their body and surroundings for the first time is beyond fas-cinating. The soul within them alive and kicking, all the while stumbling to maneuver in a strange form.

Watching twin sons do this was altogether unique and awe-inspiring. An all-knowing grace void of any learning scale was carried between them. Like well-coordinated athletes, their limbs instinctively reached out for and successfully con-nected to each other's.

There was no need for assigning the word "hand" or using my own to bring theirs together. They simply, immediately, did it on their own. Soon blankets of "there you are" and "all is good, Brother" covered the horizon.

Since the day they were born, I have placed everything for Elijah on the right, and everything for Harrison on the left, just as they were in my womb. Car seats, high chairs, beds, cloth-ing, bottles, pacifiers, jogger stroller seats, and whatever else you can imagine during any developmental phase they were in. It helped us treat each individually, keep things organized, and cater to different preferences as best we could.

We still do this today. They actually get upset if something or someone disrupts it. "Hey, that's my seat," we'll hear one say until the other obliges. Also, the twins have always been on the same sleep and eating schedule.

When they were tiny, whoever woke up first was held in my left arm and got my breast. Like clockwork, the other twin woke up within seconds. I'd rock him with my right foot and give him a pacifier until a bottle was made and given to him using my right hand. After a few minutes had passed, I'd switch their positions. It sounds complicated, but once I had it down, it worked out well enough.

Bill knew I liked finding these kinds of weird practical solutions. He saw me do the same while on the road with Diego. I deeply appreciate how he often told me he was in awe of my mothering. He also knew I hated the thought of one twin not receiving equal attention and nurturing in any given moment. He most definitely helped as much as he could during the long nights and lack of sleep.

But as the months passed and they grew stronger, we had to figure out something else with their sleeping arrangements. Not only did Bill need his sleep, the rockers weren't safe anymore, and the twins never adapted to the cribs. I can't count the number of different things we tried.

A grandmother of twins two houses down asked on a weekly basis, "So, what's happening in the sleep arena now?" knowing all too well how difficult it was for her daughter that first year.

It took a while, but soon we realized it wasn't merely a case of wanting a bottle in the night or needing "sleep training." They were actually waking up in search of direct physical contact with each other. So I converted their room into a "womb."

We placed two twin mattresses directly on the floor on opposing sides of their woodland-themed room. A thinner foam mattress was placed in between so no hard ground was reachable.

Within days, we watched how our little bunnies came together as one. It's hard to say who initiated the process. It'd be easy to claim it was Elijah. He's always on the move. But in reality, Harrison very well might've sent subliminal messages prior.

"Brother, get your butt over here. I miss you."

Elijah exerted great effort while half-asleep. Little by little, he squirmed his way over to Harrison's body. Upon arrival, the ritual would end with a tiny touch of hand or feet. Like clockwork, Elijah lay transverse at Harrison's legs or feet every morning, just as he had in my womb. They didn't just need their mommy, her breast, or a bottle. They needed direct contact with their womb brother.

**

Harrison is like one of those charming and all-convincing Precious Moments figurines, with his massive green drop-shaped eyes framed by tousled hair. His smile and massive dimples are beyond beautiful. He was on the left side of my womb and stayed in the same position the entire time. He just hung out, all chill and content as can be. He still sleeps the same way, with his arms up to the sides of his head, never really budging from that position throughout the night. His body is strong and husky, with thick limbs and wide feet. A "gentle giant" with immense sensitivity and sweetness for everything. He loves the soft and gentle things in life. Baby animals, chocolate, puppies, shells, pinks, tiny toys, and little sea creatures. But he doesn't limit himself to those either. Next hour, he'll be holding a dart gun, chasing his brother.

Elijah is like an all-knowing, quick and graceful avatar with big blue-green eyes that can pierce you like comets. He was on the right side of my womb and journeyed all around in varying positions. Head up, head down, transverse, or sideways. He still sleeps the same way, moving comfortably from position to position. A "mighty man" with immense tenacity and curiosity for anything adventurous and challenging, he adores the strong and vivacious things in life. He is outspoken and expressive. And he loves superheroes, dinosaurs, ninjas, long sticks, blues, big trucks, and deep-sea creatures. But just like Harrison, he doesn't limit himself to those either. Next hour, he'll be wrapping a blanket around his brother.

Despite all their distinct differences, there is most definitely a consistent overlap in personality traits and interests. Both are kind, giving, and empathetic. Both are stubborn and emphatic when it comes to their opinion or desire. Both love any and all pretend play, and most often, all three of us are part of the story. Both can be feisty, unwavering, and persistent. They can fight over a toy until one gets it, but then that one eventually gives it back. If one hurts the other, they more often than not apologize and hug each other. If one gets hurt by accident, the other often comforts his brother.

They never want to be apart, and for the majority of their time since their birth, they've always been together. I could count on one hand the few times they've been separated.

The twins' stroller became a "womb" too.

It allowed me to give a sense to both boys of being held and nurtured by Mommy when it was nap time. I'd cuddle each in a blanket, sit facing the stroller, hold the bottles up, rock the stroller with a foot, and sing, looking into their eyes. When heavy eyes arrived, it was time for their pacifiers, or "mimis," and a long walk.

It worked like magic. I often walked ten miles a day. While

I grew to despise leaf blowers, I deeply appreciated the human contact, even if through a neighborly wave.

Their second nap would end in front of Diego's middle school when the final bell rang. He liked showing off his little brothers and appreciated our walks home together.

Diego played the violin in the school's orchestra. I volunteered to head up his school's annual music program fundraiser and auction and often checked in with the school's music program director in person. It felt good to be part of Diego's schooling in this way. It felt good that I was finally giving shame less power.

Beautiful feathers always appeared on our walks. I began to pick them up and keep them. Every time I did, my father entered my mind. A little "hello" from heaven was heard. Looking back, I see they were actually lights being placed in front of me, spiritual messages trying to awaken me. "Hey you! Go to your home within. Ground yourself. Strengthen your armor. Maintain that source of wholeness so you can keep your mind in check. Some things are going to happen and you'll need it every day."

My sons know why feathers carry a deep meaning for me. My father's inspiration enters my heart.

Thankfully, they've gained their own personal understandings and connection to them. They think of their "Opi" and Acjachemen ancestors. To this day, whenever they see one, they pick it up and hand it to me.

Feathers. If one presents itself to you on this road of life, pause.

If you listen, it carries a tiny yet powerful message.

If you follow the messages, you just might get your wings.

CHAPTER 14

Dear Son,

if you want to go quicker, go alone.

If you want to go further, go together.

Words will never adequately describe the twins' profoundly unique bond. Reaching out to one another is engrained in them. Deep attuned listening is automatic. It's a literal manifestation out in the world of living in harmony while in the womb. They instinctively go together.

If they approach life this way, they will indeed go further and more fully. Their example will forever serve as an inspiration to me.

Since the day of my release from Santa Ana jail, when the seven-year journey began, my head said, "Go alone and get it done quickly." Just get "better," be "ok," and "fix" it. But that's not how recovery from trauma, addiction, and chronic pain is possible.

Self-sufficiency worked well during my pregnancy with the twins and their first year. My commitment to them and the pure joy of new life obliterated cravings, reduced flashbacks, and minimized body aches. All three were kept at bay for a period of time.

Life on the outside evolved, but I was still the same Nadia inside.

While fear, shame, and resentment were always lurking, what began happening was far beyond that. Psychological warfare and physical pain slowly returned to levels I could not handle. I began to feel "off" more and more frequently.

I failed to reach out to anyone or ask for help when I was feeling this way. I hadn't yet built real, honest, and consistent relationships with a therapist, a sponsor, or the fellowship in Alcoholics Anonymous.

This is dangerous territory for someone like me who often didn't even recognize when I was "off." I was flying solo on grit, straight into a full-blown crisis and a crash landing in the embankment.

Dear Son,

I want to describe the next years in a clear, orderly way.

I want it to flow with ease like a step-by-step play.

But it's impossible to make sense of all the mistakes I made.

And even harder to accept the wreckage and pain I caused you.

All I can tell you is no amount of self-will worked.

After every "failure," shouts from the universe came.

"When the hell are you going to grab a helping hand?"

"When will you finally surrender to a higher power within?"

After every trip and fall, a different block was lifted.

I am so sorry it took so long for me to finally walk together.

Love, Mommy

***

Chronic pain. I will do my best to describe what it is like to live with mine. For other sufferers out there, I know everyone is different.

For the last two decades, physical pain has been a constant. I don't remember life without it. And frankly, I am scared of what my later life will be like if I don't stay on top of self-care.

Because physical pain has always existed, my ability to accurately gauge its level is skewed. The crappy question "What is your level of pain on a scale from 1–10?" doesn't work well for me. Tolerance of pain unintentionally twists the truth in my answer.

In my "I can handle it on my own" mode, the norm was to ignore and hide its severity. I admittedly still struggle to recognize and express the severity of my physical pain to anyone. I don't know why. Maybe because I don't want to be viewed as "the broken fragile girl."

It is a good day when I make it through without letting pain modify my to-do list. It is a bad day when sudden, piercing pains strike in my hip and literally stop me in my tracks. My leg gives in, loses strength, and walking is limited. It is a bad day when neck and shoulder pain send mentally distracting pulses up to my head. And when I feel like a bony bird being placed on a bed of needles sitting or lying down.

Gravity is not your friend when you've had a crash landing.

Since the first day I returned home from the rehabilitation hospital, my mistake has been waiting until the physical pain rises to a disabling level.

About every three months or so, the entire upper left side of my body goes haywire. My shoulder and neck pulse in a rage, eventually reducing sensation in and weakening my left arm and hand. Sometimes the left side of my face tingles, numbs, and feels like I have Bell's palsy. My patience is low, I feel dizzy, and it's difficult to hear or fully comprehend things. At these times, the "off" state takes control.

Worse, physical aches can initiate psychological warfare. For years, I had no clue that there was an interrelatedness between chronic pain and PTSD. It became an absolute nightmare to navigate and find my way out of.

It doesn't matter which comes first, they equally initiate and aggravate the other. Something triggers a flashback, my neck and shoulder ache. My neck and shoulder ache, the mind takes over and taunts me.

Like a mocking song on repeat, my head chimes in.

Tap, tap, tap, remember you're just a body.

Don't you think for a second you'll ever escape SC or physical pain.

You're just a dirty, crippled, broken little brown girl.

I thought, *That man is still harming me somehow!*

The whole saga of terror, injustice, and shame would engulf me again. There was no break, and it just rang and rang in my head.

But the psychological warfare can also come at any time, from anything, and anywhere. What does that mean? A lot, but here's a little.

It means for the past decade, a bad dream repeated over and over. It went away for a little bit but returned around this time with a vengeance.

I'm in a wooded valley surrounded by deep forest. I carry one twin attached in a sling to my body, the other with my left arm on my hip, and a few belongings hanging over my shoulder in long cloth bags. Strings fly out from them that one twin plays with. A mighty bow and arrows are carried on my right.

I am on the run and hyper-vigilant in every moment, at every turn, because SC and his friends are tracking and chasing us. To feed my babies and rest, I build a temporary tree house or cave. Sunrise is clockwork, scoping and gauging the risks, checking SC's and his friends' locations before little eyes open. If far enough, I search for snippets of food, berries to feed the twins.

I pretend we're playing a game so they're not scared of what I must do. One second, I sing them a song, the other, I look behind my back. One moment, I see my son smile, the other, I hear SC laughing at me for thinking I can feel joy.

The warrior mama I was curls away in a ball. A few moments pass, I soon shun the tears, get back up, and fight. I pull out an arrow and attempt to find an aim, but all I sense is they're lying in wait. I know I have to move us again and disturb my children's peace. They're getting too close, and their eyes are on me. I try to hide the tears every time my son asks, "Mommy, why do we have to leave again?"

After I wake up, I sit up immediately, anxious, hyper-vigilant. I run to stand still in fight, flight, and freeze modes. Feeling grounded wherever I am is impossible. The home I worked so hard to make begins to feel temporary, as though something or someone is lurking around the corner, ready to pull the rug from under me.

***

What is PTSD anyways? I had no clue then.

But I do know that I'm not here when it happens.

I do know it robs me of being present and myself.

I do know it causes disassociation, often leading to regrettable choices, and that it used to scare me, knowing how vulnerable I am to it.

I initially rejected the words "victim" and "PTSD."

I didn't feel I deserved either.

Me? I was molested and bullied as a child, but blessed too. Me? I was assaulted and blackmailed, but I put myself in danger. Me? A big rig shattered my body, but I lived. Me? I'm a strong cookie and those don't affect my life. Denial is a bitch and she had me bought.

My mind's beliefs were far from the truth. I didn't recognize the severity of my condition and didn't get help until much later. Recognizing trauma's aftermath and PTSD is one thing. Admitting it is a whole other. It felt like I was making excuses for being too screwed up to do either. I felt the system would use them against me as a mother. The public thinks the "downfall" was scandal, resignation from office, and an arrest. But the real downfall was just about to happen.

***

The first time I lost it entirely was during a family trip up north.

I should have never walked back into our Hayward house without preparing myself first, and perhaps not at all. Everything came back to life in my head like a violent tornado.

Oh, I'll be ok, I said to myself, only to find my mind racing, and that I was unable to sit still.

The front mat reminded me of the stolen key. The keyboard, the note left by SC. The computer screen, the hacking. Every single room, the horror of random threatening texts. *Bing, bing, bing,* it went, visions and memories like an avalanche.

I could not breathe. *Get the hell out, Nadia!* I thought.

But I couldn't. The boys needed my care and attention. And I didn't want to disappoint Bill, who made special plans for our Fourth of July.

At first, I took the boys outside to play to get out of the house and into fresh air. It helped a little, but I couldn't stay outside all night. When it was time to cook dinner, I got so anxious I never started.

Eventually, I told Bill I was going to take the boys on a drive to pick up pizza. I tried to explain to him that I was having a hard time being back in the house because of everything SC had done. He didn't seem to take it seriously, which just made me more emotional.

I remember driving in circles on the crest. The boys eventually fell asleep. An hour passed. Still at square one, I had no idea what to do or where to go with what was happening in my psyche.

Bill called and "woke" me up, but I didn't answer. I knew I had to go back. "I have to go back," I kept saying out loud in a panic.

The third wheel, addiction, came shouting and loving every moment. *A drink will help you manage* quickly became *I must have it to make it through until tomorrow.*

I parked right in front of a small nearby liquor store next to the college and stared through the front door at the counter and bottles behind. The boys fast asleep, I went into self-destructive ninja mode, rolled down the windows, jumped out of the car, dropped a twenty on the counter, and told the man I wanted vodka. As soon as it was in a bag, I grabbed it and ran back to the car, thinking, *Ahh, now there is relief and release.*

Who does that? I did. And I am ashamed.

I ordered a pizza for delivery at home, parked in our driveway, and sip, sip, sip was my refuge.

The pizza arrived, everyone was happy, and I had a temporary false sense of relief. It worked for the night and then the disease shouted, *Ah, now I gotcha!*

Dear Son,

Albert Einstein is widely credited with saying, "The definition of insanity is doing the same thing over and over again, but expecting different results." For me, it means having a drink while in crisis and expecting that nothing bad will happen, despite knowing that doing it only makes things worse. It obliterates any chance I'll reach out for help. It crushes all ability to take meaningful action and find solutions in the rooms of my fellowship.

The only thing I can promise you today is that I take one day at a time, fully embraced in the support of the fellowship, my sponsor, and my sober sisters. There is a solution. They are living in it. I just gotta continue living in it too.
Love, Mom

Desperate to get the help I needed while being with and caring for the boys, I called every treatment center in the state asking if they would take "us."

"Sorry, we don't do that here," I heard again and again.

Thankfully, eventually I got a call back from New Directions for Women, and they miraculously said they had space for us. But my heart sank again when they told me the cost. I had no way to pay for it without Bill agreeing, or so I thought back then.

My mind raced for a solution as I packed. I took off with the boys to the treatment center, having no idea how I'd pay for it. I felt a surge of hope when a credit card worked for the down payment. I was given a quaint room in a house with mothers and children. I quickly unpacked and settled us in. I remember cuddling with the twins in bed on the first night. They were so content and calm in our cozy little safe haven. It had been months since I had felt as peaceful and in control of the future as I did there. I got on my knees, said a prayer, and made a commitment to stay as long as needed to get better.

Over the next couple of days, the twins quickly adjusted to the amazing gift of on-site daycare in the house next door. I was then able to attend treatment groups and therapy right there on site. Within days, we had our morning-to-bedtime routine set in stone.

With every day that passed, I felt more and more empowered, happy, confident, and committed to my sobriety and healing.

I was able to do so with my children happy by my side. *You are on the road to recovery, Nadia,* I thought. I had no idea how I would pay for it but made a six-month plan for us to stay, after which I would get an apartment and work.

Another housemate and her young son became good friends with me and the boys. We shared about our diseases and how much we wanted sobriety. We talked about both living in the area and the boys' future playdates. I ran into her several years later and I'm happy to say she beat her demons and, today, is a teacher. She and her son live a healthy, happy, stable life.

Thirty days is not a long time for anything, let alone recovery.

When I mentioned the cost of treatment and housing for me and the boys to Bill, he immediately said it was not possible. No discussion or options offered. I had no checks or additional credit cards, still had no access to the marital income account, and was completely oblivious to my marital rights in financial matters. I knew the funds were there, but had no idea how to access them during this time of need.

I sank into a compliant mode within seconds. But I also felt guilty for having created any financial stress at all. Even more, he had a scheduled knee surgery around the corner and said he needed me home to help. Foolish, guilt-ridden, and naive, I made the grave, life-altering mistake of returning home again without having done any real work inside nor changed anything in my life.

Today, it is so hard to acknowledge this missed opportunity in time. Had I known my rights, enforced them, prioritized my needs, and stayed there with the boys, it's highly possible everything would have evolved differently and for the better.

A month passed together in our home. Bill had his surgery and his recovery was underway and going well. But then I began bleeding profusely in what I initially thought was merely a heavy period. After a week of this, volumes of huge blood clots fell into the toilet repeatedly. I began to feel weak and faint. When I first informed Bill, he dismissed it, accusing me of having an affair and it being a miscarriage.

I did everything in my power to convince him that wasn't the case, but felt more powerless and feeble every hour that passed. I was so desperate, I took a photo of the blood and sent it via text to my sisters to ask them for help, something I had never done before.

The entire situation spawned a feeling of being tricked and trapped by Bill, whether true or not. My mind soon churned self-centered shame, fear, and resentment with thoughts like, *I was tricked into leaving the best place I'd been in months. I am powerless to get the help I need with my children. I have to stay sick with my conditions if I want to be with them. It's Bill's fault I can't get better, and he's the reason I drink in an unhealthy marriage.* All of these mental intrigues can be so self-defeating.

I entered a severe depression. A perfect setting for the disease to start screaming again, *A drink will help you get through the pain.* There will never be anything more difficult to admit than the fact I let myself get so depressingly and sickeningly drunk to the point of suicidal ideation and an attempt. But it's the truth.

My disease had convinced me that I had no way out of my afflictions. My mind thrashed messages with such intense severity, they overcame me. *You're all alone, separate, stuck, chained. You can't escape your body and brain; you'll just be a drunk, creating more suffering for everyone. They're better off without you.*

Immediately after a part-time nanny arrived, I drank alone and cried, then swallowed a bottle of sleeping pills with vodka before lying down on the bed. I do not remember it in detail, nor as real.

Bill found me later with a very faint pulse and called 911.

When I began to wake up in the ER, my sister told me that I kept repeating, "I don't know what to do. I don't know what to do. I don't know what else to do," over and over and over again.

Dear Son,

There is a section of the book A Course in Miracles *that talks about how we often do not perceive our own best interests. What we often think they are merely binds us closer to the world of illusions. The purpose I had given the world led to a frightening picture of it. I was afraid of the outside shame and unable to handle it because I forgot who we really are within: infinite spirits that are whole, perfect, and complete. Today I continue to remind myself on a daily basis, to let my mind open to the truth of who I am, the truth of light and love all*

*around us. Therein lies the solution just as it
did back then.*
    Love, Mommy

A few days after a hospital stay to recover, I was put on a seventy-two-hour hold at Kaiser's mental health center. A few of the patients there were easy to talk to. A strange feeling of belonging among the insane entered. I felt "safer" and more "seen" than I felt in my own home.

My sister visited and begged me to leave the marriage. She put me and the boys on a shelter list and said she found a way out. But I was still terrified to leave Bill. I thought I had to convince him to agree to it. I gave her a mouthful of reasons why I had to return. She left, heartbroken and dismayed.

When I was released, I stood there alone on the curb, desperate to get home and hold my sons, look them in the eye, and let them know everything was going to be ok, as though I knew how to get there myself. I called Bill, but he did not answer. I waited. Nothing. Eventually, I took an Uber home.

***

Any suicide threat or attempt is a desperate call for help. I implore all those reading to take note. Suicidal ideation can be prevented both from within someone as well as through those around them. To prevent it, everyone needs to take part.

***

When I walked back into the house, I just stood there in shock. It felt like I was in the twilight zone. Holding the kitchen counter, I waited to hear a breath of life and hoped for a touch, a hug, my son's sweet voice. Silence.

The deep bruised ditch in my arm from the IV needle called out and my mind went, *You are just a body. Your soul is gone. No one cares whether you're here or not.*

Bill finally walked in. He set a note on the counter. "Here's a list for the handyman. He'll be here in an hour," he said, then left the kitchen, not mentioning anything about what had just happened.

He gave no simple gaze into my eyes, or brief "How are you?" No touch of his hand on mine, nor "I'm here if you need me."

Just silent, empty, blank space after the heartiest, most intense, and most desperate cry for help and love I had ever made. The reality of my pain abandoned, rejected in a heartbeat. I'll never forget it.

In that very moment, I felt like a mere ball of flesh. Like a cadaver desperately waiting to be cut open by anyone, anything, just to know it was once alive. His voice on a work call in the room next door solidified the dictate. *I am not to feel, think, be anything but a walking dead body.*

I sat down on the couch in both utter shock and numbness. There were no thoughts, tears, or ability to move. Nothing. Just absolutely nothing. When I walked upstairs to lie down on the bed, scraps of medical materials from the ambulance were still scattered on the bedspread.

The one and only thing that kept my heart beating in that moment was the fact that my children's hearts were beating somewhere close by. *Breathe, Nadia, breathe. The air in their lungs, the blood in their veins will revive you,* I thought. That flicker of light and hope emanating from their very presence never faltering or failing.

My Journal Entry

Changing my twin baby boy, Harrison, a bit upset and restless. His brother is happily

*playing nearby, lying on the carpet. I kiss his
forehead and nose, rub my fingers along his
hairline. He calms, takes a deep breath, gives
me one of those "I'm ok" kinds of looks straight
in the eyes, with his so so so big set, I mean
huge, beautiful, unique eyes.*

*He does not know I've had a hard night,
a difficult yesterday. He does not know. He is
too young. I do know he knows love, safety, and
warmth . . . joy, stillness, and fun. I know he
feels adored and cared for.*

*Still, in that moment, I began to softly cry
. . . a few tears filling my eyes, one falling down
my face. And he noticed. As I buried my face in
his chest, hugging him, I silently talked to our
Creator, saw my son's eyes through the darkness of mine closed, and prayed . . . I prayed to
be held through the day, to make it a good one,
to be truly present, here and now, every second
. . . not "running to stand still," no dark memories haunting my brain, nor body aches and
pains stiffening, stifling me.*

*Wiping my tears, still looking down, smell-
ing his skin, breathing new life, I tell myself,
"I will get out of this place," one more time, as
Daddy did. Giving thanks in my heart for all
the depth of blessings and beauty before me.
Gratitude for my son, for all three, right then
and there before me.*

*"This too shall pass," I silently, mentally
chanted. All is indeed exactly as it should be,
perfect in its imperfection, perfect in its yearning and strife, perfect in its eventual grace and
glory. As I lifted and held my head high, with*

a smile big on my face, I immediately received
one from my baby boy in return.

When the twins awoke shortly thereafter, they ran into my arms with all the might of baby cubs. Sure enough, a surge of utmost strength and commitment flowed in immediately. All doubt, darkness, and despair disappeared in an instant. I was suddenly a strong tiger mama giving them brief words of reassurance and, despite my wounds, would carry on in glory for them, and for me.

I called my therapist, sponsor, and sisters, letting them know I needed and was getting help for depression and drinking. I came up with a plan and presented it to Bill. We'd live separated for a few months and go to marriage counseling. I would live in the house with the boys, have childcare help, which he had somewhat objected to prior, and thus be able to go to therapy, meetings, and Kaiser. He would stay at his friend's home and go to Al-Anon and counseling. If that worked, then maybe we'd think about reuniting under the same roof. He agreed.

It was a major step forward on the road to creating a better relationship, as well as being the best parents we could be, both admitting our faults yet committed to doing something about them.

Sadly and tragically, a week later all hopes and intentions were destroyed and nothing would ever be the same for our family. Children's Services showed up and insisted I leave. But not just leave. They required I leave without my children.

What? How? Why? There can't possibly be a
when? Nowhere in this lifetime did I ever, ever
imagine this. My heart is being gouged out.
Their hearts will be stopped. Who will care for

them? Where will they go? How can ripping their lives apart be good for them? How can this help anyone? Why do you, the system, so easily barge in and destroy families' lives? Why do you so easily break children's hearts?

The twins heard their words, grabbed my legs, and began to sob uncontrollably. I fell to the ground and embraced them, having no words or way to comfort. I could not breathe, move, or think.

The entire concept of separation from my children was incomprehensible to me. But more importantly, it was deeply and gravely traumatizing for them, their innocent minds forever etched with the memory of forced abandonment.

The twins and I were together twenty-four seven. The cells of our bodies breathed in synchronicity, from the moment we woke to the second we lay our heads down to sleep at night.

Being a mother, a good mother, was and is the single most joyous, important, and purposeful thing in my life. My children are the reason I fought to live, the impetus for finally recognizing I was suffering from depression and PTSD, the very motivation for finding strength and seeking help.

But they forced me to leave my sons. I was forced to leave them.

I was forced to give them the trauma of abandonment.

The thought of their pain, confusion, and fear suffocated me.

The world was ending. How could this be?

I drove to my sister's, sobbing. I dove into flight mode and drowned the pain away with a bottle of vodka. Bam! *Just disempower yourself a little more, Nadia!*

The next morning I had a residual blood alcohol content high enough to be pulled over and arrested for driving under the influence. Another drink in crisis adding more wreckage.

And when more wreckage is added, getting deep down into the real work of recovery and healing is further pushed out on the horizon.

Dear Son,

I have had a dream repeat itself since very early childhood. I sit on the floor near the closet with an overwhelming tangled mass of string before me. It is so big, I can't see anything else beyond it.

I scramble to find an end of the string. When I finally do, I begin to carefully, slowly roll it into a ball. But there is so much tangled string surrounding me, it feels like forever. Around and around in circles I go with one hand, meticulously crisscrossing each line over the other, the hand holding the ball tightly grasping.

Like a sewing machine in auto mode, my focus is impenetrable. It goes on and on this way until my head begins to hurt. At some point, I finally see the end of the string. I sense a forthcoming relief, sit up straight, and smile.

But suddenly in that joy, the ball bursts out into the air from my hands. The string scatters all around me in a drowning, massive, tangled mess.

I sit back and mock myself for thinking it would end any other way. I know the dream all too well and think, What else did you expect?

I used to wake up in a state of anxiety when I had this dream.

I didn't know what to do then with what was going on in my head.

*I am so sorry, dear Son, I am so very sorry I
didn't figure that out first.*

*I am so sorry I did not master that skill be-
fore I brought you into this world. Please know,
please know, your mommy found a better way
to live.*

Love, Mommy

My sons are life itself.
They are souls of love, light, warmth, and hope.
They hold the source of my life in this world.
They are the air I breathe. The light I sense.
They are the raindrops on leaves and the reason to dance.
They are the reason I survive and the reason to grow.
They are the impulse to get up again after every fall.
They are the energy itself used to dig my way out.

***

You'd think I'd get better once the system got involved. You'd
think I'd dive deeper into the real issues inside. Tragically,
the system's messages implore mothers to "Just be 'ok' and act
'normal,' dear," and, "Don't cry or flinch, else you be deemed
unstable, unhealthy, unfit, and unworthy."

While every future relapse brought me closer to the underlying truth inside, every single one of them was a direct
result of never being able to drop into the space of vulnerability in the middle. I had to go alone and quicker and be "ok"
for the system in order to prevent further separation from my
children.

The system punishes vulnerability. It rebukes diving deep
into one's psyche for wisdom. It shuns brutal honesty and
forces ignorance of the underlying truth.

No judge or social worker wants to hear, "I'm in a depth of emotional, mental, and physical pain and need a way out. Please help me stop my mind from convincing me a drink is the only relief out there." They'd simply say, "Lock her up and take her children away!" adding to the factory line of generational trauma, addiction, and shame.

If you really want an answer to the question, "Why does she/he do that?" then ask that person! Allow them to be vulnerable. Allow the truth to come out.

But can you handle it? Probably not. Why? Because then you'd have to admit that those causing hurt to others need to be permitted the space, time, and place where they can be vulnerable and heal without fear of their children being taken away and of the system's judgment and shaming.

Don't tell me it isn't possible. It can be done. Then and only then can the cycle stop.

I'm sick and tired of the system banishing vulnerability.

When will they give a mother and her children the opportunity to get, stay, and remain somewhere safely together and be supported for as long as needed?

When will judges and social workers say, "I see you. I hear you. We're sorry we keep banging your head against the wall. Here's the support and help you need to get out of hell. Go with your children and you won't go to jail. And by the way, the man that hurt you is being punished instead." Why not provide daily coaching, counseling, a mentor for both child and parent? Daily workshops where sobriety is the requirement?

I know it's insane to think this could happen.

But we can't sentence mental illness and think that will cure it.

If this sounds like pure blame, well, I include myself in it. I am pissed off at myself for all the unhealthy choices. I am pissed off that my children had to carry the toll. I am pissed off it took so long to find space to heal.

I "failed" the system time and time again. I admit it. But something about saying that doesn't feel right too. Something about it ignores the underlying truth. The important space between stimuli and response.

Whether it was the doctor's reckless actions ignored, carrying the pain of losing those I love alone, the shattering of my body by a big rig, the bad guy never prosecuted, the press's shaming, and more, I responded to each with "unhealthy" choices.

But what happened in the middle? What happened in my head, heart, and psyche? For many like me, it's called all-consuming feelings of shame, fear, and resentment. What can be done to give those less power? Being able to discover a home within us that keeps those mind-made emotions in check. But we can't get there unless we are allowed the journey. We can't force people to act "ok," to be stamped "ok" to be with loved ones.

It forces going alone and quicker. It doesn't work.

We have to go together through the middle so we can go further in the end.

Dear Son,

Please know whenever you are in pain, I am here to hold space for you to be vulnerable, acknowledge your truth, and find freedom through it. The wisdom is in the middle. You don't have to go alone, quicker, and act "ok" if you're not. Please go together, dear Son, so you can go further and wholeheartedly in your truth.

Love, Mom

CHAPTER 15

Dear Son,
truth is your identity.

Somehow, someway, my sister found a healing, safe place for me to get better. The angels of Dee's House provide a warm and empowering home for women to heal from trauma and related substance abuse. I knew I needed help, always knew it. There was always something much deeper I had yet to identify eating at my soul. I never understood why I lived life in a constant "running to stand still" survival mode.

As soon as I walked in the door, angels' wings surrounded me.

Real recovery began. *It began, dear Son. It began.*

Mariam Paul, MFT, is a wise, beautiful, older woman. She is one of my angels. She wears colorful, unique garments with grace. She is a lover of life and a giver of love, determined to help women discover who they truly are inside, what real love is.

In our first session, she took out a piece of paper and drew two huge circles. In one, she said, "This is your ego mind" and in the other "your true self."

"The ego will do anything and everything to keep you disconnected and in power." Huh? What does that mean? Aren't I the one who does the thinking?

"You are not a body, Nadia. You are not your ego mind," she replied. "You are just as God made you, whole, perfect and complete."

But I made the bad choices, and I am screwed up! What the heck is she talking about?

> I am not a body. I am free.
>
> Freedom must be impossible as long as you perceive a body as yourself . . . The mind can be made free when it no longer sees itself as a body, firmly tied to it and sheltered by its presence . . . The ego holds the body dear because it dwells in it, and lives united with the home that it has made. It is a part of the illusion that has sheltered it from being found illusory itself.
>
> —*A Course in Miracles*, Lesson 199, sections 1–3

I had a sense of believing in my heart what she was telling me. I wanted to believe it.

I had a glimpse of that deep connection to my spirit, the infinite realm I entered into near death. I have longed to return there in all the wrong ways.

But "me" was cut off the moment they brought me back to life.

Poke, poke, poke, "you are a body," the childhood memory returned in a dime so many times.

Drip, drip, drip, the morphine entered my veins and set in motion a physical disease and curse.

"Tap, tap, tap," my body screams in pain. Sometimes subtle, but too often intense. It is a constant, the way I have to live. Like a battered metal vessel reminding me, repeating, *No, no, no, little girl, not for a moment will I let you be. You are mine for the rest of time, I will make you suffer in me.*

I can't ask for another body to continue carrying this soul. I don't have the option others do to quell the pain with a pill. I'm simply a soul in a violated and shattered body that won't shut the hell up. "And you're asking me to believe I am something else?" I asked.

That's not fair, I thought. *In fact, it angers me you even think I can. But where does that get me, dear Son? Where does that attitude bring us?*

I must get past my body and see the truth beyond.

"If I am not a body, then what is it I am?" I asked.

"You are love, light, warmth, spirit—infinite and beautiful," Mariam said. Ouch, it hurt to even hear that.

"Our minds strive incessantly to be in control and shut that one truth out. Everything is a threat to it. It has to send attack thoughts like fear, shame, and resentment in order to stay in control. It seeks to be the one and only thing you think is life. But when you see what you really are, you're halfway there."

"But my body is cursed, marked, bruised and damaged," I said.

"Your body or your soul?" she asked.

"All of the above . . . and more," I replied.

"Would you say that to your son if he was hurt by someone and tried to handle the pain unhealthfully? Heck, maybe even became addicted to something? Or attracted an abusive partner?" she pushed.

How dare she ask me that. "Well, of course not," I replied.

"Then what is he?" And it is there that she got me.

"My son is love, light, warmth, and spirit—infinite and beautiful, beyond all time and space. I sense him here and all around me and send my energy and love his way," I responded, a tad feisty and protective.

"Ok then, when you shut down after the doctor molested you, when you starved yourself when your family fell apart, when you drank and got high to feel loved, escape pain, find freedom from bad memories and flashbacks—did any of that change who and what you are at the core when you were born in spirit form?"

I started to sob and could not stop.

"What would your father tell you? What does he tell you today? I know you've heard him. I know he speaks to you," she added.

The lingering question sat with me like a boulder had knocked my head open.

Daddy, where are you? What am I? Please tell me, please remind me.

"Underwater"
There you go, off to somewhere.
Here I am, standing where you were.
And the sun fell over the valley.
Found myself staring at you,
on the wall staring back at me.
And the sun fell over the valley.
In my conscious, in my dreams, flashes of
    you come in streams.
Are you by me? Do you love me still?
Took a drive off to somewhere.
There I was driving where you were.
And the sun fell over the valley.

Found myself looking for you, anywhere,
    looking back at me.
And the sun fell over the valley.
In my body, in my head, flashes of you
    come in bed.
Are you by me? Do you love me still?
I keep dreaming, I get lost, underwater,
    turned and tossed.
Can you help me? Do you love me still?
In my conscious, in my dreams, flashes of
    you come in streams.
Are you by me? Can you help me still?
I keep dreaming, I get lost, underwater,
    turned and tossed.
Can you help me? Do you love me still?
Here I am, cursing upward, at the sky.
Wondering where you are.
And the sun fell over the valley.
There you are . . . There you are . . . There
    you are.

Lyrics by Mark Phillip Davis, © 2000
    Inkling Music
(From the album *Immaculate* by Mark Davis)
Website: markdavisinklings.bandcamp
    .com

***

I remembered my father's words, "Every little victory counts," and said to myself, *Just stay on the path and you'll see,* even though it was very hard to believe.

What would my father have said to me when I was in pain and wanting to drink like him? Maybe if I was listening, trying to connect, he would have sent a gut feeling somewhere. If I was attuned and aware, I most definitely would've heard him say:

"Don't repeat the same mistakes your grandfather and I made!"

"You're almost there. Keep going, dear."

"Don't let your mind fill with shame like it did those before us."

"Go now, dear. Find out what you really are."

"You are not a body. You are love and light. I know that for sure."

"Let yourself cry now, let it all out."

"You don't have to pretend you're ok or hide."

Mariam helped me see that I am not a body. She helped me understand how my mind's thoughts, in any given moment, cut me off from my true self. Worse, how they cut me off from any connection with my father's spirit and an intuitive truth right within me. Indeed, the only real thing in the end.

If I was treated like just a body, then I came to believe I was. If I came to believe I was just a body, then I allowed myself to be treated as one.

"The only time we suffer is when we have a thought that argues with reality," Mariam said. And so the work began to discover the illusions my mind was making.

> So with the feathers we gathered, dear Son, I began to build my wings. I began to see that shame, fear, and resentment took me away from you and me. I began to see that my body's aches and pains sometimes easily let them in.

***

All the while, the pain of separation from my children intensified and became harder. The twins were too little to understand I didn't have a choice every time they begged yet were unable to stay with me after a visit. All I could say was "I love you always. Mommy will be back home soon," or something of the sort. But no words could ever really quell the confusion and fear in their hearts. It was heart-wrenching. The same went for Diego. All I could say was "I love you. I miss you. I'm sorry."

> *Dear Son,*
>
> *During those painful nights, I'd breathe and try to quiet my mind. The only thing that helped was to remember what I saw and felt that night I died. It is there where we were and are together at all times. I'd send angels' wings and envision their glow of love surrounding you sleeping. Kisses on your cheeks with a silent, sweet "Mommy loves you." That one truth and vision kept me going. I hope you felt it, my dear Son. I hope you always felt my love along the road.*
> *Love, Mommy*

***

Thankfully, during this time I found kundalini yoga and the Seventh Chakra Yoga family.

I cannot over-emphasize how the absolute beauty of this particular practice began to restore my life. It did not happen overnight. It simply remained a part of my journey from there on out. Today it is much more than that. It is everything to me.

I will forever hold deep gratitude for the beautiful blessing and presence of Priya Jain, a constant guide and light along my journey (www.seventhchakrayoga.com).

I won't try to convince you that kundalini yoga is the most brilliant physiologically designed technology to balance the mind, body, and spirit. But frankly, it truly is.

The word "kundalini" sounds funny, like a roller-coaster name. It is quite the opposite of that. "Kundalini" is a Sanskrit term from ancient India that describes the rising of an energy and consciousness, a life force, or "prana," in each of us. Since birth, it is coiled at the base of the spine.

With a combination of breath work; exercises, or Kriyas; meditation; and sound, mantra or music, anyone can tap into energy and consciousness. It is not some strange power that only the weird "yoga people" get. Quite the contrary, kundalini yoga was made for all. Everyone has access to the bridge it provides to spiritual awareness, a sense of well-being, and, ultimately, that home within.

The first time I took a class, I was eager yet skeptical. It was painful to just sit on the ground that long. My broken back would scream right in the center and I'd have to change positions. The limited range of motion in my once entirely shattered upper left side of my body made it even more difficult to hold certain positions. My once broken hip and pelvic bone would click on leg motions designed to engage my core. There were so many physical reasons I could've stopped.

But kundalini yoga's use of breath, sound, and mantra pierced through me. Blocks were broken—physical, mental, and spiritual.

Hands down, no amount of physical therapy and pain medications prior could match the immediate release of body aches and surge of endurance through pain I felt while combining breath with movement. Through the practice of "pranayama," conscious awareness of breath used to both energize and relax the body, the physical pain I experienced became more tolerable. My range of motion slowly increased. Eventually, with the use of breath, I was able to lessen and delay chronic pain flare-ups to the extent I felt more in control of my body.

And meditation? Well, it was a lost cause in the beginning. I was a mess in my head, and nothing could stop the often agonizing chatterbox. But by repeating a mantra out loud, my mind's harmful voice started to lose its reign, even if just during the actual class. Never in my lifetime had I ever attempted to put my mind in its place.

Chanting mantras is an ancient practice that calms your mind and soul. Scientific studies have found that just chanting one word for ten minutes can decrease anxiety and depressive symptoms in the human body; it can wipe out shame in its tracks. Its psychosomatic power is in one's hands just like our breath. Hell, if our ego minds are "chanting" crap thoughts over and over again, why not counter with a "screw you" saying? You pick the word or phrase. And just do it, just start.

I clearly remember having a breakthrough while chanting a mantra during this mid-phase of my healing and recovery. I was so fragile, wounded, and vulnerable, everything being thrown at me seemed overwhelming. We were guided in a class to repeat and listen in song to "Sa Ta Na Ma"—birth, life, death, rebirth. In silent yet powerful and welcoming tears, I surrendered for the first time to the turbulent chaos in my life, fully believing it all must be leading me somewhere, somehow. I didn't need to know its direction or ultimate outcome. I simply had to let go.

Dear Son,

Equally impactful was my exposure to the power of sound, the currents created both through gong and sound bowls. The song "Good

Vibrations" by the Beach Boys didn't come from nowhere.

The sound current simply broke through to my cells. Physically, I could feel it in my bones. Mentally, it brought me to a place of peace and calm. It spoke to me in more ways than one, and forced me to just shut up and lie down.

Love, Mommy

Priya,

In my level 1 training, I had an "out-of-body experience" that wasn't close to where I was, or what I saw when I "died," but was indeed a "middle ground."

In that experience, many different faces flashed before me, like a black-and-white slide-show . . . I did not know "who" they were, but I knew them somehow, as though they were my tribal ancestors. It was as if they were speaking to me without words, some saying thank you, others urging me to go on, others reminding me of who I am.

I silently cried. An understanding and self-forgiveness arose, something I had never tapped into before. It all was clear and written. I am carrying the load of my ancestors' unfinished work, and though so much is my own, I heard, "You can do both, you have thus far; go on, dear one, go on, and you will find the way."

Past, present, future, all in one . . . everything made sense, and I began to forgive myself.

Thank you for leading me to today.

—Nadia

In kundalini yoga, I also found two words that served as a bridge back to that home within me—"Sat Nam." In the ancient Sikh language Gurmukhi, "Sat" means "truth." "Nam" means "name." Together "Sat Nam" essentially translates into something deeper—"I am truth" or "Truth is my identity."

I had allowed my identity to be based on everything outside me. Titles, roles, successes, the approval of others, my marriage, what was said by the press and the system, even motherhood. As Buddha put it, my life was existential suffering by virtue of physical existence and my inability to locate myself, misplacing my identity in something or someone else.

What was my original face underneath all that? That unique authentic individual form, completely clear, a place to belong, a home within my heart? For it is in there, and only there, that I could experience real peace and joy. *I started to search, dear Son. I knew it lay in your eyes. I knew it lay in my father's. But had I ever looked in mine?*

Dear Son,

I fell in love with the practice and was later certified as a kundalini yoga instructor. Over the following years, I completed two Level 2 certifications, Consciousness Communication and Mind & Meditation, and a Master Course in the Japji language that the practice is so beautifully grounded in.

It is in this practice I eventually found the map of our existence, a daily guide to our home within. It is this beauty I seek to share with others. It is this truth of what we are that will bring us all to healing.

Love, Mommy

I had begun a spiritual journey and was finding my way back to the "Nadia" I was born to be. I set out to recreate my life with the boys.

***

After months of hard work to recover and heal, it started to pay off for things on the "outside." I finally mustered the guts to try to live under a different roof than Bill and eventually begged him to co-sign a lease for an apartment. It was close to Seventh Chakra Yoga and all my AA meetings.

The boys were returned to me half the time. I drove back and forth between two cities, sometimes twice a day to keep them on the same schedule. When they were in school, I did AA, kundalini yoga, work, and chores. Months passed in this routine.

But "I" was doing what "I" needed to do, and "I" automatically operated as though "I" didn't need anyone else to help me do it. It was me and my children versus the outside world. The tiger mama and warrior woman was fighting for her life like a vigilant loner. Self-will and reliance ran riot. Sadly, the connection to the home within me and my truth began to waiver and was replaced with that same reptilian, ego-driven survival mode.

Fact is, I was terrified to be alone in the very loneliness I had created. I still had no ability to get close to people in order to create authentic bonds in the fellowship of AA and other women in recovery, let alone a man.

I had a slew of healthy people ready and able to receive a call for help and guidance, but the "I am different" and "no one can relate to my story" beliefs infiltrated my head.

Without my children there on any given day, I was a lonely puppy dog longing for love's embrace.

If at any point in my early adult life I had a chance of

creating healthy attachments, it died along with my father's passing and all the sudden deaths that occurred thereafter.

So what did I do at this time in my life? The only thing I knew.

I tried to find unconditional love and security in unhealthy attachment. I believed I could receive those in the arms of a man. Yes, a man became my drug of choice, my disease, silly me. I thought, *Bill and I are in the middle of a divorce, so what's the harm?*

Lonely and exhausted from caring for the boys in my time alone, I justified the relationship in my head when they were with their father. I told myself, *We "connect" over long conversations about each other's pain, we actually walk together on the beach and snuggle. We help each other with practical chores and difficult days, spending nights in each other's arms.*

But this man was also unstable and a recovering addict. I was blinded to his inability to find work and stay sober, having unhealthy empathy for his core problems. I gave him chance after chance after chance, trying to save him in unhealthy attachment.

The result was disastrous. My meetings and yoga practice suffered greatly. Worse, I still had no inkling of the intense trauma work I needed and the negative effects of deep-rooted trauma on my everyday functioning and finding healthy attachment.

Every time I tried to end things, he became suicidal. He would write, "Nadia, I am sorry. I love you," with chalk on the sidewalk and streets where I lived. Somewhere in my sick mind existed a thought that it meant he really did. I couldn't see past the false belief that I had to save him.

My flashbacks and nightmares became more frequent under the stress and anxiety of the situation. It all seemed too familiar. Picture frames of finding my brother after he attempted suicide, memories of SC's texts when he threatened to take his life, visions of a razor and blood on his wrist ran rampant day and night. I should have reached out, but I was far gone in my head by then.

At one point, the man I was in a new relationship with hopped over the fence and stood peering through the sliding door. My kids were present. I insisted he leave, or I was going to call the police. He did but an hour later, when I took the boys on a walk so they would nap, he sat on the curb just a block away.

My body tightened up, mouth clenching. People started setting off leftover fireworks—it was, after all, July 5th. I did what I'd been taught and reached out to my sister, as my cell phone was inundated with texts in which he threatened to take his own life.

Was it real? Fake? Did he really mean it? Or not? I couldn't decipher things to understand what reality to hold on to. Confusion and panic evolved into an automatic drive. The boys asleep in the stroller, I crossed the street, bought a bottle of booze, went to the apartment, set it on the counter, put the boys in bed, sat down on the kitchen floor, and stared at the bottle.

I heard knocks on the door as he called repeatedly, "Please, Nadia, please!" I grabbed the bottle, poured a drink, and started consuming the devil.

After a year of sobriety, it hit me hard, really hard.

With every continued knocking on the door, my heart raced more and more. *Another drink will help you through,* my disease lied.

My phone in hand, still sitting on the floor, I called 911. After a jumbled explanation that there was a suicidal man stalking me at my door, I hung up and had another drink. By the time the police arrived, responding to my call for help, I was drunk on the floor, crying in a ball. Unbeknownst to me, the boys had woken up, opened the front door, and were on the sidewalk unsupervised when the police arrived. I was arrested, not the suicidal stalker, and thereafter successfully added a few more labels to the list.

Some may say I'm crazy to have shared so much. I do not care, unless someone ever dares to use it to shame my sons.

Today I firmly believe that having the courage to share the truth may help another woman and, most importantly, another parent recognize and hopefully get the help they need to address trauma and related substance abuse. We have to start somewhere. How about starting with our truths?

Maybe shame won't have the same power.

Maybe courage will be found, knowing another has recovered.

Six months later, I received a text from that man's roommate saying, "X killed himself." To this day, I do not know if it's true. It doesn't matter. I'll still blame myself.

***

I had not yet learned how past trauma and my unhealthy attachment system affected me detrimentally. I did not realize how I set myself up for deep, overwhelming feelings of abandonment and low self-worth.

Nor had I yet acknowledged and taken responsibility for the fact that PTSD often landed me with a drink in hand.

CHAPTER 16

Dear Son,
good and bad come in waves,
but the truth remains the same.

Dear Son,

I had climbed up from the embankment and was standing on the side of the road. I began to see my face and soul again, the path ahead of me. But I started to forget the truth of what I am. I gave my power away, seeking love and security in the arms of a man. I blinded myself to the footsteps of all the women who'd walked before. I let my diseases run wild, unaddressed.

I failed you again, dear Son, I failed you.

I am so sorry I let my self-made loneliness win.

Love, Mommy

The court gave me the same choice I had been given before.

Treatment or jail. My children suffered again greatly from forced separation.

I feel selfish to even mention how hard it was to be apart when indeed it was my unfinished work that caused it. The heartbreak was just too much at times.

I cried myself to sleep every night, obsessing about the damage done. *How would they learn to trust human connection again?* I worried about all the confusion and questions they carried in their little heads. *How would they receive full attention to their feelings that only a mother can give? All the anxiety and unmet needs they had to carry so young. How could it be that I, Nadia, had done this to my children? The woman who was obsessed with being the best mother on the planet?*

I saw them just three times a week for a few hours. Every time I saw my dear sons' innocent confusion and how they begged for me, maintaining a confident motherly stance for their benefit became more and more difficult. *If they hear and see in my eyes the belief that everything will be "ok," maybe it'll ease their pain,* I thought. Still, the moment they drove away crying, I broke down in tears and hid in my room.

To see my child suffer, but have no power to stay and comfort. To see my child hurting, while being forced to leave.

It is the deepest pain any human can feel.

What on earth had I let my unfinished work do to them?

My Journal Entry

My dear little guy. I am so sorry.

I am so sorry for my actions that caused this. I am so sorry I didn't know what to do in the panic. I am so sorry the system is so screwed up.

Why can't you be here with me as I get the

help needed? Why do they make you suffer for having a mother in need? Why am I cursed with this brain and body while I try so hard to be the mother you need?

"Too many classes, Mommy, it's too long," you say. I know, dear one. I know. I have no choice. They make me leave. They say, "Try harder, crawl more, bleed more, do more, do it again, and again, and again . . . crawl more, bleed more, cry more, bleed more, and more and more . . . until you can no longer anymore."

I say to them, "The pain always comes, more and more when you make us part. How can I focus on the work needed when you are breaking my heart? I know you try to break me, to think I've had enough. But you'll see, I will fight till the end of all pain for them . . . You'll see."

Your mother is stronger than the system will ever know.

I will never give up, dear Son, never.

No, not I.

Love, Mommy

In the ponds of tears, the tiger-mama instinct took over entirely. Anger and fear fueled a vicious fight to prove myself to everyone, for my children's sake. My entire daily life was consumed with working my way up the mountain until I received a stamp that I was "ok" from the system.

The difference this time was that I was aware of it. *Ok*, I thought, *I'll play your game.*

I knew in my heart I was a good mother and person inside despite my diseases and mistakes. I knew my diseases and mistakes could someday be a chest full of wisdom for my children and others in need.

***

For the following year, I worked day in and day out, doing everything I could to rebuild our lives. Cleaning up the wreckage and digging my way out was beyond challenging, but I committed myself to go above and beyond what was expected of me.

I completed ninety days of inpatient treatment and saw the boys three times a week. Afterwards, I enrolled myself in a ninety-day outpatient program at Kaiser and continued working with pain management.

I voluntarily had an alcohol ankle monitor installed that tested me every half hour through the skin.

I had a rigorous weekly schedule that included eighteen months of parenting classes two times a week, calling into three different entities to test every day, several months of community service hours at a local women's shelter, daily attendance at AA, and weekly therapy.

I was also approved to and enrolled in the State Bar's Alternative Discipline Program, a supportive alternative when a link between mental illness and/or substance abuse is found in the commission of a crime that does not involve moral turpitude.

I got more involved in AA. I even moved closer to the fellowship hall that would become my family and refuge. For the first time, I started to really listen and feel comfortable and accepted. I began to open up and allow myself to be vulnerable and brutally honest, even when I was fearful of judgment and no one relating to me.

Everyone knew about my sons and that motherhood was my priority. It turned out the vast majority related to my story.

Morning meetings forced my interaction with members, and I began creating healthy friendships. They would prove to be angels later. I want to thank them all here, but anonymity is sacred.

For months, I was limited to only three days a week, four hours each, with the boys. So I became a parent volunteer at their playgroup, and it added more time. I did my best to be active in their daily life, checking on the little things a mother does—the length of their nails, slight congestion in their chest, pants getting too short, and so much more.

I also moved closer to where the boys were living under Bill's roof. The practicality of visits at my place became more manageable for everyone. With the sand a block away and a huge front gated patio, we fell in love with the area and began making hundreds of treasured memories.

Perhaps more importantly, the move closer addressed a long-standing chasm in my heart, a desire to give my sons grounding in one home filled with unifying love. But I was now fully aware I would lose my mind again if I lived under the same roof as their father.

The proximity of our homes began to create a feeling of community and teamwork for them. Mommy and Daddy were just a hop, skip, and a jump from each other. We could both easily drop and pick them up from school, have direct exchanges, all the while keeping boundaries in a separate abode. Healthy coparenting began.

Still, Bill had complete control of the boys under his roof for months and months. Despite all the hard work I had done for close to a year, social services still hadn't let up restrictions or approved overnights with me. An unhealthy sense of being forced to succumb to Bill's control or inappropriateness in order to be with my children was ever present and triggering.

Thankfully, I was still working with Mariam, my therapist. Healthy boundaries and managing more minor present-day triggers became our focus. Mariam always told me relation-ships are opportunities to heal. That the actions of others trig-ger core wounds in us that need to be heard.

"What did he do? What did it bring up in you?" she'd ask after an interaction with Bill.

"He looked at my breasts then smirked at me in the midst of trying to tell him something important. I got a funny feeling in my tummy. He has control of the children and finances. I can't say anything. I must 'take it.' I can't escape it," I'd say.

"But how does it make you feel," she'd push. "What are the feelings?" Geez, I struggled for so long with that damn ques-tion. Still do. She'd push and push as I always went back to the present incident. "No, Nadia. What is the core wound?"

"It makes me feel unseen, powerless, ashamed," I said. Once tapped in, the focus immediately turned away from whatever triggered me and how. Instead, it increased my awareness of what happens in my head along with past unrelated hurtful experiences still swimming inside that I had to acknowledge and let go of.

"Listen to that hurt child, Nadia. Let her come out. The trigger will lose its power. Who is she really? What does she need? The ego mind sends messages to distract you."

The mere process of identifying the cycles inside, the truth in the middle of stimuli and my response, always helped quell and prevent minor present-day triggers from turning into im-mediate responses or disassociation. I fumbled. I do all the time. But observing became a little more habitual. It was never all Bill. It was me and my responses to him.

Mariam also introduced me to a forty-day submersion in *A Course in Miracles*, which can be overwhelming when you first see the book. It looks and initially sounds like another version of the Bible. But the shorter presentation is graspable, simple, and straightforward.

Without a doubt, its basic teachings mapped out how our

minds' illusion-making separates us from who we really are. It was added to the list of hefty efforts made to release myself from identification as "a body" and other shame-based thoughts coming from the outside world.

A morning routine of meditation, readings, coffee, journaling, and AA kicked off my day every day that entire year. It still does. Without this daily practice, life would be very different. My mind is less vulnerable to thoughts as well as others' behaviors around me when I remain steadfast in discipline and routine.

Back then, I put words like "suffering is a choice" and "I am not a body" on Post-its and placed them on my visor, repeating them throughout the day.

Dear Son,

There will always be waves on the journey. The "good" and the "bad" arrive through currents in life. Mental, emotional, and physical ebbs and flows. But if we dive into the middle between the world's stimuli and our responses, you will not only find the truth of what and why you are feeling something and react in a certain way, you will dig through it all and find that truth is your real identity.

Trust me, if hindsight allowed compartmentalization of "recovery," I'd do it. I'd make "to-do lists" and flow charts for the world in hopes it'd stop others' pain. But diving into the middle can be messy, curvy, scattered, and a ton of hard work. "Failures" suck, yet carry new revelations and direction if we look. As molten layers clear away, we can return to our home within and life alive.

Love, Mom

***

I was working my butt off in so many ways. I was "managing present-day triggers," as we called them, maintaining sobriety, and fulfilling court demands. It all became fragile when I began a newly prescribed medication for pain, gabapentin. One day I suddenly felt faint, as though I'd fallen into a black hole. The left side of my face warmed, numbed, and drooped, the Bell's palsy thing. Left hand curled up, arm weakened. Fully aware of my past sensitivity to medication, the prescribing doctor immediately advised I titrate off and go to the ER. I did. But in the midst of this, my nightmares returned.

I had opened my heart to a male friend who became a lover. This man was a good person, stable, successful, brilliant. Thankfully, also tall, dark, strong, and handsome. A long-serving special operations marine, he too suffered from PTSD and chronic pain. We understood and supported each other, never interfering with each other's internal work and progress.

Yet not even a special operations combat marine and nearly a year of sobriety could protect me from the warfare in my head.

My Journal Entry

"Wake up, Nadia, wake up . . . you're dreaming." His strong, large arms wrap around me from behind. "You're safe with me," he said. "You're safe. You're safe," he repeated from a space far away while I was in the midst of mental hell. I couldn't wake up. I couldn't wake up. Like a mocking curse, I could not get out.

In a dark hallway, an unfamiliar place, two faces were sitting with a stick or long hand. Fumblers jabbing at me, down there, way down there in my private place . . . I try to endure it, but no longer can. "Stop, please stop, please stop" . . . but I'm glued there, chained, cannot get up.

"I want out, let me out, let me out, please! This is not my creation, this is not me. Let me leave, please, oh please. I want to create my own back and forth, my own tide, my own life."

"Wake up, Nadia!" he shouts, literally picking me up, shaking me out, saving my soul.

"Please hold me, please hold me, please hold me, dear one, please," I repeated over and over.

The nightmares repeated a few times over the course of a week or so. Most often he was not there to wake me up and my sleep was disturbed. When he was there, he knew I was off and clearly understood. He would cook me dinner, then offer to stay over. One night, I found myself there again in a dream.

My Journal Entry (nightmare)

The same dark unfamiliar hallway, two faces sitting and fumbling with sticks. But this time, they did not jab me. They could no longer reach. Instead, they mocked me, laughed at my face. Tapping their sticks to the ground, I saw one was him (SC). A look on his face, maybe words, something sent a "You think you got away from me? You stupid bitch, fool, don't you see he's one of us too?" I cried and cried in a ball and they just laughed at the hole in my heart, liking it, carving it larger. Poke by poke they went now into my chest. Down there hurt less, so I begged

*them to do that instead. They refused and just
laughed, SC and his friends.*

"Wake up, Nadia!" He tugged at me and yelled.

But when I did, I screamed, "Get out! Get out! Leave!"

Confused, dazed, and pissed off, he gathered his things. I was convinced in my head he was tricking me like SC. Sure enough, he left. *SC made me lose him,* I thought. My mind said, *See, Nadia, he didn't truly care about you and all along intended to rip you apart. You'll never be loved by another person again.*

That week, I tried to go about my daily routine, probably with a little more caffeine. I became the come and go wave, just walking in and out of AA meetings, class, and therapy sessions, disconnected. Being with the children always brought relief and brought me back to the present. But my time with them was still so limited.

How could it be, he was still harming me?

I am furious that man still touched my life in my mind.

I am furious at myself for not dealing with trauma's markings sooner.

I am furious at myself for not gaining the skills to stay safe immediately.

I am furious at myself for what happened when instinctive defenses kicked in.

I am furious at myself they so often led to having a drink in hand.

I am furious my children bore the brunt of the work left undone.

My Journal Entry

Daddy, please bring me home, please, oh please. Where is my home? I can't rest with that man SC in my head. I need my base in my children's hearts. I need them with me. I feel homeless here without them. I have not felt safety and warmth since you died, ever since they took them away from me I have cried. I'm so exhausted, searching and searching for the light. I pick myself up and keep going, but that man keeps returning to mock me in nightmares . . . Oh dear Daddy, where are you to keep us safe? Where is my home and why was it stolen? Please Daddy, please, please show me the way back. I must get out from under his spell for my children's sake.

A week later, on the anniversary of my father's death, November 12, I relapsed. I had a couple glasses of wine then stopped. Proud of myself for stopping, I called my sponsor and told Bill when I arrived later to help him with the boys at the house.

Sure enough, he got hostile, we argued, doors were slammed, the police were called for domestic violence "arguing." When they arrived, I sat down outside on a bench with Elijah clinging to me and attempted to console him. The sight of police car lights and voices interfered, as I rocked him back and forth and sang into his ears.

An officer walked up, asked me if I had been drinking. I said, "Yes, earlier in the day." It is a violation of probation to drink alcohol. Another officer interrupted and said to his partner that Bill did not want me to be arrested, that "all was ok." But it did not matter. I was arrested anyways.

There is no need to give more details or place the blame on anyone but me.

It was the worst day of my life.

No prior bottom compares.

I am to blame for it all, dear Son.
I am to blame.
It is me.

CHAPTER 17

Dear Son,
the end is often the beginning.

The police took me to the hospital and held me there for hours.

In their vehicle, I had said, "Just shoot me." They took it as suicidal ideation. They handcuffed me to a metal chair and just stared at me with a "poor crazy girl" look. Apparently, that was an "evaluation."

I'm sure they thought I was drunk or crazy when I said, "Do you want to know why I cry? Why my heart is broken? Do you want to know what memories enter my mind that I wish you could cut out? Can you help me erase them? Can you bring me a cure to end a man's curse? Because that's what I need." All they did was stare and watch me cry, which made me sob more.

A few hours passed. They put me back in the police car and drove me to the city jail, where I was put in a cell, stripped naked, and placed into a large Velcro wrap that barely covered my body. An apparatus to apparently prevent a suicide, it scathed my skin bloody in spots with every slight move I made.

I attempted to sleep this way overnight while chanting mantras and prayers in my head. "You are not a body. This blood does not make you just a body. This nudity does not make you a body. Their looks of shame do not make you a body."

In the morning, officers loaded me into their vehicle and drove to the county jail in an attempt to transfer me. My entry was refused. I didn't know why at the time. So they drove me back, frustrated, and I spent another night in a Velcro dress on the ground.

I guess I'm supposed to lose it in here, I thought. *They are trying to make me lose it. Don't lose it. For them, don't lose it, Nadia, stay strong,* I thought.

The following day I was taken to LA County Lynwood Women's Jail. I sat in front for hours with my hands cuffed, trying to keep my Velcro dress up with my chin as it scratched me raw in places I didn't even know it could reach.

Another girl waiting was asked to pee in a cup.

"I want to be tested," I said out loud. I wanted to prove my outer appearance was not the cause of anything else but real internal pain. *I need help to cut that man out of my head. Please acknowledge it, Officer?*

But it seemed no one cared in there.

I was placed in a section of the jail for those "on crazy watch" and stayed there another several days alone, naked in my Velcro covering. The woman in the cell next to me literally never stopped screaming. "Get me out, please. Get me out, please. Ahhhh! Get me out!" she screamed over and over again. Heart-wrenching pain oozed out of every corner. It was beyond unbearable.

Mostly because no one was doing a damn thing about it. It doesn't take a rocket scientist to see the stupidity of a system that thinks someone will feel or act less crazy when dehumanized. When denied any response or gesture of care. When locked up all alone with their mind churning as if in hell. *Don't you see you're fueling the pain, causing her criminality?!* I wanted to scream.

After forty hours of her desperate wailing, I don't know what came over me, but I suddenly started to sing softly, "May the longtime sun shine upon you. All love surround you . . ." In an instant, she stopped. Silence. "I'm here," I said. Silence. "You're not alone." Still, nothing. But it must've been something. I continued singing all day.

When it was time to try to sleep, I sang, "Close your eyes, rest your head, feel the peace, my baby. Mommy loves you so so much, and I always will. Dream big dreams. Stay safe tonight. Remember that I love you. Close your eyes. Rest your head. Precious baby girl . . . ," my eyes filling with tears, voice cracking . . . *my sons, my dear sons* running through my head and heart in painful streams as I sent the words home to them too. The only time I stopped singing was to sob for all the human suffering around me, period.

It made me cry knowing all anyone ever needed was love, light, and warmth, safety, an ear, eyes looking into theirs to say, "I see you."

"Thank you," I said out loud. "Thank you." Then I sang on.

Her cries never resumed.

After three days, someone finally came to my cell door, peeked inside, and asked, "Do you want to kill yourself?" Just like that. "No, not this time. I never did. I want to live for my kids. I want to live."

They didn't say anything in response and left.

I just sang more, but this time the lyrics to a different song, "When you gonna make up your mind? When you gonna love you as much as I do?" And so on.

Several hours later, they opened the metal door and

ordered me to stand outside. "You're not alone. I send you love and warmth," I said, before they walked me down a cement hallway, to what seemed like an entirely different existence.

I could hear the shuffles of life and soon enough other inmates, officers, and people talking. The itty bit of human interaction and rhythmic routine was sweet breath to me.

Oh my God, I thought. *Thank you, God, thank you for this blink of light.* I had been in solitude, half-naked in Velcro, for nearly six days. Imagine those that are kept this way for weeks, months. Who knows what they go through, especially the innocent ones.

I was led into a large semicircular ward with guards' quarters set near the main entry looking out above a floor of bunks to two stories of locked cells. A little courtyard was along the wall to the left as you entered and a row of various vending machines on the right.

My jail cell was on the second floor all the way to the right, which I later learned meant I had the fewest privileges and had to work my way up. My cellmate was young but tough. A lesbian woman who longed to be home with her love and son, she struggled with poverty and addiction but had achieved sobriety. She was taken in after a warrant was released for unpaid traffic tickets. Imagine that.

She gave me one of two worn-down pencils and an old book I held on to for life. The pencil was an inch long with tiny pieces of wood shards broken off to reach the lead in order to write. How very gracious she was to me. "Thank you so much," I said over and over again. I still have the book with tiny notes to my sons written on both covers.

All I could think of were my sons hour after hour. Aching for what must've been their confusion and pain after having to watch me be taken away, their wails of "Mommy" ringing in my head. My self-hatred and shame were suffocating. I could not breathe.

I cried and cried and cried, holding my jaw so tightly, I chipped several teeth. Struggling to find the pieces in my mouth, a desperation overcame me as though pieces of my life were falling off.

Twisting and sliding my tongue against my teeth for what seemed like forever, I finally found two pieces. I felt so relieved, I saved them at the top left corner of the metal bunk so I could stare at them when I fell asleep.

I am going to be here for a minimum of six months, I told myself; after all, that is what a violation of probation means. *I have my two-inch pencil, book, and a couple pieces of teeth to keep me company.*

Be a stone, a robot, be "her," that version of you that pops up all the time. The one who is not here, but watches from outside, detached, and unalive. Look them straight in the eyes, shoulders back, and stand tall. Hold your ground. Set in your standing. This is it. This is life now, Nadia, I said to myself.

The following morning, I got as much information from my cellmate as possible. Daily schedule, how to get paper, stamps, money on the books, use of the phone. How do I make a call? "Only at this time, dial this number first, then that, then wait, then wait again, then press that, and this . . . ," she said.

My mind spinning. *Oh God, please help me remember.*

A few days passed until I was allowed outside my cell to go to the courtyard with the others. When you're a newbie, you're sized up, gazed at, and talked about under the breath. I just looked others straight in the eye as if to say "hello" and appreciated my height at this point, standing a few inches above the others and motioning for one of the gals to pass me the basketball.

That night, I fell asleep in another body and reference point. *You belong here. You're destined to rot away a failure.* Then it was, *Do your time, pay the price, and just maybe your sons will let you be their mom again.*

Later in the night, suddenly an officer stopped by with my medication, which I hadn't had in days. I begged to use the phone and it was granted.

The only number I remembered by heart was Bill's. I tried multiple times but to no avail. Maybe I was doing it wrong. I tried one more time and he picked up.

"Are the boys ok? Please tell me they are ok," I immediately blurted out.

"I am trying to keep them home," he said.

"What? What do you mean? Bill?" I begged. My head filled with black liquid. Everything fell into an abyss.

Fainting, I tried to hold myself up by the dangling phone. As it slipped out of my hand, visions of my babies' umbilical cords being severed from my body cut through my heart, and it stopped beating, once again.

I am dead, I am dead. A chilling darkness engulfed me, saying, *You're mine. You'll never live and walk to see them again.* Dr. K.'s clown face peered down, his disgusting mouth laughing at me. SC's mocking words poked my insides, enjoying my suffering.

Dirty little damaged broken brown girl. You really thought you deserved them? My head rang and rang.

Minutes passed and no one noticed me on the ground. Not even the guards within view.

There was no angel calling 911 or police officer resuscitating me.

This time, I was dead inside in a body alive.

***

Eventually, I pushed myself up to stand, walked slowly back up the stairs and into my cell. I crawled on the ground and just sat sobbing into my folded arms and knees.

I don't know what to do. What am I doing wrong?

Please, oh please, please infinite one, please show me how to live. I've tried so hard. I've tried so long. I've tried every possible way.

Please take away this pain and shame. My children need me thriving again. Please show me the truth of what I am. Please bring me back to that home within for them.

In total exhaustion, I subconsciously moved into a different state. The past, present, and future merged together, like I had once experienced in meditation.

***

Her little hands touched my slouching head.

And I looked up. I looked up.

Little Nadia was sitting before me, a formless wave.

She held my face and I held hers.

I broke down and sobbed, knowing deep down her truth.

I have searched far and long to find you, I thought.

She wiped my tears and said, *I know your name.*

I felt a touch on my left shoulder.

And I looked up. I looked up.

Arthur was standing before me in a formless wave. He reached out his hand, I took hold of it, and he helped me to my feet.

A nod of his head spoke. *They have stolen the heart from inside you.*

But this does not define you, he emphasized. *The truth is the truth, it will prevail, and set you free.*

The cell door opened. And I looked up. I looked up.

My father stood before me outside the cell, a formless presence I can't explain.

He opened his arms in a firm call to embrace.

As I walked through the thick open doorway, he spoke clearly.

This is not who you are, he stated as his eyes hit me hard.

The truth inside his heart instantly banished shame and its scars.

You know who you are, he repeated sternly, lovingly.

And there "It" came, dear Son, to break down the chains. I saw what was real, illusions erased.

"It" whispered so gently. *Wipe your tears now. Get back on your feet. Your true self and home are right there within you. Step by step, walk again. Remember, you did it before. This time, remember there are lights along the way always there to guide you. It's time to free yourself now, dear, just like you did for that kid back then.*

And as I lay my head to sleep that night, I neither tried to comprehend nor analyze the experience I'd just had. It just was, and a powerful peace overcame me.

No matter what happened from there on out, I was no longer afraid and alone. I was fully surrendered to whatever came next.

***

A few hours later, everyone was woken up.

It was Monday, court day. One by one, they hauled us out like cattle for the long ride to our future dictated destinies.

Prison buses section off each double seat with bars. Interacting more intimately with the dreary imprisoned human being sitting next to you is basically inevitable, just as it is in crowded holding cells.

I always found myself receiving and holding the desperation of others. I didn't mind. I didn't mind at all. In fact, I needed it.

I needed it to remind myself of all I had to be grateful for.

To remind me of how many desperate and disadvantaged women out there need help, are crying out for it in all the wrong ways, are in the depths of pain without their children, and who want to get better in an overwhelmingly shaming and often damaging system. I needed it to believe I could still help others someday, maybe even that day, if even behind bars. If even to give an open ear, or an understanding heart.

The woman next to me was a young mother locked up for possession of meth. Her drug dealer "love of her life" was going to rescue her and her children, she thought. Having worked in an office, once financially secure and in an apartment, she lost it all within a month after they met. She was frantic and anxious, and I could feel her mind reeling.

"It will get better," I said, then continued to just listen while slightly distracted as we drove down the freeway. But then she got my full attention when she said he "kind of" made her have sex with his "friend." "So we could stay in a hotel rather than sleep in my car," she said, and she believed him.

I turned my gaze from the window to her eyes. Shame was oozing out of them. But she saw in mine relation to her pain. No judgment. No "what's wrong with you" or "how could you do that" phrase. "You're a good person. I get it," and I did.

She said she told him no, then he beat her up, so she got high to do what he wanted. "That's not love," I said quietly under my breath, but perhaps shouldn't have. It hit a sore spot of truth. The devil's drug had merely cloaked it with fake consolation. Her eyes filled with tears and she just sat there silent a few minutes.

"I don't know where he is, I'm worried for him," she eventually said. "He wasn't there in the morning, my wallet and phone were gone, I think his friend took them, not him, he wouldn't do that." She went on and on, as my heart ached with every word coming out of her confused and defrauded mind.

"How did you end up in jail?" I asked when it seemed ok. After she fled him, she said, police found her and her daughter sleeping, cold and in a tight embrace, in the back seat of her car near the Long Beach Port. They flashed lights into the car and ordered her out. Without an opportunity to say goodbye, her daughter was ripped from her arms and placed in another police vehicle, screaming and crying. They arrested her for possession and child endangerment. "I don't know where she is, I'm so worried," she broke down.

I despised all the pain in her soul and the scrambled crap in her mind. I wanted to shake her and shout, "Wake up. Break free!"

I wanted to tattoo "he drugged and exploited you" on her brain so she'd never return to the same.

"You have to get sober if you ever want a safe and healthy life," was all I could say, from my own disgraced place. "You can't see clearly otherwise. You can't see the truth underneath all the chaos inside. Your child is waiting for you." Tears fell down my cheeks, thinking of my own.

Soon she joined me, and we fell into the middle space together, letting some of the shame and pain roll out. With gratitude like no other in my heart that I broke free from that devil drug many years prior, I just kept repeating over and over again, "You have to get sober first. To see the way out, you have to get sober first, hon." I also finally acknowledged how far I'd come since the day I was assaulted by SC.

***

Who will be there for this mother with a child who needs her well? Who is going to say to her child, "I'll walk your mom through and never judge?" Who will hold her hand when she has to dive in and be vulnerable to get out? Who will keep her and her child protected from the shame the system gives?

Her story is another mother's story and another woman's story and until all their stories mold into one, it will continue to be a massive, large, forgotten, and ignored epidemic.

Mothers have suffered from childhood and adulthood trauma which causes pain that blocks them from their truth inside. It manifests in their seeking false refuge, falling into addiction, and hundreds of other self-destructive behaviors. But for God's sake, these are the mothers of the sons and daughters of the world! And so I ask again, who will be there for them?

Stacked like puzzle pieces of flesh without souls in cells, branded, dehumanized, and shamed, don't we realize we are eroding the sanctity of motherhood and the children that depend on it?

Some mothers are silent and numb, just going through the motions. Others are sick and nervous, going through each second like torture. Some have remorse for crimes committed. Others have none and only point the finger.

Does it matter which way a mother is responding if there's any chance we can save her so she can be there for her little one?

The souls they brought into this world are begging us to try a different way and a little harder.

The souls they brought into this world need us to hold their mothers' hands, to show their mommies the truth of who they really are within, so we can walk them home to safety and so they can feel their mothers' love again.

***

We arrived at the courthouse and were unloaded bus by bus into large cells so overcrowded most of us had to sit bunched together on the ground. As the day slowly passed, groups of six inmates or so were called one by one and taken down a hall. Upon return, many shared what happened in the courtroom. A sentence, a transfer, a new date. Some got answers, some didn't.

Reality hit, and my mind went to work. My anxiety rose to

a heightened level as my hope hit the ground. I began to panic for my sons' pain. As I rocked back and forth with my head between my legs, the other ladies tried to console me, saying things that only made it worse.

"It's not so bad. You'll still get to see them in jail," and "Time will go by. You'll be fine. You'll do ok in here," and more. I could not believe what I was hearing. My destiny set in. So I started repeating phrases in my head to get through.

I am not alone. Sat Nam. I am not alone. Sat Nam.
You know who you are. Home is within you.
You know who you are. Home is within you.
Angels surround them with my everlasting love.
Angels surround them with my everlasting love.
"It" will show me the way. Walk ahead with grace.
"It" will show me the way. Walk ahead with grace.
Surrender, surrender, surrender to "It."
I surrender, surrender, surrender to "It."

On and on they went in my head as hour after hour passed.

By the end of the day, everyone's name had been called but mine. As they loaded us back in the bus, the gal next to me queried a guard. "Hey, what's up with her? She was never called." The officer flipped through a clipboard, was distracted, then paused. "Huh, you're not on here," she said, then continued about her duties.

All my unanswered questions quickly turned to blank as we went through the motions of the long drive back "home." Brown bag dinners and all, there is a quiet yet powerful understanding among most female cellmates that you're in a struggle of some sort against the pain in this world together.

As I lay my body down to sleep on the metal bed, I distinctly remembered the all too visceral x-ray tables after the car accident. The scathed open wounds on my bony body wouldn't let me forget it even if I tried those nights.

But I didn't mind it, strange as I am. They brought my head

back to planet earth, where I actually needed to be, in preparation for whatever news I'd hear next regarding the months
ahead.

Mentally, physically, spiritually, I was ready to face whatever came my way.

In the wee hours of the night, clanking keys on the door
woke me up and a guard directed me out. I had no idea what
was happening, so I quickly touched my cellmate's shoulder,
kissed her forehead, and whispered in her ear, "Don't give up."
She threw me a nod and we gave each other an unspoken gesture of hope.

I was directed to walk down corridor after corridor, further and further away from my cell until I couldn't have made
my way back to it if they'd asked me to.

As soon as I saw the same front cement bench I had sat on
in the Velcro dress, I had the inkling of pending release. Sure
enough, there were no grounds to press any new charges.

After going through the formal motions, I walked back
into the darkness of early morning into the "unreal" world
and saw Bill waiting outside in the car. I was terrified as I sat
down. For the first time in months, I stayed completely silent.
Given no information whatsoever regarding what would happen next, I eventually burst out in tears, expressing my worries
for the boys and extensive remorse.

"Just be quiet," he said. I crumbled all over again in his
presence.

He was scared too, we did not know at all what the next
hours would bring. "I'm sorry about it all," he said minutes
later as he parked the car.

"It's not your fault but mine," I said. "It is all mine."

I immediately ran and fell into the boys' bodies as they
slept, wishing I could just stay there forever in the womb. But
I knew I had to report to my probation officer in a few hours.
I knew my short stint at the Lynwood Women's Jail was just

the beginning and something more horrifying was around the corner.

As their innocent eyes opened, I kissed their foreheads and tried to give them all the reassurance I could muster in my state. There was nothing I could say to make a very awful memory go away, to erase it from their brains.

All I could do was walk into the future fully surrendered.

All I could do was take any and all direction from a higher power I now heard. All I could do was walk myself back into the fellowship hall and beg for help.

And that's exactly what I did. Everything from there on out evolved in a way beyond any human power.

I immediately left a message with my probation officer, informing her I'd be turning myself in for a probation violation as a result of drinking and being arrested. I drove to my apartment, packed as many things for the boys as possible, and dropped them off at my sister's just in case she was called to help.

Yes, I was a "criminal probationer." Yes, I, Nadia Maria Davis, the daughter of civil rights champion Wallace R. Davis was that. *I don't give a damn what you think or say about it. Why? Because my daddy loves me the same.*

I absolutely knew what was going to happen to me. I was going to be taken back into custody and face up to a year in prison for the violation. I owned my actions and had to take full responsibility. So I called Beth, my attorney, and a bail bondsman then walked into the department with my head held up.

When my officer opened the door and called my name, I walked straight down the hall, she told me to turn right, and sure enough, a group of deputies were there waiting.

"Put your hands on the wall and spread your legs," my officer said.

"Yes, ma'am," I said. Calmly and with respect to the

all-female deputy team, I directly owned up to my relapse and apologized for disappointing her, as she had gained confidence in me. She said she hated to have to take her people into custody, but something "has to change."

I was taken back to Santa Ana jail, exactly where the journey began seven years prior. I spent another night in a crowded cell, having no idea what my future or the children's would be.

I repeated over and over again in my head, *Nothing can touch infinite love and I send it now to my sons. God is with me, helping me. Home is within you. You know your truth. Keep moving forward.* I mumbled it softly one time, moving my lips, until one woman asked me what I was doing. So I told her. She said, "Where did you learn that?"

"Well, that's a loaded question," I said. Half of them laughed, or more like woke up from internal hell. I tried to muster up a summary of all the efforts I had made to stay sober and healthy, but the practical efforts were just the beginning of the journey. I had to attempt to put into words a spiritual journey that one could possibly swallow under such circumstances as we were in at that moment. But how?

"Treatment, jail, hospitalizations, you name it, nothing I did worked. I forgot the truth of who and what I am. Stay sober, that's the first step. You have to stay sober, then you'll see the power shame has over you, and you can break free."

I thought they'd all burst out laughing like I was some Jesus freak. But no. It was more like a "huh?" and a curious "really?" on most of their faces.

One woman said she was homeless and happy to have shelter for the night. A few minutes later, another woman, restless and clearly frightened to death, said it was her first time in jail. "I'm not supposed to be here."

They just kept coming, one by one, story after story, over multiple hours. Same thing over and over again. Abuse, a man, a drug, more abuse, desperation, arrest, no way out, self-pity, self-hate, self-harm, and the cycle goes on. We can't get out of abuse until we see we are the ones abusing ourselves too.

"You have to get sober first before anything else," I repeated, the only piece of advice that made any sense in the web of messes among our lot.

There I was again, in the midst of my own wreckage, somehow believing I could share words of encouragement. But I think it mattered to them.

"I see you. I hear you." I was a human being merely saying, "I believe in you. You can do it. I'm trying too. I've made some progress, and may fall again, but I'll never let it be because I let shame win again."

A bit later a guard stopped by with our bologna sandwich dinners, smiled at me, and said, "Lockyer, looking and sounding much better these days." I merely smiled back, knowing exactly what she meant.

A couple days later, I was released on bail alone into the heart of downtown Santa Ana. I had my whole life ahead of me to recreate for our sons, Bill, and me.

Still, I had a level of hope and conviction in my heart I had never had before. I smiled in the direction of the school named after my father, felt his presence, and merely told myself, *Just take one day at a time. You are not alone. You know your truth inside. Now go fight for those boys and your life.*

I called Lyft and got a ride home. On the way, I called Bill, my sponsor, and my sister, and told them, "Thank you for loving me."

That night was the first time I'd slept in a soft bed in a dozen days. As I awoke in the morning, alone and feeling like I was in the twilight zone, my mind went to work again right away.

I started to feel more imprisoned than I had behind bars. Thoughts became full of shame as a mother and woman almost immediately. *They will forget me. I will lose them. I will*

be all alone, I'll never forgive myself. Bad woman. Bad mother.
Tears rolled down my face as I curled up in a ball.

While I was more aware of how our minds work, even so, I feared the thoughts in my head would continue for days to come as I committed to stay sober.

A panic began to set in, so I jumped to the floor, sat on my heels, breathed, tuned in, breathed again, and then said out loud, "I am an infinite soul, and no shame can overcome me," repeating it over and over again until my mind quieted to a calm.

Then, and only then, was I able to move into a different space. I can only keep my mind in check by staying connected to the home within me. I imagined a circle of love, light, and warmth, that all-consuming sacred place I know, surrounding me and my children.

Sat Nam, my true self is not here in this body form. It is with infinite wholeness, my children's souls. I surrender. I am listening. Please remind me of the truth of what I am.

"It" spoke, it speaks to me.

Just breathe, just breathe, and you'll know the way.

CHAPTER 18

Dear Son,
courage is often a verb.

In *Rising Strong*, Brené Brown wrote how we do not always sign up for a hero's journey, but that the second we fall down, get beaten up, have our heart broken, or make a terrible mistake, it automatically starts right then and there.

Her words spoke to me, saying, *The only decision I get to make now is, Do I want to write the story this time? Or hand it over to someone else?* I chose to write mine, which meant I had to get deeply uncomfortable, I had to "choose courage over comfort," as she said.

It is not easy to have courage to be vulnerable, to see vulnerability as a positive thing. I was not made that way.

Courage is painful, messy, and marred with ups and downs.

It's never a one-way street up to the mountaintop.

I've learned that "courage" is not a noun but a verb.

I've learned to "courage my way through" by doing

everything wrong first and feeling the pain and suffering in the process.

I've learned to "courage my way through" by falling into the depths of shame and fear, being vulnerable enough to talk about it.

I've learned to "courage my way through" by proving to myself over and over again that I am powerless over the effects of trauma on my psyche and using alcohol when in crisis.

I've learned to "courage my way through" by finally admitting I need help and can't do life and manage my conditions alone.

***

The day after I was released, I walked straight back into the arms of my AA fellowship, albeit with my tail between my legs and glowing shame. I disclosed everything that had happened and asked for everyone's help to stay sober and walk through whatever was next.

A woman walked immediately up to me after the meeting, looked me straight in the eyes and said, "You're mine now." She gave me no choice.

"You can't spiritualize sobriety!" she insisted. "You're going to meet with me tomorrow morning here at 6 a.m. We'll get started."

Now, this woman isn't just any woman.

To me, she was like the godmother of AA in Southern California.

I knew who she was for years prior. She always sat in the same spot with an aura of strength, confidence, and grace. In fact, she intimidated me.

But over that past year, she referred now and then to stuff from *A Course in Miracles*. I felt an unspoken connection to her despite the fact we had never really conversed one-on-one prior.

I had no inkling she would one day be my sponsor. But it was no coincidence that she came to be mine toward the end of my seven-year journey. She was exactly what I needed in order to fully surrender to the program of AA and the support of the fellowship.

Then another miracle happened.

Various members of that fellowship, led by a man named Rooney, volunteered to write letters of support for me to the judge. No words can express the depth of gratitude I hold for these people. I felt a gust of strength enter my heart as I read their words.

Before this, I always felt like all my efforts to stay sober went unrecognized. Healthy or not, I always had a desperate need deep down in me to have someone, anyone, recognize my daily hard work and long lengths of sobriety over the past years, despite the falls.

Little Nadia screamed inside, *But, but, but if you only knew all the things I've done and tried, all the to-do lists I've made and checked off all the months I was sober, and that I've honestly tried my best, you might feel I am worthy of another chance.*

But this time I didn't do anything. A higher consciousness and power worked through the fellowship. On the day of my criminal court hearing, I entered the courtroom and various seats were filled with members of my fellowship holding letters of support in their hands.

My attorney handed the judge a stack full of meeting attendance cards and completed programs, including Kaiser outpatient, chronic pain management, mandated classes, and volunteer hours. The judge reviewed them, looking up at me a few times.

Then he handed the judge a stack of support letters. Minutes passed as the judge read and contemplated. By this time, I had mentally prepared myself to spend up to a year in prison.

The judge began speaking, first with the formalities, then directly at me standing with my attorney at the podium. She delivered a much-deserved heavy load of reprimands for my past actions then looked back down again at the letters in her hand.

"Mrs. Lockyer, you have one last chance. I am ordering you to 180 days of AA meetings where you are to write in a journal about how something someone said affected you. I don't want simplicities. I want details. I don't want stuff like 'It was a good story,' I want to know how you related to what was said and how it will help you stay sober. I don't want one excuse for one meeting missed. Even if it's a holiday, an earthquake, or you're in the hospital. Do you understand?"

"Yes, Your Honor," I replied, my heart pounding.

***

I hadn't done a single thing but surrender all my efforts to something beyond me. Everything changed from there on out. The home within me could finally help me keep my mind in check.

Not in some big bang that swept away all the crap.

But in a perfectly sloppy and vulnerable strength.

I was still on the road but now held others' hands.

I was still walking forward, but now diving into the pain.

There were highlights, hopes, disappointments, and tough lows.

Bad days and good days. Triumphs and falls.

Yet this time, dear Son, it all seemed to make sense.

This time I let something else guide the way.

***

I taped large monthly calendar pages to the walls behind my desk. Each day included a checklist. Morning medication, calls into drug testing, daily readings, AA, kundalini yoga, mandated class. I followed it religiously on a daily basis no matter what.

The visual was soothing to me. I could see the road ahead.

I began seeing the boys four times per week. I made a conscious effort to give them and only them my complete attention every moment we were together. I aimed to give them my eyes looking straight into theirs with the ability of speaking with or without words, "I see you. I love you no matter what. We will always be together. You don't need to worry about Mommy. You are the most important thing to me."

My head still carried so much intense shame and fear.

I told myself, *Well, at least I'm better aware of them when they creep up. My mind isn't so easily running me to the ground, nor can it when I say to it, "Shut the hell up." At least I can better recognize when I'm projecting that crap onto my sons whenever I see myself overcompensating with "I'm sorry" and "I love you."*

The storms in my head had a watchwoman, if not in me, then in my sponsor and therapist. I had no chance of getting away on the train with another conductor in control. That mere fact alone gave a sense of being more securely fastened in the car of life.

"Where are you at today?" my sponsor would ask.

"Well, I went to China last night, was in Australia by morning, then arrived in the North Pole. I'll be heading down south on the Polar Express, ready and willing with some coffee in hand."

We met regularly before and after our 7 a.m. meetings.

She walked me page by page through the first 164 pages of the *Big Book* that holds the entire foundation of the program.

She directed me to attend a twelve-step workshop. For the first time in my entire seven-year journey in and out of the rooms of AA, I truly committed myself to completing the twelve steps of AA, being as rigorously honest as possible in my newcomer state.

I admitted I was powerless over alcohol, that my life had become unmanageable. Did I want to say it was just for the time being? Yes. All honest alcoholics want to believe they can drink again and keep it under control. Did I want to say I was powerless over the one thing that reliably gave relief from pain and panic? No. But after I made a list of all the ways drugs and alcohol had harmed my life, I couldn't deny it.

It was never the loss of loved ones, childhood and adult trauma, depression, or PTSD that was to blame. What I had to admit to was allowing my disease to take control in response to them.

I came to believe that a power greater than myself could restore me to sanity, and committed to turning my will and my life over to "It."

Dear Son,

Remember what I saw the first time we met. Before any human idea of you ever came to be, "It" was the truth of what we are—infinite spirits whole, unchanged, unmarked by anything that happens here in this physical life. That truth is your identity.

"It" is a home within you that time can't take away. That is real life. Not this one our

minds define. That is the one truth. Not the thoughts that draw us away.

If I can't do this life, "It" can because it is it.

If I can't be rid of the pain, "It" can because it sees it.

If I can't be rid of my disease, "It" can because it made it.

Love, Mom

***

Self-will and self-reliance are some of my worst enemies. One day, I'll be and feel deeply spiritually connected. But the next day, I can jump onto my high horse, thinking the connection is all that's needed. That's never enough. It's about literally taking my hands off the outcome of any given issue, surrendering control, and getting the hell out of the way.

Next was doing the real dirty work in Step Four.

I had to identify my "character defects." I call them mental, emotional thoughts that lead me astray. Oh, so let me guess, shame, fear, resentment, pride, selfishness, self-pity? And so many more.

My sponsor was relentless about being "brutally honest," not only with her but myself. Well, I didn't quite know what that meant, and I'm still trying to figure it out, but my intentions remain good, so I just try my best.

Shame. The hardest thing about dealing with shame is that I had grown so used to it, I barely recognized it was there. Shame is epidemic and egocentric. Our mind twists and turns it in multitudes of ways until we eventually succumb to its complete control, forgetting the truth of who and what we really are in non-finite form. The first hurdle was to identify where it came from, how, and what it did to me. Then and only then did I see how self-defeating and self-centered it made me.

It wasn't until my sponsor hit me with one simple truth.

"Do you realize shame is actually pride in reverse?" She said, being on the depressive side, we addicts are "apt to be swamped with guilt and self-loathing." Worse, we will let ourselves swim in it and forget others around us.

"That is cruel. I was publicly shamed! You don't get it," I said.

"Oh yeah, well, how has focusing on that helped you?" Bam!

"You don't understand what I went through. No one ever will. You don't understand how hard it is to feel judgment in a stranger's eyes, to feel powerless over recreating life, to lose people close to me because of it. You don't understand the pain. You don't understand. It made me suicidal."

"Really? You're going to tell me I don't know what it's like to be self-centered?"

"Self-centered?" *Wow! What the heck? Is this woman speaking to me?*

"Yes, Nadia. Shame causes selfish self-pity and you lolled in it daily, only harming yourself and those you love. You know your truth. That's all that matters. Who gives a crap what was said about you? The more you cared about it, the more you let your mind and the disease win. What people think and say about you is none of your fucking business. Wake up! There are no more excuses here, no, not with me! Wake up, now! Or else you're damn sure to get drunk again and cause more wreckage!"

"But, but, but . . ." I wanted to scream at the top of my lungs.

But then she interrupted, seeing the tears welling up in my eyes. "Have empathy for yourself . . . you have gone through more than any one of us could handle. I don't know how you made it through. Get the pain out somehow, you have to, with a professional, somewhere else. But here with me, as your sponsor, I will not allow you to wallow."

I wasn't going to get an ounce of sympathy from this woman.

Resentment. I once believed I had none. Ha!

It just never came naturally to me. The only hate I thought I held was toward hate in the world. To those who spread hate to others. Me? I hate hate. I despise it. I hate to hate. Thus, whenever I held it, I also hated myself.

Unbeknownst to me, resentment held me down like a wicked weed. I not only projected the shame and pain outward, I pointed the finger at everything outside of me instead of truly taking responsibility for my actions.

First, I had to make a list of all the "people, institutions, and principles" I was resentful toward, the causes, and how they affect my life (self-esteem, security, ambitions, personal relationships, etc.). Then I had to ask myself whether I had been selfish, self-seeking, dishonest, or frightened. Where was I to blame?

"Really?" I said to my sponsor when I first read the worksheet. *Whoa! Seriously?*

"Yes, dear," she replied. "Resentment is not necessarily a sin. It's what you do with it. We didn't learn as children to express it, to get it out in a healthy way. All we heard was 'No!' whenever we had a tantrum. What is a tantrum? A fear or resentment a child doesn't know how to express, right? Resentments often have a good reason. But it is destructive if you stay bonded to it," she said.

"Put one foot in front of the other, Nadia. If a resentment ever comes up again, and they often will, acknowledge the underlying pain or fear that caused it, pray for that person, and do your best to let it go, one day at a time," she added.

The very definition of resentment is "a bitter indignation of having been treated unfairly." Well ok, crap, I was! But every time I held on to the resentment, I felt the hurt all over again. I recycled the negative feelings by revisiting the old wrongs done to me by others, whether Dr. K., the bullies in elementary school, the man that raped me, the big rig, death, Bill, SC, or the local reporter.

I had PTSD. It was not by choice. But with resentment, I did have a choice.

In other words, much of my suffering I had made on my own. Resentment did nothing to change the past, nor what people did or did not do. Rather, it allowed those very things to dominate my thinking and drag me down in emotional bondage.

If I worked on ridding myself of or even lowering resentment, I could possibly begin to clear away repeated traumatic scenes in my head as a result of PTSD. What a relief that would be. It was the first time in my life I had heard of such a concept.

Mariam, my therapist, told me that "anything anyone does is either an act of love or a cry for love." It has nothing to do with me. When I can embrace this basic idea about human existence, I am better able to step back, not react, become an observer, and see the person either as hurting or sick themselves.

I do my best. Some days are better than others. Things often still get messy. I don't always get to this perspective quickly. But I strive to eventually get there, whether at a meeting, in meditation, or with my sponsor or a friend or my therapist. Today I try to give others love without fear or judgment because of their own wounds, to recognize when my own are triggered, then commit to healing them on my own.

Ultimately, dark clouds of anger prevent my adequately hearing the guidance of my true self and spiritual directives.

The beauty of this layered, connected, very diverse personal work is endless. I could never have put it in an order. It had to happen this way.

Love holds no grievances.

To hold a grievance is to forget who you are.

To hold a grievance is to see yourself as a body . . . Perhaps you do not yet fully realize just what holding a grievance does to your mind . . . If I hold grievances, I am attacking love, and therefore attacking my Self.

I am determined not to attack my Self today, so that I can remember Who I am.

—*A Course in Miracles*, Lessons 68–69 (online)

***

I release all grievances I've held toward SC, the media, and the former Attorney General's office. I send all of you warmth, healing, and love, and pray you'll do better with how you treat others in the future.

I release all grievances I've held toward Dr. K., the elementary school bullies, the man who raped me, and the big rig driver that hit me.

I release all grievances I hold against my father, Priscilla, Arthur, and my baby for dying too early.

I release all grievances I've held toward Bill for presenting a drug, for marrying me for perceived wrong reasons, whether imagined or not, for not protecting me from SC or the local reporter, imagined or not, for not defending me in the press, for being controlling, imagined or not, and for wanting to be intimate when I had flashbacks.

I release you from all the illusion- and non-illusion-based things I've held against you. I release and forgive you entirely, with all my heart and soul.

***

Dear Bill,

I'm so sorry you carried the brunt of my shame, fear, and resentment.

You did nothing but try your best with what you were given.

I know your own fears made you do things you regret.

But please, please, let go of that now.

You gave me three sons with all the love in your heart.

You gave me our children to love for all time.

You made me a mother and you said I was the best.

You believed in my intelligence and supported my dreams.

I love you more than I'll ever be able to say or show.

We will co-exist in a way that is healthy and safe.

Thank you for working with me to get to this place.

Please, let me be there as your best friend when you take your last breath.

We will live together again in the divine infinite.

Love, Nadia

***

Shame and resentments are indeed deeply rooted in fear.

Fear is epidemic in the world and runs rampant in my mind.

I had fears of abandonment, rejection, being defrauded, duped, or blindsided. Fear of losing something I already have, mainly my children and loved ones. Fear of not getting something I really want, like lasting true love and forgiveness.

If I'm not vigilant in awareness of my fears, everything can fall apart. For this woman, it requires a ton of consistent spiritual practice, step work, and continuous connection with healthy, safe people.

If I recognize my fear or someone points it out to me, I try to sit quietly and go to that home within me, asking for clarity regarding a certain situation.

I often get instincts to just sit back and observe myself and others that may be involved. Somewhere within me, I have built more confidence I'll know what to do because I am no longer leading but rather listening to a higher guidance.

I try to share it with my therapist, sponsor, and fellowship. Sometimes, just getting them out of my head is enough to stop the horses from running wild and doing something unhealthy, like prematurely pushing someone away or trying to prove I am worthy.

I once was consumed with fear I had lost the bond I shared with Diego and the twins. Based in a fear of abandonment, the thought of having my role as a mother stolen from me once brought me close to taking my own life.

Sick as I was, motherhood and my children were the last source of hope I had to hold on to. I let my fear of the system break me for much too long, when all I really had to do was own up to my unhealthy choices and make better ones in the future.

I knew Diego had been put through so much since his early teen years. Broken promises, disappointments, unnecessary and overwhelming stress while carrying the load of taking all accelerated classes and leading his sailing team in high school.

I now know depression and anxiety disturbed his sleep and focus, while fears and pain caused dissociation and withdrawal. I could see it, whether or not he recognized it at the time.

My fear-based self-centeredness drove an obsession to make him feel better and "fix things" between us right away. Motherly instincts would kick in and there was nowhere to put them. I could sense when he was sick, only to be told I could not go to the house. I could smell the vanilla chamomile tea with honey and milk I would've handed him. I could feel the foot rubs I would've given him.

I wanted nothing more than to look him straight in the eyes and see his soul inside. To hug him, hold him, tell him everything would be ok. To be convinced he still loved me, and healing would come in time. To be reminded that physical separation cannot dissolve our mother-and-son bond.

Scared to death he was hurting alone, confused in solitude, and escaping the anger in technology, I ended up writing three pages of an amends letter to him. But when I read it to my sponsor, she immediately told me to rip it up and throw it away. I was flabbergasted and offended. "What? I worked hard on this letter and completely owned up to every bad choice I made," I said.

"Nadia, that's the problem," she said. "It isn't about you. It should be about him. He is a teenager and has his own life. Simply tell him you love him, you're working hard, and ask him what you can do for him. Leave the rest up to your higher power and give him time."

It was the best parenting advice I'd ever received.

From there on out, I'd drop off fresh homemade cookies with a simple note on top, saying only, "I love you. I'm here for you. Keep your head up and shine! Love, Mom."

After a couple months, Diego came out and gave me a hug, saying, "Mom, you don't have to try so hard."

I thought, *But, yes I do, yes I do. I owe you a life of amends. I need to know I haven't permanently negatively marked you. I have to know you will not hurt later in life like I did. I am scared to death you are hurting alone. I need to believe you have forgiven me, that I'll never disappoint you again . . .*

"I, I, I, I, I, and I . . ." It was all about me and my fears. I was trying hard for me, not necessarily for him. Yes, I'm grateful he'll always know how hard I tried to mend things, but that is still about me.

What did he truly need? What did he want to receive from me?

The freedom to live without the distraction, projections, and burdens of the adults around him. He needed to see me continuing to be in touch with my true self, owning my mistakes, embracing vulnerability, and diving into healing and growth.

He needed me to reflect back to him his innate nature.

He needed a mirror manifesting the home of love, light, and truth within him.

Diego chose to set his own boundaries with me those first months. The pain was intense, but I walked through it and allowed him to walk on his own road.

I found gratitude in knowing he had gained the wisdom and willingness to communicate his limits and needs. That he didn't believe faking it and pretending everything was "ok" were indeed ok. "No, no more," he clearly expressed without words. He did what I should've done.

Hi Mom,

Been a while since we've talked, but I wanted to let you know that I am supportive of your

efforts and hope you can get through this triumphantly.
   Sincerely,
   Diego

***

Eventually, I too had to learn how to set healthy boundaries with people. If they accuse me of being the bad guy because of it, then so be it. Enforcing my right to decide who and what energy I permit into me and my children's circle is pertinent.

Setting boundaries with someone I care about is difficult. I tend to put myself in the other person's shoes, have compassion, ignore any discomfort I may have suffered, say it's "ok" and move on, completely disregarding the fact that something indeed was not ok. On the other hand, setting boundaries with someone I am attracted to will be a lifelong challenge and process. Admittedly, I am only attracted to a small set of the male population. But if one arrives, I'm in trouble. Ultra-intelligent, driven, strong, manly, handsome, and unfortunately avoidant men used to draw me in and are drawn to me like magnets.

It's like I wore a sign saying, *If you're also a phenomenal lover and broken inside, come over here so I can blow your mind.* They often ended up addicted to me. I felt a false, sick sense of control, worthiness, and "love" where fears of abandonment subsided. All the while, the risk of negative consequences waited around the corner.

Today, things are very different. I take pride in nurturing a quality communicative and mutually supportive relationship. While it takes consistent awareness and hard work to prevent falling into old patterns, I finally have true joy in love, and I get a natural high every time we regularly step back from moments of heightened emotions or words to see the big picture, to recognize that every action or word of the other was either a cry for love or an act of love, arising from a core wound and having really nothing to do with the other. Getting to that safe, judgment-free space within me on a daily basis enables me to offer that space to others as well.

Setting healthy boundaries and enforcing them has become easier. I am better able to gauge the risks. It used to be a pain in the ass. But the pain prevented far outweighs the work. And let me be clear, there's no perfection in practice and it is not the goal here. It is absolutely a process. At least today the process is present, and fear of abandonment has lost its hold.

> You are not in this world to create relationships.
>   You are in relationships to find your Nam,
> or true self.
>   If any relationship does not serve your Nam, you must say goodbye.
> —Priya Jain, Seventh Chakra Yoga
> Institute of Spiritual Sciences

***

After a year or so had passed, the blessings of forgiveness and healthy communication began to flourish between Bill and me. We eventually built a mutually supportive coparenting existence for the boys, which is by no means always perfect. But as his former wife, there is nothing I am prouder of than the friendship and relationship we have today. There certainly are bumps in the road, but we walk through them together and communicate in a way I never imagined would be possible.

Bill indeed remained someone, often the only one, I could rely on for over two decades. He never gave up on me and the person he knows I am inside, even if it was in some unhealthy, co-dependent way. Eventually, he even expressed empathy and acknowledged the challenges of living with chronic pain, PTSD, and untreated substance abuse. Most importantly, he always supported and praised me as a mother to his sons.

He will remain a source of strength and support in my life and our children's forever in time.

We are infinitely united through our sons. I will stand by and care for him with all my heart when it is time for him to walk to the other side in infinite life. Not only because that will be what is best for our sons but also simply because he is owed that depth of gratitude, amends, and respect.

***

Today living with chronic pain is dramatically different. Routine trigger shots, spinal epidurals, lidocaine cream and patches, glutathione shots, turmeric, and intravenous non-narcotic anti-inflammatory hydration sessions help a ton. While it requires a regular investment of time and money, in no way, shape, or form do I underestimate how privileged I am to have these.

But what honestly impacted my pain management the most was gaining a deeper understanding of the circular relationship between physical pain, emotions, and PTSD. Like a ping-pong machine, one propelling the other. It was a double curse and mere shots would've never been enough. If I have a bad memory, I do my best to check in with my body. If my body aches, I try to be on the lookout for bad memories. It's never perfect, but the more open I am about both, the more likely I am to do something healthy to quell them.

***

Over the next following years, I was relentless and unwavering
in every aspect of rebuilding my life for my children's sake as
their mother, knowing how inextricably linked it is to my own
happiness and health.

This sounds crazy but here it is: I completed ninety days as
an outpatient at Kaiser, a year and a half of parenting classes,
three years of probation, testing for three different entities,
a behavioral health group, weekly individual therapy, weekly
group therapy through the State Bar with other struggling
lawyers, six months of AA journaling for the court, a forty-day
Course in Miracles program, and a total of fourteen months
of voluntarily wearing a locked twenty-four-hour alcohol-
monitoring device on my ankle.

***

With enough sobriety and sanity, I was able to ask myself,
*What transformed in me? What was I asked to let go of? What
resolved in me? And, most importantly, how can I break down
more blocks to that home within me?*

I immediately was called to sign up for another level 2 kundalini yoga training at Seventh Chakra Yoga, this time it was
"Mind and Meditation." I not only began to teach the practice,
I began to seek additional guidance from Priya, the founder of
the studio.

It just happened, and at the right time.

I said, "Ever since I 'died' in the car accident and was in a
vast infinite clarity and consciousness, I tried in every and any
way to make peace with knowing that space while existing in
this finite body and world. I did everything 'wrong' and it was so
painful for so, so, so long, both for me and those I love the most.

"All along, I felt 'apart,' 'different,' and I know others sensed
me 'out there' sometimes, that I was not fully present here. I'm
sure you've observed me struggling to use my words and calm

my head, to ground myself, over the past two years since we met. This happens a couple times a year when in a flashback or disassociated mode and mental intrigues take control.

"So my question is, How do I stay grounded here?" I asked. "How did Guru Nanak walk grounded in this life after he nearly died? How did he center himself in the middle ground you talked about? Did he struggle in the beginning? For as long as I did? Did others see he was not completely here? What did he do about it? I'd like to know, if you do. That has always been my life's challenge."

"Suniai," Priya simply said. "Deep attuned listening to the frequency of anything and anyone around you. By listening you will see the truth behind it all. By listening you will be able to retreat into a room within yourself. To become the observer and not allow mind and body to react."

Through deep attuned listening, the pain of sorrow, suffering and errors all disintegrate.

Through deep attuned listening, one can arrive at pure contentment, gain genuine wisdom, and know the nature of the ultimate reality.

Through deep attuned listening, one can locate oceans of merit and worthiness within yourself.

Through deep attuned listening, you can recognize royalty, wisdom, nobility within yourself.

Through deep attuned listening, those stumbling blindly can locate the right path.

Through deep attuned listening, you can grasp the unfathomable.

Oh Nanak, devote yourself to the Nam and live in playful bliss.

Through deep attuned listening, all your
sorrow, suffering and errors disintegrate.
—Parts of pauries 8–11, Japji Sahib

"But it takes practice, a lot of daily practice," she reiterated. "I promise you, it is the answer to all your suffering. 'It'
lies along our path, guiding us in and often back to our Nam,
our true authentic selves. If you were called to this, then you
are already there. And so, my dear, what is your Nam? It is 'It'
in you. Your one true home within. Your purpose here you've
always known."

*Oh dear Priya, thank you for your amazing guidance and
beautiful glowing light.*

A few months later, I stumbled upon a Seventh Chakra
Yoga Institute offering of a Master Course in Japji Sahib. I was
drawn to it immediately. Priya, my spiritual mentor from years
prior, said, "If you come to the study of Japji, it means you are
done with suffering. You are asking the 'Ek,' the divine infinite,
'Show me the way.'"

A man named Guru Nanak wrote Japji Sahib, a sublime
set of verses describing an enlightened state of consciousness,
following his own near-death experience while submerged for
hours in a lake. It is not a "bible" or organized doctrine. The
verses can be read and appreciated simply as wise philosophy
and one of many great literatures of the world. They eventually
came to be revered as sacred texts by the Sikhs, but are not
part of an organized religion.

In Priya's words during a live training, "For those who can
truly tap into Guru Nanak's experience and receive the essence
of the core reality that hides in plain sight, Japji Sahib becomes
a sure guide of the highest goal of life, self-realization.

"Even though the event of Guru Nanak's awakening occurred more than 500 years ago, the state of his consciousness

is imbedded in the words and sound current of the Japji Sahib. His experience is as alive today as it was back then in these words.

"It carries the message that all religions, philosophies, belief systems, and traditions become redundant, irrelevant, and unnecessary when we recognize and bow to the divinity that resides within our own soul.

"Anyone who tunes themselves into the ecstatic power of Japji Sahib will be offered the portal to come home to themselves."

Sound, frequency, and vibration serve as gateways to this bridge. Meta-data emanated from them can indeed be translated. The brain just needs time to do so. One just has to let it happen. What it means and what its meant to do through you will reveal itself, sometimes quickly, sometimes slowly.

> "Shabad Guru"
> Words uttered in an elevated state of consciousness. When patterns of sound and thought in a Shabad like Japji are repeated, the frequency inherent in the sound current counters the direction and intensity of habitual thoughts, inducing a release of established patterns, emotional wounding, trauma and fears. If you allow yourself to surrender to the sound of the Shabad, new healthy patterns begin to replace the old. The mind clears, you are able to perceive everything from a fresh set of eyes.
> —Japji Sahib, An Owner's Manual for the Soul, Priya Jain

Priya looked into what scientists were saying about sound

and discovered a renowned string theorist named Machio Kaku, who said, "The subatomic particles we see in nature, the quarks, the electrons are nothing but musical notes on a tiny vibrating string.

"Physics is nothing but the laws of harmony you can write on vibrating strings.

"Chemistry is nothing but melodies you can play on interacting vibrating strings.

"The universe is a symphony of vibrating strings."

In other words, physicists are also experiencing what spirituality has always known. The only difference is that physicists have never inquired as to the source from which this music is coming from.

***

Oh how I desired to cultivate a stronger spiritual capacity to see, hear, and follow the bread crumb trails of lights that are placed before me. Priya implored me not to stop. "Dive deeper, Nadia."

From that point on, I began my days more frequently with morning Sadhana, a traditional practice that includes chanting the Japji Sahib, a Kriya or exercise, and meditation with the Aquarian mantras. I now teach it and hope to share this great blessing with so many more. The mere twenty-seven words of the "Mool Mantra" say it all for me, "an expression of our core reality."

> "The Mool Mantra"
> Ek Ong Kaar
> "'It' is a singular waveless consciousness,
>   nothingness and everything (Ek)
> that manifests into multiple forms (Kaar)
> through a vibrational frequency (Ong)."

Sat Nam

"'It' is the underlying identity within us
  all."

Karta Purahk

"'It' itself is the doer and experiencer of
  everything."

Nirbho

"Without fear."

Nirvair

"Without judgment, blame, revenge, or
  bias."

Akaal Moorat

"Eternal and ever present."

Ajoonee

"Without form, color, gender, or body."

Saibung

"Self-sustaining, whole, and complete
  within itself."

Gur Prasad

"Recognition of this divine guiding consciousness is the most blessed gift."

Jup

"Meditatively repeat this realization."

Aad Such

"'It' was the only reality in the beginning."

Jugaad Such

"Through all the ages this consciousness
  has been the only reality."

Hai Bhee Such

"Even in this moment 'It' is the only reality."

Nanak Hosee Bhee Such

"O Nanak! This consciousness is the only
  perpetual reality."

This wholeness is all there was and has remained since. Do we know how long existence has been in existence, pre-earth, pre-galaxies, what was there? This consciousness is the only reality.

Everything else is false, a thought my mind created. That's why it disappears. Anytime a fear arises, I remind myself of Priya's words, "Only that which is real will stay, everything else will shed off. So give it permission, acknowledge it, and let it go."

All the branding, shaming, and force to be "ok" in the system's eyes were and are not "real." Those identities and "I-ness" are actually not here. Even though it was written or required in this physical life, it cannot touch or change the true self of me in non-physical form.

Priya said in the training, "It takes a while to digest this truth. This is why daily practice is so important. Repeating the words over and over again as much as possible until you and your memory can retain the truth.

"This world is changing at a pace faster than any other time in the history of humankind. If we don't remind ourselves that there is a larger reality at play, we will feel so much tension, pressure, and stress that our minds will not be able to sustain it. We are going to feel like time and space are pulling us whether we like it or not.

"But it is all happening as it needs to happen. We are part of those waking up to this reality and will have to hold space for others who are not yet ready to wake up."

***

No, I am not a hippie or "guru." I am merely a woman seeking to live my truth one day at a time.

That's what a person who has lost it all and is willing to do everything and anything possible to fight for their life and the lives of their children does. To be healthy and happy, no matter what is thrown at you along the road, no matter if you fall flat on your face, and your body is bloody and bruised.

You just don't give up. You never give up. You keep moving forward into the light around and within you.

***

Life evolved in the most subtle yet beautiful way leading up to this point. Most importantly, the children settled into a healthy schedule and routine, sharing time between Bill and me as our communication, friendship, and boundaries strengthened.

I have never felt more serene, empowered, and true to self.

"It" is indeed guiding my way.

CHAPTER 19

Dear Son,

never stop growing or

striving to live wholeheartedly.

Perhaps it was the result of hard work, clearer thinking, and healthy boundaries. Perhaps it was the inevitable end of a seven-year journey.

You see, dear Son, something drove me to do more.

I had to go back to the beginning to understand the middle.

I had to understand the middle to create a new end.

I had to do deep trauma work to fully exist in my true self.

I had to turn inward toward the memories, pain, and defenses.

I had to do it without symptoms overwhelming me.

I had to discover, listen to, care for, and calm all my parts.

I was called to do the work when many never get the chance.

*Dear Son, this was the last unturned stone
when I thought I'd done it all.*

***

I heard through the grapevine that Kimmy Hunkle, MFT, the founder of Dee's House, was now focusing entirely on specialized trauma treatment for women. I instinctively called her one day and said, "It's time." She knew exactly what I meant, having helped me years prior on the journey.

She made one thing vehemently clear to me from the beginning. "If you're going to do intensive trauma therapy, you must commit to a massive load of work. Hard work. Exhausting work. Work that requires everything in you as though you are learning to walk again."

"Kimmy," I said, "I've had to learn to walk again before, remember the accident?"

"Yes, I don't give a damn. This is harder, much harder. Most give up and aren't willing to continue. You will feel cut open, deeply vulnerable, and often unstable, distraught and pissed off, confused and angry. People around you may judge your mood and behavior. It is critical you shelter yourself from such negativity. You'll make it to the other side, Nadia, resolved and lighter. Everything, and I mean everything, in your life depends on you doing this work. It is the best commitment you will ever make to yourself and, ultimately, your children."

"Ok, I'm in. I'm fully in. But that doesn't mean I'm not scared to death," I said.

Over the first several weeks, she introduced me to the basics of trauma therapy, as well as new strategies and skills to incorporate into my daily life. I learned about the goal of staying in a "window of tolerance," and how trauma survivors spend too much time above and below it in "hyper-arousal." This can manifest as panic, pain, terror, rage, agitation, overstimulation and more. Trauma survivors end up shutting down, ashamed and exhausted, finding it difficult to accept happiness and live in the present.

It felt as though my "twilight zone" existence was abruptly exposed without my consent, while I never knew it was screwed up in the first place. "I am not crazy after all," I said.

"No, Nadia, no," she responded. "In fact, your survival instincts are so strong, you mastered living that way." Then she continued: "Now is the hard part, honey. You have to dive into traumatic memories and resolve them in order to stop them from disturbing your life. This will help you learn how to stay in that window of tolerance."

"But how?" I asked.

"Create a new ending and they'll lose power," she said.

I most definitely initially had my doubts about EMDR. I had heard of it before. It sounded like a gimmick and I wasn't standing in line expecting some magic cure-all. "Eye Movement Desensitization and Reprocessing," huh? What?

Kimmy explained that EMDR therapy is an interactive psychotherapy technique used to relieve psychological stress. It is a clinically proven effective treatment for post-traumatic stress disorder. During sessions, you relive traumatic or triggering experiences in brief doses while the therapist directs your eye movements.

Recalling distressing events is often less emotionally upsetting when your attention is diverted. It allows exposure to the memories or thoughts without having a strong psychological response. Over time, this technique is believed to lessen the impact they have on you.

Ok, I thought. *I'll give it a try, what the heck.* At this point I had nothing to lose but a lot to gain and I was ready to create a new ending.

First, she asked me to write a list of major experiences for every five-year increment of life. I filled three pages of grid charts. Among approximately twenty-five, three or four were selected. Then, I had to create a "safe place" to go to in my head. This took longer than expected. *Yes, I could see, feel, and sense a place. But it was all in front of me. Behind me was nothing but darkness.*

So we tried again. I pictured half a dozen women who had positively impacted my life holding hands in front of and facing me. Priya, Mariam, Kimmy, and my sponsor. Behind me, Diego was placing his hands on a force field, reminding me without words that I was in a bubble of love. I could actually sense a cushion behind me for the first time ever. This alone was monumental.

Ok, I had my "safe place." Now we could start.

***

She chooses to work on my very first memory as a child and often the only one. *Oh crap*, I think, then say, "This is the 'room' I've 'lived in' my entire life. It is where I exist, I can't explain it."

She smiles, says "Let's begin," then turns on a device with a red light moving left to right.

She asks me what the room is. I say, "Dr. K.'s office . . . the exam table was placed diagonally."

"Follow the light with your eyes," she says, then nothing more.

I do not like it. The back and forth scatters my thoughts, impedes focus, and feeds anxiety. A minute goes by. I go in and out of that place in my head.

Then I am there, but not her, she is about five years old, stuck within four walls and complete blackness surrounding it. A ravenous rat peers down at her, his meal, a piece of meat. The shape of his mouth makes her feel sick. I am nauseous, stuck in there, anticipating . . . something. It seems to last forever, the apprehension and unease.

"What are you feeling in your body?" Kimmy asks.

I clasp my hands as little Nadia places hers on her tummy. "We are going to throw up." Breathe. Breathe. Breathe.

I close my eyes and watch her, tiny, innocent, brown, and afraid.

Unable to move. She doesn't know she can. Unable to call for help. She doesn't know who will respond and how. She looks up and away, desperate, grinds her teeth. The wait, the wait, thoughts run frantic, heart beats fast, frightened to death, feeling faint.

He walks in, gives a sick grin, and pulls her legs to hang halfway over. Standing, he begins brushing his prong against them. Rubbing, rubbing, rubbing, he quietly says, "Yes, you like it?"

Abandoned, alone, unheard and unseen.

I begin to sob for her, feeling it all. Yet I am not her, nor me. I am outside, in no body, not really living.

This is the first "me."

He frantically begins poking and prodding. *Shut it out. Shut it out,* she thinks. I see her surrender, numb. Eyes, ears tight. *Don't hear, don't move, don't see.* But fingers ricochet in her, making it much harder, you see. *You can do it. Just do it. Don't move a bit. Take it. Just take it. It will be over soon.*

I am with her, but see no relief.

This is the second "me."

She tries earnestly to maintain her grit. Her body tightens and shivers. He gets angry, annoyed, then holds her legs down. Now it'll take longer to get what he wants. *It is your fault,* she thinks. *You're stupid and weak.* She is enraged at herself. *You stupid little girl.*

I am her, she hates me, and will suffer more in the end.

This is the third "me."

She finds a solution and recites in her head, *If I have to do this, I'll be his best one.* She switches her face, relaxes her body, consumes what he gives, escaping reality. *I'm in control now and aware of his hunger.*

She is shaken, awakened, disgusted at herself. Shame consumes little Nadia then steals her soul.

Her innocence lost, she feels dirty and broken. *What can help me endure this?* She searches and searches, almost falls off the cliff. I must find something to relieve all the pain.

This is the fourth "me."

I see all my parts. I see how and when they come out.

I see my world and false understanding of this finite self.

It has always been parts of me trying to survive alone in a box. Disconnected, people-pleasing, shame-filled, or high. The robot, high achiever, depressive, and addict.

That session lasted several hours.

This is how my mind and body survived.

This is how character defects identified in step work arise.

This is how living in my true self gets blocked.

Today I can do my best to notice, stop, and listen to "her." I can tell her, "I hear you, I am here now and will keep you safe."

A week or so later, I mentioned the work I was doing to my mother.

"Now I know why you screamed every time we went there," she responded, nonchalantly, sending a dagger straight into my heart. She said the doctor told her to leave the room, that it would help me stop crying.

Ouch.

I had absolutely no recollection. I only remember the silent drives home, without a word. I only remember curling up into a ball in the closet to feel safe afterwards.

I was just a little girl! I screamed in my head. *Where were you, Mommy? Where did you go? Why did you leave me so all alone? Why didn't you grab me and run out? How come you left me with him? Why oh why, Mommy? Why am I the way I am?*

But I knew she'd have no answer. I knew she did the best she could. I knew she couldn't hear me then nor can she likely now. I knew she meant no harm and was clueless all along.

It is not your fault, Mommy, you didn't know.

I cry for that little girl today. What did she really go through?

Dear Son,

I am so sorry I became her time and time again.
Little Nadia, I am so sorry I brought you
back there in my head.

During the following weeks, more and more details of incidents emerged. I cannot put them all down here in words. The more I went to that room and closet, the more I discovered. The more I discovered, the more I wasn't just watching her. I returned to her, became her, and finally am me again.

It got to such a profound point that I stood up, placed her behind me, then beat the crap out of that man. He shriveled into a tiny creature then melted away, only his stench remaining.

I had never known nor seen an anger like that in me before. I am sure it came out a few times in drunken rages later in life, either directed inward causing suicidal ideation, or outward toward Bill. This is where having learned to make a living amends in step work helps.

I was now ready to take her the hell out of there.

I pulled her in close and hugged her tight.

I could feel it as real, dear Son, sensing our embrace.

I told her she wasn't alone anymore, that she didn't have

to hide in the closet ever again. I told her I'd protect her from now on, like I tell you now, "I got you."

We jumped on the back of a massive eagle, its feathers once laid on my daddy. We flew off and far away, the dark box behind us falling. The air upon our faces filled us with breath beyond our understanding.

We knew we were free now in our home within us and surrounding us.

Together we thanked our eagle and stroked its beautiful feathers.

She looked back at me and said, "I knew you'd come back someday." I smiled and held her closer, "Thank you, dear one, for saving my life."

***

When it was time to address more recent adult dramas, it proved to be layered, confusing, and exhausting in the very beginning. This phase of trauma therapy is very difficult to adequately describe here. Basically, I did not know where to start when it came to traumas inflicted by SC and, in turn, by myself as a result of unhealthy choices made. There were simply too many psychologically complicated and crappy things that SC did. As a result, I also couldn't stay in one "scene." They kept overlapping each other.

Some things that SC did were fraudulent acts, but I experienced them as real regardless. You see, it wasn't until years later that I learned his suicide threats were phony, including the time he sent a picture showing a razor blade at his wrist and what appeared to be blood, as well as the times I drove, full of fear, to the Golden Gate Bridge to prevent him from jumping off. Having found my brother after his own attempt, these moments were absolutely frightening and real to me to the core. On the other hand, the actual abuse and crimes, delineated prior in this book, were committed against me and my family and were equally experienced as real. Still, according to my therapist, the differentiation did not matter. She reiterated over and over to me that all of it was equally traumatizing, the fraud being one of the worst parts. I had to process it all as though all of it actually happened. If I could do that, if I could just do that, she emphasized, then and only then could the actual fraud be understood and healed from.

So where to begin? "Where to begin, Nadia . . . where to begin?" I'd ask myself over and over. The memory of his slit wrist, words in blackmailing texts, laughing at me in agony, lies and pictures in the press? It was terribly overwhelming. But ironically, thanks to flashbacks and nightmares, we eventually found a "starting point." The last contact, yet the most marking of them all: the physical assault itself. Nothing, and I mean nothing, has ever affected me in every way more. *At least I can start there,* I thought. *At least I can start there.* And so we did.

I had to go back into that restroom and relive his hand grasping my neck and seeing the sheer rage in his eyes. Writing it down here sends shivers down my spine. At least I could be there with my therapist by my side. At least I could hear her guide me, knowing I'd get out from hell.

I know now what to do when a reminder of the assault enters my head or wakes me up at night. I close my eyes, take a deep breath, and remind myself I am not in that bathroom and the assault is not happening today. Only then am I able to connect to that awesome place of truth, clarity, and warmth in that home within me. If I am with someone close to me when it happens, they are healthy enough to say "You are safe, you are ok." That is how life is lived today and I am full of gratitude. This will be a lifelong process.

Dear Son,

Today, I do believe it gets easier and easier to live with the reality of that man's abuse and the system's treatment of it as time passes by. I work hard every day to ground myself in the here and now. Your mom reminds herself and others daily of the truth of what we really are. Please never forget, my love, you are infinite warmth and light. Please listen to your internal instincts around others as to whether they are good for you or not. Protect your privacy online in every possible way, if you can. Should anyone in any way violate or harm you, you have a tiger mama here who'll do anything and everything to keep you safe and sound.

Love, Mom

***

Part of trauma therapy also involved learning about the different "parts" of me. We all have parts. You know what I'm talking about. Just sit back and watch yourself for a minute. Heck, do that for a day. It's not rocket science that our warrior sometimes transforms into a frightened child in a heartbeat, or our angelic guru becomes a wild animal at the drop of a dime. Those might sound extreme, but the feelings often aren't. Sometimes it happens quickly, in the case of a flashback, other times it's slow, in the case of interactions with different people. Yet when we can observe ourselves well, it is actually quite fascinating to see how our minds work.

If I listen to, care for, have gratitude for, validate and calm the parts of me, it creates a sense of connection, well-being, and belonging. I do not stumble or fail to reach out and ask for help as much. But if I ignore these feelings and habits and attempt to just be "ok" in others' eyes, I'm never truly living in the present, growing, learning, and welcoming in the happiness. It is constant work, yet I am fully committed to it.

I was also introduced to a variety of Cognitive Behavioral Therapy (CBT) techniques I can use regularly. I even made acronyms for them. That's just how my brain remembers things.

"MTP" stands for "Meaning, Truth, Projection." I ask myself, what Meaning am I giving the situation? Can I really know if it is completely True? Or is my subconscious Projecting that meaning onto the situation because I am triggered emotionally?

Remember the marine I dated? I believed he was intentionally "tricking" me, but did not know whether it was true or not, and my subconscious projected fraud because something he did triggered past trauma by SC. Unfortunately, the trauma of being framed and defrauded will always set in motion a strong reaction to dishonesty and non-disclosure. But at least today I am able to talk about and address it. Today it actually can create a deeper intimate connection with another. It serves a purpose beyond me.

After those weeks of intensive trauma therapy, I truly left with a different ending to the most significant traumatic experiences in my life, plus a stack full of inspirational memoirs written by others having completed similar work. There is an entire worldwide community of professionals and trauma survivors that speak this language and demonstrate an immeasurable depth of strength and wisdom. There is so much more that can be learned through a plethora of techniques and materials. It is truly a different way of life now, free and released from "the twilight zone."

***

In my experience, the system often discourages and even punishes displays of vulnerability, suggesting trauma work should be the last on the list. It can disable any real dive into the truth behind our feelings and responses. When I went through the process of EMDR, frankly I was a mess and felt scattered for days. Sleep was disturbed, chronic pain flared up, and my appetite was low. That's the same thing that happens when in flashback or disassociated mode.

Let us not be "ok" for a bit. Let us dive in and do the work without fear of judgment. Or would you rather continue imposing your way of doing things, and repeat the same mistakes over and over again?

We must put a stop to the ineffective ways our system deals with trauma and addiction. We must protect the children who suffer from unnecessary separation. Mothers and sons all over the world need to be allowed vulnerability.

For God's sake, let them dive into core wounds in a safe place.

Let us cry, weep, scream, replay it over and over again, to then create a different ending. Let us trip and fall, get up and try again, however many times it takes. Because maybe, just maybe, that wounded child will go back to their true home within and be able to show their own children how to get through this life healthy and sober without having to be "ok" all the time.

***

Dear sons of the world, we are here for you.
   Dear sons of the world, we know you are
there.

Dear sons of the world, we know you suffer too.

Dear sons of the world, who is telling your truth?

I don't mean the biographies. The "this, then, and that."

I mean the yearnings, discomfort, and hurt.

What happened to you back then? Was there lack of love?

What did you have to bear, too often, too much?

What did it teach you about living this life?

What did you learn about how to treat others?

What causes your fears, avoidance, and rage?

What causes you to touch us after we say, "No"?

Did your father, your brother, your son learn the same?

Do you know you deserve love, comfort, and safety?

Do you know you can ask for and not force what you need?

Do you know you don't have to suffer and place blame on me?

Do you know you can rid yourself of the shame?

Please help us understand how to prevent you causing more pain.

Maybe, then maybe, things will begin to change.

***

Dear Son,

I also learned that we are hardwired to connect! Our survival depends on our ability to be and feel close with others. When caretakers are warm, loving, available and reliable, our attachment system flourishes. When our attachment system is healthy, we feel comforted and relaxed being close with other people. Being close with others helps build emotional resilience.

Healthy attachment helps us stay in what is called a "window of tolerance," that space where we are able to think and feel at the same time.

If healthy attachment gets stronger and stronger over long periods of time, it creates positive feelings about us and the world around us. Those feelings act as a comforting buffer between traumatic events and our sense of well-being. Basically, we are less likely to feel bad about ourselves when bad things happen.

Having healthy attachment helps people recover more easily from traumatic experiences, whether disappointment, tragedy, loss, fear, abuse, or violence. It transforms hardship into wisdom, adaptability, connection and resilience. I will do my best to heal and strengthen the attachment we share every single day. I promise you this, dear Son, I promise you this every day.

Love, Mommy

"Reminder"
Goodbye to all the familiar
It's a crumbling cage.
Goodbye to immortal illusions
And to my youthful age.
I am no longer a slave to sorrow
Now she can only release me.
For when she comes the progression re-
    minds me that I belong to you.
Goodbye to the reign of the intellect
I set him free.
He stole my beliefs and emotions
And he put his reins on me.
I am no longer a slave to reason.
Now he can only release me.
For when he comes the possession re-
    minds me that I belong to you.
I give myself to the river that takes me.
I give myself to the sea.
I give again to the rain cloud that brings
    me,
to dry land that dreams about me.
I am no longer a stranger to freedom.
Now you can only receive me.
For when you come the recognition re-
    minds me that I belong to you.
When you come the recognition reminds
    me that I belong to you.

Lyrics by Mark Phillip Davis, © 1994
    Inkling Music

(From the album *You Came Screaming* by
Mark Davis)
Website: markdavisinklings.bandcamp
.com

CHAPTER 20

Dear Son, I got you.
You got me.
We got we.
Family.

You are healed and you can heal.
The light has come.
You are saved and you can save.
You are at peace.
You bring peace with you wherever you go.
Darkness, turmoil, and death have disap-
    peared.
The light has come.
I have forgiven the world.
I have forgiven you.
    —*A Course in Miracles*, Lesson 75

Perhaps the most profound thing of all about having committed myself to do real trauma work is that it instilled in me the most important question I could ever ask myself as a mother. How did my own trauma and bad choices affect my children? How might they continue to affect my sons' own relationships? Is there any way to truly know or prevent it?

I wanted and needed answers so I could at least try to do something about it. I dove into materials and asked a lot of questions. But deep down inside, I know it will be a lifelong process. There is no quick fix, or magic potion. All there can be is my commitment to help them through it.

***

Elijah had bad dreams.

Upon awakening together one morning, he says, "A bad guy was trying to take you and I tried to stab him."

Wow, he said "stab," I think.

"Oh honey, I am so sorry. That must've been scary."

"But Mommy, you don't like stabbing," he says.

"No, I don't, but the dream was not real," I say.

"I know, Mommy," he says.

"How did you feel?" I ask.

"Mad," he says.

"I get it," I reply. "I understand."

"How did it end?" I ask.

"They didn't take you away," he says . . . my heart breaks at the thought of what he had to experience during our separations.

"No, they didn't. That's the ending now. We are here together."

"Ok, Mommy," he says, but I know it will take time for him to heal and grow a full garden of deep, healthy attachments.

I remind myself of all the people in his life who love and are there for him. I know today I will remind him of that too.

Harrison sits nearby with a book on his lap from the night before. It is one of our favorites, so I sit up and snuggle next to him, drawing Elijah closer to both of us, and begin to read so we can best start the day in love, light, and warmth.

They listen to me read, "Will you be my sunshine on a cold and frosty day? Yes, I'll be your sunshine on a cold and frosty day. With warm smiles and great big hugs, I'll chase the clouds away."

***

There was a time when the twins' outbursts and tantrums were common, complicated to navigate, and even more difficult to watch them go through.

There was one incident I'll never forget. It was a moment of pure and innocent revelation. A moment of truth.

After a simple "no" was given in response to Elijah's request to do something, he burst immediately into a full-on protest. I gave him a warning, but it didn't stop him a bit. He screamed, threw things, smacked me, and knocked down furniture. It was all surprising to me.

His twin brother Harrison plugged his ears and began to cry for him to stop. Elijah responded, "You stop it," and then tried to hit him. I blocked it and tried to comfort Harrison while also keeping Elijah under control.

I tried everything. No words, distraction, or incentive worked.

I was at a complete loss. Out of ideas, I gave up, I surrendered.

I sat on the floor and breathed.

Eyes welling up, I hid my tears with my hands.

This is all my fault, I thought, then said, "I don't know what else to do."

The room was suddenly, utterly, completely still.

Nothing but the truth filled up that space in seconds.

Only the untouchable was in that moment in time.

Only the middle between stimuli and response.

Only the feelings and core wounds behind it all.

I will not project this guilt upon them, I thought.

Reassuring them, I said, "Mommy's ok . . . I'm ok. I'm just sad Eli is sad . . . and it's ok he's sad . . . it's ok he's mad. You can be sad and mad here whenever you want. Please just try not to hurt yourself or your brother. Do you need a hug, dear Son? Will that help you through?"

He immediately fell into my arms, we held each other, and he heard, "I get it," without a word, unconditional acceptance and love received.

> *Dear Son,*
>
> *I saw behind the tantrum to the real you inside.*
> *I saw your hurt. And your hurt is seen.*
> *Let it out, dear Son. It is important to me.*
> *Thank God you're getting the hurt out here and not stuffing it away.*
> *Thank God you know that you can cry in a safe place.*
> *I will always be here to listen with open ears.*
> *We are in this together and always will be, dear.*
> *Love, Mommy*

The next day, Mariam asked me, "What did it trigger in you?"

"Truth is, I didn't want him to hurt. It hurt to see him hurt.

It hurt to see his hurt causing his brother's hurt. It hurt knowing he would hurt more when he realized he hurt his brother.
It hurt knowing his hurt was causing the behavior. It hurt to
know he can't yet put his hurt into words. It hurt not being
able to do a goddamn thing about it. I didn't want him to hurt."

I didn't want him to hurt like I did.

I didn't want him to hurt like I did and never share it.

I didn't want him to hurt like I did and have someone only
focus on what he did because of the hurt rather than the hurt
itself.

I wanted to somehow say to my young son, "I see you."

Later, I also realized that shame was sending energy, affecting the parenting of my sons. I turned to Priya for guidance. She asked why I chose to create more children with their
father. I dove into my heart and realized it was because I was
overflowing with love to give. She asked me to close my eyes
and tap into that.

"Your ego mind tries to hide that simple truth with layers
of guilt and shame. Your sons can see the doubt in your eyes,"
she said.

I began to cry in the sheer bliss of pain turned joyful
realization.

"You love them with all your heart. You were the chosen
one to carry their souls into this world. Look your sons in their
eyes with all the confidence and clarity you can muster cen-
tered in that one single truth shining through," she said.

I began to do this more and more. It drastically changed
everything. And I mean everything. When my children saw
the absolute resolution of a confident, shame-free mother, they
felt more secure, had less separation anxiety, and reduced op-
positional behaviors.

If I stay connected to that one true home within me, even
shame as a mother cannot hurt me or my children anymore.

***

It is Thanksgiving. Months of social distancing have passed and continue. But I am closer to others and myself than I've ever been. After cooking a yummy traditional meal, my mother, Diego, Harrison, and Elijah all head up the hill where my father is buried. Diego stands with his Omi as the boys run around in the cool fresh air. Gratitude overwhelms me. We return home, eat our meal, and give thanks.

Having waited all morning to begin an epic Nerf gun fight outside, Elijah eventually loses his patience. When I tell him it is "almost time, but not time," he says something he does not mean and is about to grab something and throw it.

"Eli, are the lavalings winning?" I ask.

The "lavalings" come from a handheld game with a heart monitor that stops whenever the child's heart rate gets too high. It only resumes after they breathe and calmly lower it.

Elijah runs to his room, pouting. I decide, this time, not to follow him and to give him space. I half anticipate a full-fledged tantrum and to hear things being thrown in frustration. But I hear nothing. A couple of minutes pass and I head toward his room.

Suddenly he walks out and says, "Mom, I just needed some time alone," with a tilt of his head and sweet-silly tone.

"Ok, glad you got it, Son," I say, as Diego and I chuckle, looking at one another in the "Oh my goodness, did you see that?" kind of way. And that is that. He hadn't even started kindergarten yet!

Yes, there will still be tantrums when a "no" isn't liked.

Yes, there will still be anger and hurt that needs to come out.

Yes, there will also be a ton of joy, laughter, and release.

Things are not perfect, nor can they be.
But they are perfectly imperfect to me.

***

As a mother, I often wonder how much "spirituality" or big-picture understanding of existence I've imprinted thus far in my sons' heads and hearts.

One day, a simple confirmation of some level of understanding arrived. When we eat dinner, I sometimes place a small dry-erase board at the end of the table so we can play hangman together. It has been a great tradition, fodder for great memories, and a way to get the boys to calmly sit in their chairs and engage.

One of them will whisper a word into my ear and I'll write down the adequate blank spaces for it. As they begin guessing letters, even the one who chose the word has to think about how it is sounded out and spelled. I just love the process! Sometimes words are silly, like "fart" or "Milo loves poo poo," other times they are more subjective, like "Daddy loves Mommy."

Elijah whispered words into my ear, and it said it all.

"Angel, Opi, God." Opi is what they call my father, even though they never met him. My son had an inkling of a spirit he could not see, of something beyond him and me. *Has he learned this from observation, things I say to him, and how I live my life today?* I asked myself. *Of course he did and it's ok to take some credit. It's ok to remind yourself you're a good mother.*

On a Tuesday morning in late June, I woke up to the twins' angelic faces and calm breaths snuggled up next to me. Like three spoons cuddled in a perfect puzzle, the truth is crystal clear in this space. The outside world seems so far away. It cannot touch us with the having to be "ok." We are "us." And for today, us is all we need.

If I could put moments like this in a chest and lock it away, I would. But I don't have to anymore. It is now untouchable in that home within us.

***

Diego and I spent innumerable hours working on his college applications together. I will treasure those moments forever. We read the personal essay questions and he asked me, "What do you think I should say?" in his answer to a particular question, "What has been your greatest challenge and how did you overcome it?"

"Well, dear Son, think about the last couple of years and all you went through at home."

"Yeah, I guess, Mom," he says, as the brutal honesty cuts through the air. "I don't know."

"Sometimes we don't realize the challenges we've walked through until they are over," I say.

"Yeah, that's true," he says.

Together, we try to summarize the hardships placed on him. When he struggles to find words for his feelings, I slowly throw out "anxious, lonely, depressed, angry, disappointed, stressed out, abandoned, afraid, brokenhearted?"

"Wow, Mom. Wow," he responds, cracking open into the middle. The truth was in that moment.

No ignoring it, stuffing it down, or pretending he was "ok."

"Yeah, it was hard," he finally says.

I write the first line of the essay onto the screen: "It took someone else to point out to me what was my most difficult challenge . . . ," then push the laptop his way.

He starts writing, and writes some more. Several minutes pass and he pushes the screen my way to see what he's written.

It is beautiful. And I see in his eyes a full-circle realization, as though someone finally put words to, acknowledged, and validated his experience. Not necessarily me, though. He did it for himself. And that matters a lot.

All the apologies in the world couldn't have purchased that moment.

As we're about to close the screen, he sees a document with "Dear Son" at the top.

He asks what it is, and I share with him that I am writing something like a memoir and that every chapter begins with that, that I hope it will help other mothers and sons out there. That I am afraid of having revealed so much to the world but had to be brave. That all the pain and hardship caused must have a bigger purpose.

Diego smiles broadly. "That's awesome, Mom," he says, then he gives me a big hug. "I can't wait till it's done."

A month later, he told me a friend of his "has gone through some hard things, Mom," and he wanted to always show her respect. "I can't believe what women go through," he said.

"Everyone does, dear one. Everyone. Life brings 'good' and 'bad,' so to speak," I said, making quotes with my fingers.

"Yeah, I know." He shrugged.

"It's about discovering a golden nugget of truth behind both," I attempted to explain. "There's always a lesson in how the mind works, how it responds, that can be so freeing. It's beautiful you hold space for her to be vulnerable, that she can talk to you."

"Yeah, she does," he said, as the most gentle, sweet, kind young man he is.

Then he showed an unbelievable kindness. "Mom, I learned to do that from you. I feel like I can talk to you."

I felt deep within my heart all the internal peace as a mother I could have ever asked for. It seemed "It" had brought everything full circle, the good, the bad, and ultimately the truth within.

My son is attempting to allow himself and others the

courage to walk through vulnerability, to see it as strength, to discover all the layered colors of wisdom in it, to dig in deep and discover the truth. And as a result, my son is hopefully sensing and connecting to his true self and home within. He is learning to live authentically, wholeheartedly.

A few weeks later Diego said, "Time isn't linear, Mom," with the graceful confidence all mothers wish to instill in their child. His had sometimes lingered and needed a little nurturing when he was younger. But in that moment, it was in high gear. I remember it crystal clear.

"Tell me more, dear Son, tell me more," I said energetically.

In his element, the concept flows in and out of his beautiful brain. He shines so bright, with a mound of magnificent ideas in the blink of an eye.

"Well, our minds aren't made to understand it. I can't really put it in words," he said, with his intelligent good looks and black glasses framing his face, just like my father's did.

"I get it, dear Son," I said, and I do.

He attempts to explain it to his dad with several man-made ideas like string theory, quantum physics, opposite directional movement of atoms and more.

But it's his own concept that says it all. "The past, present, and future are simultaneous," he says, as he looks into my eyes. "Our existence is," he adds. "It just is," we say in perfect sync, and smile together at Bill.

Today, Diego and I share a bond I could never imagine. We speak of past core wounds of his. When his feelings arise, we acknowledge them and use those moments as opportunities to better embrace today. We even have live online discussions as a parent and child so others can grow from our experience as a family on the road of recovery. This is one of the best miracles of sobriety and finding a home within.

Later that evening, as I was snuggling with the twins, Harrison played with our tiny dog, Bella, on my lap.

"She's restless and a bit stressed, it seems." He leaned down and whispered in her ear, "Breathe the lavalings out. They don't belong there. Doesn't that feel better, Bella? We got you."

***

As a mother, I have learned that the concept of "we" must be repeatedly learned, taught, and embraced in all its magnificent, varying forms. Like a wolf pack journeying across the plains, bound together by love, loyalty, and respect for one another, I have only made it this far by doing my best to turn to the "we" in life.

I'll always remember my sponsor clearly saying to me, "Nadia, when you do step one, it is the 'we' part that matters the most. 'We' admit 'we' are powerless. If you just say, 'I am powerless,' you'll end up at the bottom again in a heartbeat. Together 'we' have the power. 'We' are in this together. 'We' are walking one day at a time together. You cannot and must not ever forget this."

"Ok," I say. "That should be pretty easy for me." But it isn't. Every day I have to remind myself that I cannot successfully continue on this road living wholeheartedly and healthily if I try to do it alone.

It is my children that fuel the internal wolf-pack instinct.

The twins love their electric go-karts. Like a kid myself, I love to follow them on a scooter as they trail blaze down the boardwalks and alleys, spinning and laughing with glee. Neighbors often enjoy just sitting back and watching their silly, unabashed daredevil ways. One day, after an hour or so of stunts around town, we return home, and Bill has arrived to pick up the twins. The boys smile and run to give him a warm embrace. Bill and I chat about the schedule, and all is good. Ever so quietly, the boys observe our interaction. I notice. Then, spontaneously, Elijah walks up, takes Bill's hand

and then mine, and joins them. I surrender to the intimate moment, smile at Bill, and then ask both twins to join us.

"We are in this together, ok?" I say.

The symbolism is priceless.

"We" are family.

It was a seven-year journey to get to this place.

From darkness and despair, there is freedom from my mind's trickery and bondage.

With daily spiritual and recovery-focused practices, the love of true friends, the fellowship, and my kundalini yoga family, I can do this life, one day at a time, and stay healthy, safe, and grounded.

There will be hard days. Painful memories will still come.

But they no longer choke me.

There is less fear, shame, and blame.

Life is no longer a struggle but rather an adventure.

Life is no longer lived in the past but in the present.

Today, I hold my children living wholeheartedly, connected to the truth and home within me.

May the longtime sun shine upon you,
all love surround you,
and the pure light within you guide your way on.
Sat Nam.

NOTE ON SOURCES

Certain sources are noted in the book text itself, but as an overview, the main sources I quote from include articles from the *Los Angeles Times* and *OC Weekly*; a lecture given by Yogi Bhajan that was transcribed in his book called *The Mind: Its Projections and Multiple Facets*; the book *A Course on Miracles*; other yogic texts; a blog post from the blog *Angry Daddy*; and direct quotes from court transcripts, letters, and formal legal motions. There is also a short quote in chapter twenty from the book *Will You Be My Sunshine*, by Julia Lobo (2015: Cottage Door Press, Barrington, Illinois). The specific articles referenced are as follows:

"The Kid Is Innocent," by Bob Embers, *OC Weekly*, September 17, 1999.

"Building on a Legacy, Nadia Davis Brings Father's Voice of Latino Activism to Santa Ana's School Board," by Tina Nguyen, *Los Angeles Times*, February 1, 1999.

"Hang in There, Arthur, It's Not Over Yet," by Dana Parsons, *Los Angeles Times*, January 12, 2000.

"Carmona Freed from Prison: 'Take Me Home,'" by Dana Parsons, *Los Angeles Times*, August 23, 2000.

"Can Justice Be Blinded by Eyewitnesses?" by Dana Parsons,
Los Angeles Times, May 7, 1999.

"In Question of Accused Teen, There Are No Easy Answers,"
by Dana Parsons, *Los Angeles Times*, May 9, 1999.

"Sometimes a Stacked Deck Is Really a House of Cards," by
Dana Parsons, *Los Angeles Times*, May 12, 1999.

"Reexamining Prosecutor's Eyewitnesses," by Dana Parsons,
Los Angeles Times, May 16, 1999.

"One Man's Word Could Clear Young Convict," by Dana
Parsons, *Los Angeles Times*, May 21, 1999.

"Things Now Look Different to Witness," by Dana Parsons,
Los Angeles Times, May 26, 1999.

"Calling D.A. to Stand in Carmona Case," by Dana Parsons,
Los Angeles Times, May 30, 1999.

"A Guilty Plea to Obsession with Injustice," by Dana Parsons,
Los Angeles Times, June 6, 1999.

"Vote to Convict Haunts Carmona Juror," by Dana Parsons,
Los Angeles Times, June 9, 1999.

"2nd Carmona Juror Says She Felt Pressured," by Dana
Parsons, *Los Angeles Times*, June 18, 1999.

ACKNOWLEDGMENTS

Thank you, Bill, for your unwavering belief in me and unbreakable commitment to our children.

This memoir would not have been possible without the love, support, and guidance of several incredible individuals: Mariam Paul, LMFT; Kimmy Hunkle, MFT; Priya Jain; Bethzabe Martinez; Maryann Tanedo; Angela DiDonato; Veronica Toole; Monica Balderrama; Alan Diamante; Fahi Takesh; Umberto DelAlcazar; Jane Jenson; Sharman Haversack; Charlotte Burns; Heather Cordova Perkins; Laura Jelin; Dodie Brewster Martynec; Brian Gilles; Rooney Daschbach; Anjie Whitman; Twila Ingram; Jackie Izzo-Moses; Loretta Baptista; Cherri Allison; Nancy O'Malley; Dr. Michelle Martin; Deanne Rocchietti; Kimberley Baird-Lyon; Ron Rale; my entire "Thursdays Fellowship"; my Seventh Chakra Yoga Institute of Spiritual Sciences family; the entire Kaiser Integrated Pain Management Team; my dear sisters and brothers, Anja, Mark, Luke, Marisa, Sabrina, and Erik; and most of all, my mother, Irmgard.

From the depths of my soul, thank you, Sabrina and Ron Eversole and Brian and Celina Friday, for being there for my family when we needed you most.

ABOUT THE AUTHOR

Nadia Davis is the mother of three sons and is a writer, attorney, and kundalini yoga instructor. She graduated from UCLA with a degree in sociology, and from Loyola Law School with a Juris Doctor. Nadia became the youngest Latina and Native American in local office when she was elected to the Santa Ana Unified School District Board of Trustees in November 1998.

A passionate advocate for youth justice, Nadia worked for some of the largest pro bono law firms in the nation, including Public Counsel, the Center for Human Rights and Constitutional Law, and the Mexican American Legal Defense and Education Fund. Most notable is her leadership in obtaining the freedom of Orange County's son Arthur Carmona, a wrongfully convicted sixteen-year-old. After nearly three years of legal filings, lobbying, petitions, press coverage, fundraising, and securing top investigators and legal representation, Arthur was eventually freed.

She has received numerous awards for her work improving the lives of others, including the John F. Kennedy Jr. Award, the National Women's Political Caucus Woman of the Year award, and LULAC's Hispanic Woman of the Year. Her journey of recovery from trauma, a near-death car accident, public shaming, and addiction is an inspiration to anyone seeking a way out of darkness into the light of knowing their infinite true self. Nadia lives in Southern California.